Critical Essays on Nadine Gordimer

Critical Essays on
World Literature

Robert Lecker, General Editor
McGill University

Critical Essays on Nadine Gordimer

Rowland Smith

G. K. Hall & Co. • Boston

First published 1990.
10 9 8 7 6 5 4 3 2 1

Library of Congress Cataloging-in-Publication Data

Critical essays on Nadine Gordimer / [edited by] Rowland Smith.
    p.   cm.—(Critical essays on world literature)
   ISBN 0–8161–8847–5 (alk. paper)
   1. Gordimer, Nadine — Criticism and interpretation. I. Smith,
Rowland, 1938- . II. Series.
PR9369.3.G6Z64   1990
823—dc20   90–31945
                                                 CIP

The paper used in this publication meets the minimum
requirements of American National Standard for Information
Sciences—Permanence of Paper for Printed Library Materials,
ANSI Z39.48-1984. ∞™

Printed and bound in the United States of America

CONTENTS

INTRODUCTION

The first extract in this collection was published in 1953, the last in 1988. Their subject, Nadine Gordimer, has been publishing fiction since the age of thirteen, when, in 1937,[1] a story of hers was printed in the children's section of a Johannesburg newspaper. Her first book appeared in 1949.[2] Since then she has produced nine novels and eight volumes of collected short stories. That fiction has relentlessly chronicled the life of the society in which she still lives, South Africa, and in particular the intellectual, political, and spiritual condition of its white ruling class. Even when she writes about events elsewhere in Africa, as in *A Guest of Honour* (1971), several short stories, and *A Sport of Nature* (1987), her discussion of the role of whites in Africa, and the nature of their opportunity for political commitment, grows out of her continuing debate on those topics as they relate to her native land.

The years between 1949 and 1988, two boundary dates already mentioned, are those in which the South African apartheid state flourished (after the Afrikaner Nationalist victory in 1948), and white English-speaking intellectuals found themselves increasingly marginalized in relation to the opposing forces of white state domination and black National consciousness.

White liberals tried to forge a nonracial alliance against apartheid in the 1950s; the Sharpeville Massacre occurred in 1960; open political resistance to the state was crushed in the 1960s, as were sabotage and the first campaign of violence; black consciousness challenged white good faith in the 1970s and rejected white cooperation even in opposition to the regime; in 1976 the Soweto riots shook public confidence in the possibility of endless white armed control; urban violence since the mid-1980s, and the State of Emergency declared in 1986, seemed to presage a lengthy period of rebellion; the long-awaited revolution had (or had it?) begun.

This is the stuff of Gordimer's writing. She has consistently acknowledged that because politics affects all aspects of life in South Africa, her writing, even in its apparently most private and personal

1

moments, deals either implicitly or explicitly with the politics of that society. And a distinguishing feature of her attitude towards the political role of writers in such circumstances is that they should write not "politics," but the "truth." This belief, that a writer's only commitment—even in a political context—is to the "truth" rather than to a political program or "solution," goes hand in hand with Gordimer's conviction that fiction itself enjoys a "truthfulness" superior to that of nonfictional analysis or political proselytizing.

Her own political position has grown increasingly radical over the years, but she has not advocated political solutions in her fiction. The essential detachment of her fictional style has resulted in both admiration and criticism. Too detached for some, she is seen as a cold and impersonal analyst afraid to leave her privileged, white middle-class ivory tower. Celebrated by others for her nondoctrinaire subtlety and truthful ambivalence about political virtue, she has been seen by certain members of that same group to espouse a political cause to the detriment of her art in her latest novel, A Sport of Nature. In either case, the loneliness of her position is remarkable.

One of the most perceptive of her critics, Stephen Clingman, treats both her insistence on the truthfulness of experience and the resulting marginalization of her position in his introduction to The Essential Gesture, a recently published collection of Gordimer's nonfictional prose. His comments, made in 1988, represent the latest word on Gordimer's austere role; and that latest word comes from a cosmopolitan, white, English-speaking South African particularly close to the world Gordimer reflects. Clingman quotes a well-known passage—"I remain a writer not a public speaker; nothing I say here will be as true as my fiction"—from Gordimer's essay, "Living in the Interregnum,"[3] and goes on to place this trait in the context of her artistic life:

> Underlying all Gordimer's changes, the flexibility of a mind growing stronger and more radical as it grows older, is the firmness of conviction. In politics, as in writing, Gordimer's sustained attempt, following her great example, Turgenev, is to see and then to relay "life as it happens to be." There are to be no lies, no party line, no propaganda for the sake of a good cause. If anything is to help a good cause, it can only be the truth. . . . neither society nor the self is to be left immune from her uncompromising scrutiny.[4]

The consequences of such an unblinking examination are not comfortable. As Clingman points out, Gordimer belongs to a minority within a minority. The larger minority in South Africa is formed by the whites who oppress and exploit the majority black population. The smaller minority is formed by those whites who oppose the system controlled by the ruling white minority. But even here, the desire of that tiny group of whites to somehow link up with the black majority is confronted with rejection, contradiction, and ambivalence. Clingman offers a compelling analysis of the consequences for Gordimer of this set of circumstances:

> What reservoirs of intellectual and emotional strength are required to confront the facts of one's own privilege while seeking ways to undo it? How does one deal with the daily compromises and contradictions explicit and implicit in one's situation? These problems are nothing as compared to the suffering experienced by starving children in South Africa's "homelands," or families divided and kept in wretched poverty by the social and economic exactions of the migrant labor system; and this too is something the white in Gordimer's situation must recognize. But these are the problems she deals with, and there is perhaps a particular heroism in doing so; more than that, in continuing to attempt, despite these odds, to make one's way towards circumstances in which these realities will no longer apply. For there is a *solitude* here, an existential loneliness which accompanies commitment.[5]

Gordimer has not always been blessed with criticism of this calibre. These extracts from Clingman's introduction to *The Essential Gesture* represent the latest critical word on a controversial figure whose concerns and practices involve her in passionate debate (as both subject and object) on profoundly serious issues. She is now a writer with an international clientele; her work commands instant attention from major English-language publications on both sides of the Atlantic, and she is herself a frequent contributor to the columns of such newspapers and magazines. For a South African white, who chooses to stay on in South Africa, this in itself poses problems of critical response within the country. An interesting facet of the history of Gordimer criticism is that although she is commented on by reviewers and critics around the world, the most penetrating comment on her work frequently comes from South Africans or ex-South Africans. At the same time, some of the most hostile reaction to her work comes from South Africans or ex-South Africans.

At all times there has been a strong variation in the attitudes towards Gordimer's simultaneous stylistic detachment and her personal ideological commitment, particularly in later life, to change in South Africa. Typical of that variation are the following two reactions to her novel *Burger's Daughter* (1979), which treats Communist attitudes and policies through the medium of their effect on its protagonist, the daughter of a well-known South African white Communist. The first is taken from a review entitled "The Politics of Commitment" that appeared in the *African Communist* in 1980. While arguing that any book *should* be welcome that discusses the relationship between the Communist Party and the African Nationalist

Congress as well as the 1946 miners' strike, the Comintern, and "many other thorny problems in our history," the reviewer continues: "Regrettably, this proves to be a book that, once taken up, is difficult not to put down. Nadine Gordimer's passionless prose is, as usual, exquisitely sculptured but excruciatingly remote, and the reader is always conscious of the artist at work, polishing the last phrase, carefully selecting the right word after rejecting many others—but to say what?"[6] The assertion that the readability of the novel is to be regretted is part of the reviewer's demand for revolutionary content. The ultimate "banality" of *Burger's Daughter*, Z. N. continues, "would have been more effective if said bluntly without the artifice and even occasional artistry which, because it holds the reader at arm's length, becomes in the end merely irritating."[7] This is quite a mixture, but apart from the paradox of "more effective" "banality," the general drift of dislike in the passage is related to any element in Gordimer's style that mitigates her doctrinal impurity. The final paragraph of the review makes explicit the grounds for all other uneasiness about the novel: its absence of "revolutionary content": " 'Burger's Daughter' is the third novel of Nadine Gordimer's to have been banned. In a way this is a tribute to be valued more highly than the Herzog or CNA prizes [South African literary awards], even though, if, like the authorities, one is searching for revolutionary content one might feel it is undeserved."[8]

In the face of such a contorted presentation of quite a simple position—*Burger's Daughter* is banal and unrewarding because it does not advocate the correct revolutionary doctrine—the positive comments of Stephen Gray, writing in Johannesburg, seem to represent a prelapsarian order of humanist tolerance. He praises *Burger's Daughter* for the very detachment that is so offensive to an *African Communist* committed reviewer:

> It has been a commonplace criticism of Gordimer's earlier work that she, supposedly, lacks feeling, that the work is stylistically glazed and therefore distant and impenetrable. One supposes that it is possible for a reader to work through "Burger's Daughter" as well and not feel a thing. But, although Gordimer often writes about people in whom feeling is numbed or eclipsed, that is not the same thing as the work itself being unfeeling.
>
> The new realms of feeling here, the new details of the human dilemma revealed here, the new Gordimer onslaught against unfeelingness, would seem to gainsay any opinion that her work itself is without human responses.[9]

Both reviews illustrate the passions evoked by Gordimer's work and the subjects she deals with. An example of what Stephen Gray calls the commonplace criticism of her earlier writing shows much more sophistication than the lines quoted from the *African Communist*, but also reveals a similar rejection of both artistic detachment per se and the culture that such detachment appears to represent. The passage is by Dennis Brutus, the politically active South African poet who has been in exile for many years. It is taken from a book published in 1969, and his comments are therefore limited to early Gordimer, or at least to the works preceding the major novels of the next twenty years: *A Guest of Honour* (1971), *The Conservationist* (1974), *Burger's Daughter* (1979), *July's People* (1981). Brutus argues:

> There is in her the kind of impersonality that you find in a micro-scope. She does not herself react to feeling. In her books even the emotional relationships are forced, are conjured up, are synthetic. Though Nadine Gordimer would say that she is condemning South African society for being dehumanized, I would say that Nadine Gordimer, who is one of our most sensitive writers, is also the standing, the living example of how dehumanized South African society has become—that an artist like this lacks warmth, lacks feeling, but can observe with a detachment, with the coldness of a machine. There is in her, herself, no warmth and feeling.[10]

While acknowledging there is a case to be put for Gordimer's "cold" style—that, in Stephen Gray's words, she is depicting people in whom feeling has become numb or eclipsed—Brutus cannot divorce his own political passion from a demand for similar passion in the texture of Gordimer's writing. The ambivalence is all-pervasive. She is acknowledged to be "one of our most sensitive writers," but that sensitivity is somehow connected to absence of warmth—which would, surely, be a sign of *insensitivity* if it were really inappropriate?—and finally to a personal failing in the writer's personality, quite distinct from her writing. The complexity of response is typical of what Gordimer provokes from those close to the issues she depicts.

As her reputation grew with the novels of the seventies and eighties, Gordimer's writing was celebrated by a wide range of international critics who did not share the insistence on "revolutionary content" to be seen in the *African Communist* review. They could claim that Gordimer's work showed a passion for truthfulness even when that truthfulness led to ambivalence.

Her topics altered even if her treatment of them did not. As the political scene in South Africa darkened, so did the subject matter of Gordimer's fiction turn more consistently to revolution itself, and to the possibilities for significant revolutionary commitment in that society. This was a change from her earlier depictions of the uneasy contradictions and compromises of white, suburban "liberal" life in a milieu that was still basically colonial. Nevertheless, her later work would not satisfy a reader searching for programmatic "revolutionary content" as advocated by the *African Communist* reviewer. It certainly dealt with revolutionary action of one kind or another, but offered no comforting dogma.

In the fiction of her later period, Gordimer does not abandon the penchant for surgical analysis that distresses those critics who call her cold. She consistently blends her closely focused observations of "normal" white, middle-class life with depictions of revolutionary commitment or activity. In "Something Out There," the reactions of white suburbia to an escaped ape run in counterpoint to the planning and carrying out of an act of sabotage by a mixed guerrilla group living in the midst of the white community distracted by the predatory ape. In *A Sport of Nature,* the female protagonist who successfully "links hands," politically and sexually, with the black revolutionary movement, is constantly placed in the context of her adolescent life in affluent white Johannesburg, where her two aunts offer the stifling alternatives of respectable white materialism or liberalism.

This last novel, published in 1987, while not satisfying those who demand doctrinal revolutionary purity, has also provoked the charge—from the other camp—of too distorting an attachment to the cause of revolution.[11] In their reversal of the commonly held earlier view (Gordimer is now seen as not detached enough), these liberal critics once again show how close to political conviction or taste is the critical reaction to Gordimer's writing.

In the late sixties and early seventies—to return to Dennis Brutus' much-quoted charge—the unease provoked by Gordimer's controlled distance from her subject was not limited to those who themselves held a revolutionary position, or—like Dennis Brutus—were racial victims of the apartheid system. Two white critics, writing in influential British publications in the early seventies, were remarkably cool themselves in their assessment of Gordimer's achievements to date. Both were native South Africans who had emigrated to the United Kingdom.

Ursula Laredo, writing in *The Journal of Commonwealth Literature* in 1973, quotes from the well-known passage by Dennis Brutus about Gordimer's coldness, and argues against him: "Brutus obviously does not like the 'impersonality' he finds in Miss Gordimer's work. But, it is precisely this quality, the ability to remain detached, to view her characters and the situations in which they are involved from more than one point of view, that is one of Miss Gordimer's great strengths."[12] Laredo makes the "correct" liberal judgment, but the tone of her essay is at best lukewarm; at times it is close to that of Brutus: "It is in her short stories that the detached observation, the 'microscopic' quality of the writing is most effective; in the novels it can become intensely irritating, and does, in fact, conduce to the coldness of which Miss Gordimer is accused."[13]

At least part of the unsympathetic attitude of these ex-South Africans towards Gordimer's tone is related to their rejection of the life "back there." Their irritation can be crudely oversimplified as a shuddering and bewildered repetition of their own acts of rejection: "How can anything sensitive emerge from so hideous a situation? All that remains in South Africa is tainted." Laredo does not articulate this view herself, and does stick to her liberal guns: detachment is to be valued in a writer. But there is an unexpressed intolerance underlying her argument about what it is that makes Gordimer's work "cold," and, in spite of her overt disagreement with Brutus, she does tend to accept his judgment, at least in part:

> Brutus links Miss Gordimer's coldness with the fact that she is a white South African. It is obviously not a remark which one can accept at face value. But it is possible that the nature of her particular commitment to South Africa does influence the way in which she writes. It is a not unfair generalization to say that most English-speaking white South African writers fall into two categories: those who leave the country and continue to examine their South African experience from self-imposed or voluntary exile; and those who choose to live in South Africa with its privileges (for whites), its daily enforced participation in a system one is powerless to change, and its restrictions on freedom of expression. . . . Miss Gordimer . . . has decided to remain in South Africa, and thus belongs to the privileged section of the community, a fact she has never denied. At the same time she has made no secret of her opposition to *apartheid*, and has been outspoken in her condemnation of the abhorrent system. . . . Her own novels, however, are not used as vehicles for protest; they are rational examinations of a society she knows, which happens to be South Africa. . . . This balance between her political opinions and her literary life is similar to the balance reflected in the novels themselves. On the whole, her characters accept the limitations imposed by their condition. Possibilities exist—how does one achieve them?[14]

Stephen Clingman's comments in 1988 deal with the same issue as that raised by Ursula Laredo, but they are much more sympathetic: "What reservoirs of intellectual and emotional strength are required to confront the facts of one's own privilege while seeking ways to undo it?" The magnanimity of tone is partly a personal trait of Clingman's as a writer, but it also stems from a recognition of Gordimer's steadfastness of purpose while continuing to live in the increasing turbulence of her white privilege. Laredo's remarks were made in 1973, Clingman's in 1988.

The second ex-compatriot of Gordimer's who produced, in the seventies, a lukewarm survey of her work for overseas readers was Christopher Hope, at that point newly arrived in London and not yet an established emigré commentator in fiction, prose, and poetry on the South African scene. His short survey, "Out of the Picture: The Novels of Nadine Gordimer," appeared in the *London Magazine* in 1975. In it he does little more than summarize some of the themes (and plots) of her writing to date, but his own tone is extraordinarily dismissive in passing comments such as:

> South Africa is palpably there in all Miss Gordimer's novels: the Greek corner cafes, the bleak little mining towns of the Transvaal, the great mining camp itself, Johannesburg, with its black townships squatting at its feet like unwanted children, and the extravagant idiocies of the well-heeled white madams and masters. . . . One might say that she perceives how deadly dull so much of it is, and she can sometimes be boring with it. At best there is her admirable fidelity to the landscapes she describes, at worst she drives home her points, tediously and sententiously, leaving nothing to the imagination.[15]

All this was in the seventies, when to remain in South Africa was seen by those outside the country to entail the inevitable taint, whatever one's politics, of privileged luxury and ease. In the late 1980s that luxury is less obviously associated with ease. But the frightfulness of staying on to comment without flinching on the steady polarization of the situation, with its descent into the constant violence of a continual State of Emergency, is a topic that has not superseded the exile-alienation of the seventies. There is frequent awe in contemporary overseas comment about Gordimer's continued presence on the scene she depicts so skillfully, but only Clingman has tried to express the cost of such an internal scrutiny.

For the revolutionary cause itself, Gordimer's topics are mostly irrelevant. If the future of South Africa/Azania is to be found in its black majority (a position Gordimer would not deny), then only literature dealing with that people's struggle is relevant to the revolutionary cause. At least so the argument runs. The neuroses and dishonesties of whites, their flawed attempts at political comradeship with the majority, and the nuances of their restricted endeavors to come to terms with a "black" future, these are, to those committed to revolutionary change, the decadent remnants of a doomed bourgeois culture.

The world Gordimer inhabits and describes now is a far cry from that which she first recorded in her writing. The still-colonial ethos of her English-speaking childhood and young womanhood is both the subject of her earliest fiction and a constant element in the local reaction to her earliest successes. That milieu is vividly captured in an account of the launching of her first collection, *Face to Face*, published in Johannesburg in 1949.

"Amelia's" column in the Johannesburg *Star* on September 5, 1949 opens with an account of the preparations for a ball, "the first of three important events being organized to celebrate the golden jubilee of this famous Johannesburg regiment [the Imperial Light Horse]." The columnist warns that "Table reservations have been heavy, and only a limited number of tables in the main hall are left," and she imagines the scene to come: "Colourful couples, the men in dress kit, or the 'undress blues' of the Imperial Light Horse, service dress, or evening dress—their attire possibly eclipsing in brightness, for once, the evening gowns of the women—will dance in the City Hall on Friday night at the fiftieth anniversary ball of the I.L.H." The second item on which Amelia comments is headlined "Publishers' Party," and this event has actually occurred before she writes about it:

> Now that new writers are being discovered in South Africa and publishing has become an established industry, the "publishers' party" to welcome new books has become a regular event.
> On Friday, Silver Leaf Books, Ltd., entertained in honour of Miss Nadine Gordimer, the writer from Springs whose first collection of short stories, "Face to Face," has just been printed. Guests were given a presentation copy on arrival, and those who had not previously met Miss Gordimer, were surprised to discover that the author was quite the youngest-looking person in the room.[16]

It is this world, in which the glamour of a dress-uniform ball suggests the excitement of more secure imperial days, and in which the quaintness of the new phenomenon of local publishing requires the phrase "publishers' party" to be used in quotation marks, that Gordimer records in *Face to Face* and her first novel, the bildungsroman, *The Lying Days* (1953). And yet even in local reaction to her first collection there is a wide range of response. Not all Johannesburgers were more interested in a regimental ball. Although dated in manner, some of the first reviews Gordimer received in Johannesburg were remarkably perceptive and open-minded. The reviewer of *Face to Face* in *The Forum* of September 17, 1949 is unequivocal: "The stories in this volume are not the exercises of a beginner. They have a definite and distinctive literary quality—they need no concessions or encouraging clucks. The promise implicit and explicit in them is the promise that Nadine Gordimer will become a writer of stature."[17] He goes on to state the concern that would be central to Gordimer's work for the next forty years. Although "some of the stories could be set anywhere," he argues, "some are South African. It is to these that one's attention must turn, contrary perhaps to the more austere canons of criticism." The centrality of Gordimer's South

African stories lies in her depiction of the gap separating white and black (in 1949 the terms were European and non-European):

> It is the separation of European and non-European which is, in my opinion, the factor most inhibiting the growth of a South African literature. . . . every European artist must feel bitterly that the imaginative chasms are huge, that he cannot, however sympathetic, get inside black misery.
>
> What Nadine Gordimer has done is to make this separation the subject of some of her stories. Four very different stories each in its own way adds up to the barriers, the tension, the fumbling in relation to the nonwhite which most Europeans conscious of the problem and free from the statutory prejudice carry with them as a heavy, inescapable load.[18]

The fact that Nadine Gordimer dealt with the "tension, the fumbling in relation to the non-white," and did so with a very sharp eye, conditioned much early response to her work in the locales that she describes. Apart from constantly glutinous comment on her appearance and social manner, there are opposing reactions in the 1950s and 1960s to the recognizability of Gordimer's settings or characters, and the incisiveness of her political themes. Very much one of us in the way she knows the Johannesburg scene, she can nevertheless be irritatingly knowing when dealing with "the political problem."

The local press could treat the writer as a social phenomenon. There was a gossip-column approach to interviewing the young Nadine Gordimer. In an article in the *Cape Argus* in 1954 entitled, "Two Years to Write a Novel: Nadine Gordimer is a Keen Observer," Lucy Bean writes:

> At a first meeting, Nadine Gordimer seems little more than a girl, certainly not a woman of 30 with a literary reputation and the mother of a three-year-old daughter. Bird-like in her movements, she is small, with dark eyes intensely alive and observant under arched brows.
>
> The oval of her face is emphasized by her dark hair swept back from a high forehead and gathered into a knot. Shy and almost diffident in her manner, she would listen rather than talk. But once she joins in a conversation the childlike quality fades out and a quick, intelligent mind and a definite personality come into play. . . .[19]

This revelation that the thirty-year-old author has a quick, intelligent mind and a definite personality, comes in a discussion of her recent second marriage and imminent trip to Europe following the successful publication of *The Lying Days* ("a story that many like and some dislike") in the previous October.

South African journalists could not refrain from commenting on

Gordimer's appearance in the 1950s and early 1960s. A familiar cameo finds its way into a short article in the Johannesburg *Star* in 1960 on the decision by the B.B.C. to turn *The Lying Days* into a television play: " 'I can't claim any hindsight,' said Miss Gordimer, who is dark and slim, with typical modesty."[20] In an excited appreciation of *A World of Strangers, The Star* columnist, "The Man on the Reef," acknowledges that "she has given what is probably the most penetrating, incisive account of Johannesburg and its people ever written. . . . Although a popular party game in Johannesburg just now is identifying the characters in 'A World of Strangers' with this city's socialites, Miss Gordimer denies that her characters are real." And the obligatory description (dark and slim) makes its way into his account: "In private life, Miss Gordimer, short, dark and slim, is Mrs. Reinhold Cassirer with two daughters and three dogs . . ."[21]

This last comment mixes social information with an assessment of the accuracy of Gordimer's writing. That accuracy could be disturbing. Local unease with seeing oneself in fiction takes a muffled form in reviews of the first three novels. "The novel, however, lacks drama and movement," writes L.S. in the *Rand Daily Mail*, reviewing *A World of Strangers:* "Miss Gordimer seems too much preoccupied with detail. The story is a long time getting under way, and the direction for long is uncertain. But the writing is always highly intelligent."[22] Owen Williams mixes praise and disquiet in his review of the same novel:

> The overwhelming impression from this book—Miss Gordimer's second novel—is that she has, in a sense, over-reached herself. The attitudes are "liberal," the language is impeccable, the reasonably taught construction in agreeable contrast to her other novel, "The Lying Days," her eye for observation and intimately-observed description of detail as delicate and convincing as ever, but the novel as a whole leaves an impression of superficiality, of a good work that has somehow, avoidably, misfired.[23]

The vagueness of complaint is typical. Williams acknowledges that there are passages with "a touch almost of a Johannesburg Jane Austen," and that her "description of the Transvaal veld, too, is magnificent, in a delicate, pastel-like way." But the core of his criticism is that her genre is "the wider and more dangerous pastures of the sociological novel."

> In spite of its faults, "A World of Strangers" is a significant and vital book. It is written with sensitivity, with a feeling for words and for people, which though only on a social level, makes Miss Gordimer into a potentially major novelist.[24]

It is not clear what the limitation is in his reservation "though only on a social level," but the sense of qualification, of doubt and hesitation, dominates the commentary in spite of its moments of praise.

The grounds for the unease in these early reviews are not clearly argued, although the unease itself is openly stated. Mary Morrison Webster, writing in the Johannesburg *Sunday Times,* closes her review of *Occasion For Loving* (which deals with the corrosive effects of a love affair between a white English woman and a black Johannesburg artist) in this way:

> In the concluding scenes, Miss Gordimer evades the real issues of her theme (but are there, or can there be, any real issues?) by a succession of platitudes on the race question, dropped by one or other of the Stilwells.
>
> For the majority of readers however, the theme and the incidents of the story will seem less important than those stretches of "interior" writing in which the author's still, small voice is heard above the sounds of ordinary living and the common day.[25]

The opting out of the obligation for a reviewer to comment in any significant way on the theme of the novel "(are there, or can there be, any real issues?)" is what the blur is used to camouflage. This is not a conscious evasion. It is simply a shrinking from the experience of the fiction; rather take refuge in the realm of the "interior," away from the (oh horror) "sounds of ordinary living and the common day."

Why bother to document this pattern of reaction in the commercial reviews of the daily or weekly South African press? Because this series of critical essays sets out to present a historical survey of reviews or comment, and the ephemeral nature of the kind of reviews from which these passages have been taken makes it inappropriate to reprint any of them in full as items in this volume. At the same time, they are invaluable indicators of the cultural and intellectual tone of the world in which Gordimer matured. Her writing records the political moods and cultural assumptions of the Johannesburg scene, and these reactions to her work are part of that scene.

South Africa in the second half of the twentieth century is a complicated place. Like Spain in the 1930s, it is the locus of viciousness, distortion, prejudice, constant violence, and—extraordinarily—imaginative daring, intellectual exhilaration, and generosity. Gordimer's own work is testimonial enough to this. So are the South African essays, dating from this period, that open this collection. As commentary on Gordimer's early fiction, they are difficult to beat, and they are contemporary with the foggy local pieces about her appearance and travel plans.

After the publication of *A Guest of Honour,* which won the James Tait Black Prize in 1971, and *The Conservationist,* which won the

Booker Prize in 1974, Nadine Gordimer's status as a novelist of world-interest was assured. Up to that point it was fashionable, among certain critics, to praise her as short story writer, and point to problems of form in her novels. In a sense this was a muted criticism of the more sustained political content of the novels (although the political themes are also there in the short stories, inescapable to any but the most blinkered reader). R.F. Haugh, for example, in his book on Gordimer in the Twayne series,[26] prefers the short stories to the novels and also finds the novels marred by an over-emphasis on politics.

After *The Conservationist*, there was as much interest paid to Gordimer's work in the world at large as in South Africa. Not only was considerable space given to reviews and interviews in the world press, but articles on her also appeared more frequently in academic journals outside South Africa. The articles already discussed by Ursula Laredo in the *Journal of Commonwealth Literature* and Christopher Hope in the *London Magazine*, are examples of the spreading interest in her work. South African critics continue to write about Gordimer, and their work is published both within and without the country. They are now joined by at least as many scholars and critics who are not personally connected to South Africa and who publish their work internationally.

The strange bitterness in certain kinds of South African reviewing did not evaporate with Gordimer's international acclaim. All writers, in all countries, receive their share of inappropriate comment, but a disproportionate amount of wildly inappropriate comment on Gordimer's fiction continues to appear, almost irrepressibly, in major South African publications. The review of *The Conservationist* in the Johannesburg *Sunday Times* is a paradigm of deep-seated hostility, surfacing side by side with obligatory praise (she is celebrated overseas, isn't she?) and an implacable obtuseness. "This novel—if you can call it that," writes A. B. Hughes, "is hard going, but readers should stick at it. There are rewards."[27] He proceeds to paraphrase the plot, mechanically, and without any insight into what the book is actually about, and concludes:

> From a Press interview, I gather that the writer regards it as important that an unidentified Black man is found dead on the farm at the beginning of the story, that the body is hurriedly buried by the police and then, at the end, is properly interred with due ceremony by the farm servants. But if this is supposed to be a unifying thread, most readers will probably find it so slight as to be almost invisible.
>
> There is one irritating little affectation which the author should abandon. Instead of the conventional inverted commas to indicate

direct speech, she uses a dash throughout. This is quite unnecessary and only adds to the general confusion of the writing.[28]

General confusion indeed. It was Stephen Gray who answered back in the correspondence columns of the Johannesburg *Sunday Times*, and once again showed how inaccurate it would be to regard Hughes' review as typical of all South African comment. Gray writes:

> His synopsis of the book is almost wholly inaccurate, if not mean-ingless, yet he has the nerve to go on and praise the book which he clearly cannot stand, or even understand, because presumably he is very concerned to maintain English South African cultural standards.[29]

The Conservationist is a novel that has received its share of literary comment in academic journals throughout the English-speaking world. The extraordinary review in the Johannesburg *Sunday Times* is not significant as an example of criticism, but rather as an example of the strange relation in the press between Gordimer and her fellow white South Africans. One last extract will suffice to indicate the degree of hostility she can provoke. To quote the letter in question is indulgent; it is so clearly less than serious literary comment. Once again, however, its degree of hostility and confusion is worth recording because the righteous obtuseness of the writer is a trait of the society that Gordimer investigates. "Gordimer trumpets her own virtues," is the heading given to a letter from S. M. of Lone Rock in the correspondence columns of the Johannesburg *Star* in November 1982. "There is nothing wrong with being a liberal," writes S. M., and continues:

> It's listening to Miss Gordimer's self-satisfaction being trum-peted whenever the occasion presents itself that makes me ask her to turn the volume down a bit.
> After all, she might want to hear something instead of being heard. In that case she might like to hear that literature which sets itself up to fight the sordidness of politics has never been great shakes and certainly isn't great shakes in South Africa.
> That sort of literature is saturated with egoism. Its admirers are people who themselves would like to get into the liberal lime-light.
> Liberal literature in this country concerns itself with the oppres-sion of black people. What do the black people think of it?
> I can't say. But I can guess. My guess is that it gives them a giggle.[30]

Gordimer's analysis of the failure of liberalism in the South African context is one of her most insistent themes. Robert Green's essay on *A World of Strangers* in this collection represents an early study of this aspect of her work,[31] and Stephen Gray's retrospective discussion,

written in 1988, of the same novel is even more outspoken about
the problem of liberal assumptions of the 1950s. S. M. of Lone Rock
has missed more than one point by insisting, in 1982, that Gordimer
wants to get into the liberal limelight. Limelight with Liberals was
not lacking in her life, but it was not of the kind supposed by S. M.

In January 1969, Gordimer published an open letter in the
Johannesburg *Star* to Andre Brink, the Afrikaans novelist who had
returned to South Africa from Europe. The letter is an encouraging
one—she opens it with the words "Welcome home," and closes with
"Greetings Brother"—which reflects a belief in the necessity, if not
necessarily in the efficacy, of speaking out:

> Our literature in both official languages is mealy-mouthed or
> banned. Welcome to the thin ranks of writers living here at home
> who are not afraid to broach subjects which, in your own words
> "really cause pain and penetrate," writers prepared to challenge
> the White man's smug self-righteousness, writers who have always
> been prepared as you now avow yourself, to accept the consequences
> of what they say.
>
> You know that even if you publish in English, this will put you
> among the Nkosis, the Mphahleles, the Gordimers whose books are
> banned, and the Patons and Fugards who have been deprived of
> passports.[32]

Although there is no explicit political message here, the general tone
is liberal—at a time when Gordimer's fiction had long since begun
to analyze the inappropriateness of liberal gestures and responses to
the political situation in South Africa. Gordimer's letter to Brink, with
its suggestion of a non-racial alliance against censorship of all kinds,
antedates the mood of Black Consciousness. Not all her black writers
listed, let alone white Liberals like Alan Paton, would continue to
carry the "correct" political connotations into the seventies.

By 1974 her tone is very different. In an interview with Michael
Ratcliffe in *The Times* of London she makes a bleak assertion: "It is
no longer possible for blacks and whites to act together for reform:
we're all distrusted now."[33] This is a significant change from what
she said (and implied) in her letter to Andre Brink of January 1969.
The most significant comment in the interview was not this remark,
however, but what she said about Liberals: " 'I am a white South
African radical. Please don't call me a liberal.' Liberal is a dirty word.
Liberals are people who make promises they have no power to keep."

Alan Paton, who had been national leader of the Liberal Party
before it was forced to disband in 1968, took exception to her
comment, and a notorious row ensued in the pages of the South
African press. "Paton slams 'ivory tower' Gordimer" reads the head-
line in the Johannesburg *Sunday Times* of 1 December 1974. Paton

is reported as saying that his reaction to Gordimer's statements is one of "intense anger," and that "Miss Gordimer is a gifted and intelligent woman, and I am astounded that a person with her understanding of language should permit herself such a vulgar generalization about a group of people. . . . Miss Gordimer should return to her ivory tower and avoid these interviews at all cost. This one has done her great harm."[34]

Gordimer's reply was both guarded and unwavering. In an open letter, she argues that "the word 'liberal' has changed its connotation in South Africa," and that she was not referring to the old-time members of the Liberal Party, but to present-day opportunists. On the other hand, she is unrelenting in her analysis of what liberal actions offered in the past: ". . . What White South Africans who bore the once honourable name of liberal offered to Blacks—in all sincerity and in some cases at personal risk—was in terms of hard political reality an empty hand. Liberals (whether with small or large initial letter) had no hope of coming to political power in South Africa and therefore no hope of extending political power to Blacks."[35] Andre Brink became involved in the dispute the day after this letter was published, and supported Gordimer's redefinition of the word *liberal*. "It is a very valid distinction she is making and, like her, I think there is an enormous difference between the term as it is used now and its previous usage."[36]

Alan Paton had a steely final word in another open letter in the *Sunday Times* a week later. "Let us face the fact that we have wounded each other," he writes, ". . . both of us can make better use of our time."[37] His defence of the liberal position is unqualified; he was its vanguard:

> It both wounded and angered me to find that you thought that people like myself could be dismissed as those who made promises they had no power to keep; and that you claimed that this was their distinguishing characteristic.
>
> I note that you exclude the Browns, Marquards, Suzmans, Sinclairs and others from your castigations. You consider it an insult to them that others should claim the title liberal. You may leave it to us to decide it. I for one, and many of my friends, are proud to be called liberals. We have no desire to climb on any anti-Liberal bandwagon. Black Power or otherwise. (7)

The issues in this kind of fratricidal bloodletting are real. The stakes are high for serious writers inside South Africa, and the relentless tone of the Paton-Gordimer exchange reveals much of the tenor of a writer's life in that milieu. Gordimer found herself in another public disagreement with a major South African novelist in 1988. In a local South African furor that anticipated the international

outcry over Iranian death threats to the author of *Satanic Verses,*
J. M. Coetzee criticized the decision of the Congress of South African
Writers, including Nadine Gordimer, to cancel a public appearance
in South Africa by Salman Rushdie after extensive threats were made
by Islamic fundamentalists against Rushdie himself and the audience
at his proposed talk on censorship. "I am very surprised," Gordimer
is quoted as saying, "that my friend and colleague has sprung this
public attack on us but that is his democratic right, and I am here
to defend it."[38] Whatever else Alan Paton was right or wrong about,
he was wrong to claim that Nadine Gordimer inhabited an ivory
tower.

International critical comment on Nadine Gordimer is necessarily
less charged than that in the South African press. Apart from serious
and lengthy reviews of all her works in major publications, there
have been four books devoted entirely to her work since the appearance of Haugh's volume in the Twayne series. Michael Wade's
Nadine Gordimer in the Modern African Writers Series appeared in
1978, and discusses the novels up to and including *The Conservationist.*[39] Much more significant are three works published in the
1980s, John Cooke's *The Novels of Nadine Gordimer: Private Lives/
Public Landscapes* (1985), Stephen Clingman's *The Novels of Nadine
Gordimer: History from the Inside* (1986), and Judie Newman's *Nadine
Gordimer* in the Contemporary Writers Series (1988). Cooke's book
is a wide-ranging study tracing broad thematic issues in Gordimer's
fiction, and placing significant emphasis on the interview published
in the *Paris Review* in 1983.[40] In that interview Gordimer describes
the crucial effect her mother had on her, in particular by keeping
her out of school on the pretext of a heart condition. To Cooke, as
a result, one of Gordimer's major themes is "the liberation of children
from unusually possessive mothers."[41] The section of his book dealing
with landscape in *A Guest of Honour* is reprinted in this volume.
Stephen Clingman's is the major study of Gordimer to have appeared
to date.[42] He discusses the political history and climate in which each
Gordimer work was written, and relates the cultural ethos of the
times to the issues in the fiction. The detailed knowledge of political
background which he brings to the novels and short stories is invaluable because in Gordimer's writing a finely tuned political debate,
occasionally using the actual words of political figures of the times,
is as much foreground as background. Only one extract from Clingman's book could be reprinted in this collection. His final chapter
on "Deep History" that closes this volume is a discussion of Gordimer's role vis-à-vis both her audience and history that has not been
equalled in Gordimer criticism. Judie Newman's study is shaped by
the aims of the series in which it appears: "to illuminate not only
those works [of major postwar writers] but also in some degree the

artistic, social, and moral assumptions on which they rest." Arguing that neither John Cooke nor Stephen Clingman makes enough of the conditioning factor of gender in Gordimer's novels, Newman sets out to show that: "In her novels, the interaction of private and public, the complex investigation of the connection between psychological and political, draws upon an awareness of the relation of genre to gender."[43] The essay by Judie Newman on *Burger's Daughter*, reprinted in this collection, is a "pilot version" of one of the chapters of her book.

Abdul R. JanMohamed's lengthy discussion of Gordimer in *Manichean Aesthetics: The Politics of Literature in Colonial Africa* (1983) has been influential in shaping attitudes towards her work in the context of colonialism and the issues affecting writers, both white and black, in a colonial milieu.[44] His section on *Occasion for Loving* is reprinted in this volume.

Special issues of major North American journals have been devoted to Gordimer. In 1984 there was a special Nadine Gordimer issue of *Salmagundi*,[45] from which the essay on *July's People* is reprinted in this volume. Unfortunately Robert Boyers's wide-ranging essay on *Burger's Daughter* as a political novel, also first published in the *Salmagundi* special issue, had to be omitted from this collection in the interests of space.[46] In 1988 *Ariel* devoted one issue to Gordimer;[47] Stephen Gray's essay on *A World of Strangers*, and Richard Peck's on *A Sport of Nature*, are reprinted from that special number.

The essays in this volume have been selected to suggest both the historical development of criticism dealing with Nadine Gordimer's writing and to offer "coverage" of most of her major works. Limitations of space made it impossible to include general articles on South African political attitudes—and Gordimer's place in them—of the kind written by Paul Rich;[48] and this is a lack. Furthermore, only two essays on Gordimer's treatment of women and women's roles are included, and this is an area of increasing critical attention, although Gordimer herself is wary about her appropriation by the feminist movement. A notable omission from this collection (again on grounds of space) is Elizabeth Gerver's "Women Revolutionaries in the Novels of Nadine Gordimer and Doris Lessing," published in *World Literature Written in English* in 1978.[49] Only one discussion of Gordimer's short stories is included, and that means that Martin Trump's "The Short Fiction of Nadine Gordimer"[50] has been omitted. In the same vein, only one essay by Judie Newman is included, which means that her much-quoted and influential piece on *The Conservationist*[51] is not in these pages. Finally, a stimulating recent discussion of *July's People* by Barbara Temple-Thurston[52] was omitted in favor of the editor's own, earlier comments.

As Nadine Gordimer continues to write both fiction and nonfiction, so will the range of comment about that writing continue to grow. There is a great deal written about her already. This Introduction has discussed some of the complexity of that response, particularly within South Africa, where her work is obviously of immediate relevance. The collection of essays that follows includes the best that has been written about her work since 1953, and in its range of contributors—from Africa, Australia, North America, and Europe—also illustrates the breadth of interest in one of the major novelists, in any language, writing today.

ROWLAND SMITH

Dalhousie University

Notes

1. Nadine Gordimer, "The Quest for Seen Gold," *Sunday Express* (Johannesburg), 13 June 1937, 38.

2. Nadine Gordimer, *Face to Face* (Johannesburg: Silver Leaf Books, 1949).

3. The William James Lecture, New York University Institute of the Humanities, 14 October 1982. Published in *New York Review of Books* 29 (20 January 1983), 21–22, 24–29.

4. Nadine Gordimer, *The Essential Gesture: Writing, Politics and Places*, edited and introduced by Stephen Clingman (London: Jonathan Cape, 1988), 5.

5. Ibid., 6.

6. Z. N., "The Politics of Commitment," *African Communist* 80 (1st quarter, 1980), 100.

7. Ibid., 100.

8. Ibid., 101.

9. Stephen Gray, "Gordimer's boldest bid for greatness," *Star* (Johannesburg), 29 November 1979, 22.

10. Dennis Brutus, "Protest Against Apartheid," in Cosmo Pieterse and Donald Munro, eds., *Protest and Conflict in African Literature* (London: Heinemann, 1969), 97.

11. This has been a fairly common reaction, but see particularly Bernard Levin, "Art Must Wait Until the End of the Struggle," *Sunday Times*, 5 April 1987. For an opposing view see Richard Peck's essay in this volume. See also Rowland Smith, "Leisure, Law and Loathing: Matrons, Mistresses, Mothers in the Fiction of Nadine Gordimer and Jillian Becker," *World Literature Written in English* 28 (Spring 1988): 41–51.

12. Ursula Laredo, "African Mosaic: The Novels of Nadine Gordimer," *Journal of Commonwealth Literature* 8 (June 1973): 44.

13. Ibid., 44.

14. Ibid., 45–46.

15. Christopher Hope, "Out of the Picture: The Novels of Nadine Gordimer," *London Magazine* (April/May 1975): 52–53.

16. *Star*, 5 September 1949.

17. L. R., "South African Writer," *Forum*, 17 September, 1949, 28.

18. Ibid., 29.

19. Lucy Bean, "Two Years to Write a Novel: Nadine Gordimer Is a Keen Observer," *Cape Argus,* 20 February 1954.

20. "Nadine Gordimer Novel For TV," *Star,* 17 September 1960.

21. " 'I'm Not So Observant,' Says Nadine: But Johannesburg Sees Itself in Her Book," *Star,* 11 July 1958, 15.

22. L. S., "An innocent in the townships," *Rand Daily Mail,* 26 June 1958.

23. Owen Williams, "A Fine South African Writer's Novel Misfires," *Contact* 1 (31 May 1958): 17.

24. Ibid., 17.

25. Mary Morrison Webster, "Gordimer's New Novel a Perceptive Study," *Sunday Times Magazine Section,* 7 April 1963, 4.

26. R. F. Haugh, *Nadine Gordimer* (New York: Twayne, 1974).

27. A. B. Hughes, "Conservationist Hard Going, But Rewarding," *Sunday Times Magazine,* 26 January 1975, 7.

28. Ibid., 7.

29. Stephen Gray, "Review of Gordimer Book Inept," *Sunday Times,* 16 February 1975.

30. S. M., "Gordimer Trumpets Her Own Virtues," *Star,* 23 November 1982, 16.

31. For another comment see Kenneth Parker, "Nadine Gordimer and the Pitfalls of Liberalism," in *The South African Novel in English,* ed. Kenneth Parker (New York: Africana, 1978), 114–30.

32. Nadine Gordimer, "A Sestiger for the Seventies," *Star,* 17 January 1969.

33. Michael Ratcliffe, "A South African Radical Exulting in Life's Chaotic Variety," *Times,* 29 November 1974.

34. Ray Smuts, "Paton Slams 'Ivory Tower' Gordimer," *Sunday Times* (Johannesburg), 1 December 1974, 12.

35. Caroline Clark, "Gordimer vs Paton," *Sunday Times,* 22 December 1974, 2.

36. "Author Agrees with Gordimer," *Rand Daily Mail,* 23 December 1974, 7.

37. Ray Smuts, "New Blow in 'Liberal' Row," *Sunday Times,* 29 December 1974, 7.

38. Carolyn McGibbon, "Top Writers in War of Words," *Sunday Star,* 6 November 1988, 22.

39. Michael Wade, *Nadine Gordimer* (London: Evans Brothers, 1978).

40. Jannika Hurwitt, "The Art of Fiction LXXVII: Nadine Gordimer," *Paris Review* 88 (Summer 1983): 83–127.

41. John Cooke, *The Novels of Nadine Gordimer: Private Lives/Public Landscapes* (Baton Rouge: Louisiana State University Press, 1985), 10.

42. Stephen Clingman, *The Novels of Nadine Gordimer: History from the inside* (London: Allen and Unwin, 1986).

43. Judie Newman, *Nadine Gordimer* (London and New York: Routledge, 1988), 17.

44. Abdul R. JanMohamed, *Manichean Aesthetics: The Politics of Literature in Colonial Africa* (Amherst: The University of Massachusetts Press, 1984).

45. *Salmagundi* 62 (Winter 1984).

46. Robert Boyers, "Public and Private: On *Burger's Daughter*," *Salmagundi* 62 (Winter 1984): 62–92.

47. *Ariel* 19 (October 1988).

48. Paul Rich, "Tradition and Revolt in South African Fiction: The Novels of Andre Brink, Nadine Gordimer, and J. M. Coetzee," *Journal of Southern African Studies,* 9 (October 1982): 54–73. Paul Rich, "Apartheid and the Decline of the Civilisation Idea: An Essay on Nadine Gordimer's *July's People* and J. M. Coetzee's *Waiting for the Barbarians,*" *Research in African Literatures* 15 (Fall 1984): 365–93.

49. Elizabeth Gerver, "Women Revolutionaries in the Novels of Nadine Gordimer and Doris Lessing," *World Literature Written in English* 17 (1978): 38–50.

50. Martin Trump, "The Short Fiction of Nadine Gordimer," *Research in African Literatures* 17 (Fall 1986): 341–69.

51. Judie Newman, "Gordimer's *The Conservationist:* 'That Book of Unknown Signs,' " *Critique: Studies in Modern Fiction* 22 (April 1981): 31–44.

52. Barbara Temple-Thurston, "Madam and Boy: A Relationship of Shame in Gordimer's *July's People,*" *World Literature Written in English* 28 (Spring 1988): 51–58.

Danger from the Digit:
The Soft Voice of the Serpent
Anthony Delius[°]

One turns with relief to Miss Nadine Gordimer's "The Soft Voice of the Serpent" (Gollancz), a revised English publication of the book of short stories published in the Union four years ago under the title "Face to Face." She is a professional writer in the class of Miss Lessing and Professor Butler. Her prose has both greater body and greater spirit than the novelist's and her imagery, in originality and aptness, is not far behind that of the poet. She is some way in advance of both in one great respect, she writes as one deeply interested in the uncatalogued humanity of human beings. Indeed the very furtiveness of Miss Gordimer's presentation of this crepuscular vivacity, its half-seen activities and stifled gestures, seems to be the author's comment on more explicit literary enthusiasms.

Her descriptions of the conception and growth of interior human incident have almost the quality of foetal development. Her language flickers and glints like some lymphatic fluid lying in the obscurities and cavities of some undergrowth of personalia. Even when her eye runs over the human exterior she has such exact attention for its remoter protuberances and depressions—notably armpits—that a fervent psycho-analyst might find it suggestive. Her style is to mass meticulous imagery and observation until the story ends in a swift emotional blow or the snapping of a tiny nerve or a dull disillusion. Throughout, her interest in the person or persons of her story is constant and unrelenting. But it is even more than this. She is as eager to get the reader to see the curious humanity of her people as Lewis Carroll was to introduce Alice to such strange and delightful creatures as the Mad Hatter, the Dormouse, Humpty-Dumpty or the White Knight.

A good example of Miss Gordimer's detailed interest in her characters and her aptness of image can be seen in her description of "The Watcher of the Dead":

> The synagogue sent an elderly gentleman who dwindled from
> a big stomach, outlined with a watch chain, to thin legs that ended

° From *Standpunte* 27 (April 1953):80–92. Reprinted by permission.

in neat, shabby brown shoes, supple with years of polishing. He wore glasses that made his brown eyes look very big, he had a small beard, and his face was pleasantly pink and planned in folds— a fold beneath each eye, another fold where the cheek skirted the mouth, a fold where the jaw met the neck, a fold where the neck met the collar. There was even a small fold beneath the lobe of each ear, as if the large, useful-looking ears had sagged under their own weight and usefulness over the years.

It can be seen again in the picture of Sarah in "Ah, Woe is Me":

Sarah worked for us before her legs got too bad. She was very fat, and her skin was a light yellow brown, as if, like a balloon that lightens in color as it is blown up, the fat swelling beneath the thin layer of pigment caused it so stretch and spread more and more sparsely. She wore delicate little gilt-rimmed spectacles and she was a good cook, though extravagant with butter.

The world Miss Gordimer conveys so precisely is that of those outcrops of urban development about the gold-pits of the Rand, those slightly shop-soiled coral isles of progress poking through the fathoms of veld from their financial seabed of basic reef. She is the delicate, quivering sea animal one finds so surprisingly beneath this hard, horny outer shell, building up her pearl in secret. The bare places with bare names like Bezuidenhout, Brakpan, Randfontein, Benoni and Jeppe conceal a life as subtle and as seeking as anywhere else, and Miss Gordimer has arisen to reveal its presence. Some of the human faults one notices more recurrently in these areas are also to be found in Miss Gordimer's writing. There is here and there a slightly spurious sophistication, a tendency to functional monotony and lack of grace, a hint of barren nervousness, and a faint female smugness. But they are only the irritating by-products of her great virtues as a writer, her inexhaustible thoughtfulness, her tireless effort to convey exact shadings and colourings of emotional discrepancy, her continuous exploration of nerve-paths, and her endless feminine sensitivity. This last quality is so overpoweringly omnipresent in Miss Gordimer's writings that even Virginia Woolf might be a little alarmed at it. It certainly makes Miss Lessing's writing look almost too masculine— perhaps, even, a comparison of this nature demonstrates a certain grave lack in Miss Lessing's equipment, not at first apparent. However, as Miss Gordimer continues to grow as a writer, I believe her faults will become, at any rate, less obvious, and her virtues will strengthen further, become sharper in expression and lose their tendency to sprawl through her work. As a matter of fact, in a quite brilliant story published in the February Forum, one of Miss Gordimer's latest, she shows already an astonishing advance in suggestive power and cleanliness of even the most delicate outlines—though perhaps her weakness for emotional irrelevance still persists.

Of course Miss Gordimer's very wealth of imagery and circuitous concentration lays traps for her. And she falls into them. Sometimes whole stories like "The Catch" and "The Talisman" read as if Miss Gordimer is laboriously trying to get out of the bottom of some game-pit of plot and style. "The Catch" is dull and long-winded, and "The Talisman" is pretentious. Even the more successful "Monday is Better Than Sunday" seems unnecessarily to labour a point. They are not in the same class as "The Defeated," "A Watcher of the Dead," "Present for a Good Girl," "Woe Is Me," and "The Train From Rhodesia." The following are examples of how wrong Miss Gordimer can go in her writing if she does not exercise iron discipline and economy:

> By the afternoon they had had enough of the beach, and wanted to play golf on the closely green course that mapped inland through the man-high cane as though a barber had run a pair of clippers through a fine head of hair, or to sit reading old hotel magazines on the porch whose windows were so bleared with salt air that looking through them was like seeing with the opaque eye of an old man.

> Out of her eyes, that seemed as if sleeping (I remembered her eyes that day at the florist's), life, the grip of living people on everyday things came and currented that quiet, inert body, long ago folded away into resignation like a set of neat faded clothes.

> She looked across at her lover. Head down, the stain of the sun beginning to show along the ridge of his nose, his was the tempered flesh of the *religieux*, who does not feel the gibes, jeers, or the silent mocking of the commonplace because he has too much faith to see even momentarily, his belief as others see it: simply one of a thousand crackpot cults from Jesus to Yogi.

All these sentences, in addition to being overbearing in their context, show a failure to judge both the most fitting colouring and the quantum of imagery that they could take. The final example demonstrates that above-mentioned sophistication, pretentiousness and laboriousness with which Miss Gordimer occasionally sets the reader's teeth on edge. This lack of judgment is only occasional, but evidence of it should not be allowed to remain after revision. In general it might be remarked that Miss Gordimer's stylistic problems are those of a very wealthy man who has to ration himself in defence of his own waist-line.

Nadine Gordimer:
The Transparent Ego
Lionel Abrahams[*]

Eleven or twelve years ago—far back enough for one not to be unduly fanciful in describing it as her literary début—Nadine Gordimer won a short story competition conducted by The *South African Opinion*. When the judges made their decision known the magazine's literary editor, Herman Bosman, telephoned to her home in Springs. Her mother took the call; Nadine was out, at the hairdresser's. Bosman took the hairdresser's number and telephoned there. So it happened that Nadine Gordimer came out from under a hair drier in order to hear this news.

The story bears telling because what it represents is importantly characteristic: Nadine Gordimer carrying on with the ordinary business of womanhood, while in the wide world her work commands excited attention.

The acclaim she has won can hardly have been paralleled for distinction and volume by that accorded to any other South African author. A consequence of this is that her writing is a source of income and she is able to make it her regular occupation. Her masterly prose bespeaks her art as a vocation in the religious sense. (Indeed, she tells me she began writing as a child and writing has been the one thing uninterruptedly present throughout her life.) But my impression is that she has made it also her vocation in the workaday sense— the job she carries out as steadily and unspectacularly as if it were just an ordinary business.

At any rate, her pursuit of it falls into place alongside what I call in no irreverent spirit the ordinary business of her womanhood— her functions as a mother and wife. She is Mrs. Reinhold Cassirer and has two of her own children and a stepchild. I have watched her making a custard for a baby's supper. I have met her in town when she was taking her little boy to the barber's and the dentist's. It is considerations of the effect upon the children of being brought up in a society dominated by racialistic ideas which may determine the family to settle in another country a few years hence, although she herself feels particular attachments to this soil.

This integration of the professional and domestic life is part of a pattern of containment. The excitement of Nadine's authorship is contained in her work. To follow the pattern further, her social intercourse is not marked by any vibrant creative overflow. Fresh, authoritative, precise and concrete as her conversation is, generous

[*] From *English Studies in Africa* 3 (September 1960):146–151. Reprinted by permission of the author.

and thought-provoking as are the things she says, she is not the commanding, transporting, memorable conversationalist one somehow expects (illegitimately, of course) an outstanding writer to be. She has no playfulness, no urgency, no drama, no theorizing, nothing risible, oracular, tentative or lyrical in her conversation. It is all meant, all straightforward and common-sensical. And apart from conversation, there is no marked personal efflorescence from this extremely neat, delicately turned, *petite* young woman. There is no aura, no special air, no pose or gesture.

I am bound to put in here two strokes that will score across the impression I have been sketching. There were, about eight years ago, four or five occasions on which I visited Nadine Gordimer in the company of a close friend of hers and mine with whom she shared particular literary enthusiasms—I remember Rilke, Lorca, Yeats, Virginia Woolf and, especially, Proust. I seemed each time to enter a world of heightened aesthetic meaning, a world in which things inanimate seemed to have fallen anew delicately into place. In truth, a little too delicately for me, *gauche* and ignorant as I was. I was a little intimidated in that world of fragile perfection. It was the world of Proust.

The second thing recalls the conference held some years ago on South African English writing. It was there that an intelligent and sensitive acquaintance of mine saw Nadine Gordimer and was completely overwhelmed by her looks. Days later he told me that he was still haunted by her face.

What lies behind the essential quietness and passivity of mien I have been trying to describe? My guess is a peculiarity in Nadine's make-up which I would describe as a transparency of the ego. It is a quality which I believe also conditions the character of her art to a great extent.

Mrs. Millin came to a session of that literary conference and delivered an address from the floor during which she declared: "I am bulk." Nadine did not speak once. (What strong evidence in support of my case this is: imagine how often the discussion must have touched upon her nearest interests during the three days.) Had it been possible for her to speak in Mrs. Millin's vein, I imagine her declaring: "I am light."

Hers is essentially an illuminating intelligence: its central function is to render visible, or be rendered visible by, the physical, social and emotional phenomena of experience. That, and not to impress upon the world the shape or even the lantern-slide shadow of a self. As in the case of Toby Hood, the narrator in her novel, *A World of Strangers* (whom I see as Nadine's portrait of the writer as a young man), the slide of her ego is almost blank. Toby has no commitments, no prejudices or illusions, no passionate convictions, no abiding desires: there is hardly more to him than his intelligence, quiet curiosity and readiness to partake. He is not a hero, directing, acting upon life, but a spectator, who is acted upon.

It is this that in my view accounts for the weakness of this novel despite its brilliant ideas and splendid writing, for Toby is the only link in the plot between various parts of the book. As a result it is something of a satirical social travelogue of Johannesburg. It lacks an emotional structure.

In Nadine Gordimer's case the more or less expunged ego is a source of powers and limitations. The magic lantern becomes a search-light—one with x-ray properties. You do not get fantasies, romances, metaphysical projections, jokes or *bobba meises* in her writings. Their substance is phenomena, facts, things as they are. For accuracy, minuteness and sensitivity I do not think her recording of experience is surpassed in modern literature: I cannot see how it could be improved on. The richness which makes art of this recording is largely the result of her comments in which she groups and compares particles of experience. The drama which makes fiction of this art is hardly ever the result of action—a movement through time—but usually the result of a penetration through emotional space—the poignant revelation of "the reality behind the reality" (to adapt a phrase of Uys Krige's).

Mention of the lack of movement through time (the concern with the states rather than the processes of experience) brings me face to face with a paradox. Notwithstanding what I have said about the transparency of Nadine Gordimer's ego, it is also true that she is present in her own guise, or in that of a narrator who is not a "character," just about constantly in all her writings. Every incident or part of an incident in the narrative is hedged about with comments, explanations, the adjustments of getting the facts into focus. The result is that the flow of time is frozen and shattered into the moments which are peculiarly this writer's *métier*. That is why she is best at short stories. And at this stage of her development plays are com-pletely beyond her range, as she said during her enthusiastic com-mendation of *Summer of the Seventeenth Doll:* that was the sort of play she would write, she felt, if she could manage the form.

To go still further in contradiction of my "transparent ego" idea, this constant overt presence of the writer in the writings results in the more or less overt communication of the writer's attitudes to her subjects. Let me be sweeping: broadly Nadine Gordimer's work expresses two mutually contradictory attitudes to life: compassion and cynicism. There is a rough division according to time. In her earlier stories, collected as *The Soft Voice of the Serpent,* and her first novel, *The Lying Days,* compassion predominates. But some of the stories in *Six Feet of the Country,* and many parts of *A World of*

Strangers set my teeth on edge with their unlaughing satire. The more important division is according to subject-matter. Toby Hood says: "I hate the faces of peasants," but it is for the equivalent of peasants in Nadine Gordimer's world that she has expressed her compassion: the immigrant Mr. and Mrs. Chaitowitz in her magnificent story *The Defeated*, the old derelict, van As, in *The Last Kiss*. Generally the people with whom she can more readily identify herself socially bring out her cynicism.

To this extent Nadine Gordimer seems to be emotionally wielded, that is, she regards her characters with a sort of automatic sympathy or antipathy according merely to the socio-economic classes to which they belong. To disprove the romantic notion of the artist's dependence on "experience" she once cited the case of Jane Austen who managed so admirably without "experience." But precisely where Miss Gordimer is constrained Jane Austen is free—free to make us respond to things according to the needs of her artistic concepts, instead of being committed to either patience or scorn according to mere external categories. Miss Gordimer, on the other hand, is either warmed or chilled, sweetened or soured, opened or closed, by whatever scene she confronts, before her imagination can begin to come to grips with it. And since the subjects that elicit the best in her seem to be those she encounters some distance out of the way of her daily life, she has something like a duty to do a kind of adventuring, a hunting of "experience." (Questions about the value of "experience" are, indeed, implicit in several of her newer stories, *A Style of Her Own*, for example, and more pertinently, *The Gentle Art*, which tells of two women, one of whom enthusiastically accompanies the men on a crocodile hunt while the other is content to wait in camp for their return, to the complete mystification of the first.)

There are some signs in *Friday's Footprint*, Miss Gordimer's newest volume (which includes "A Style of Her Own," "The Gentle Art" and "The Last Kiss"), that she may be drawing herself free from the emotional wielding I have described. In the longest piece, "An Image of Success," she approaches as near as she ever has to tragedy: at least she provides the first prerequisite of tragedy, a hero who elicits admiration (however qualified) and sympathy (however mixed). And this Mr. Butters is by no means of the "peasantry."

That hair drier I mentioned at the start—its shape also is significant: reminiscent as it is of a cocoon. The other day Nadine and I chatted a good bit about the idea of being closed in, and about cocoons. Someone growing up in a country like this had a whole series of cocoons to break out of, she said: cultural, racial and so on. She herself had broken out of the cultural cocoon relatively early, forced to it by another sort of confinement: that due to her years of seclusion in childhood and early adolescence, during which her energies turned to "the exploration of self." (Interestingly, she explained that by this phrase she did not mean "contemplating the navel" but reading, listening to music, and so on.)

As I see it, those years of removal from much of the rough-and-tumble of ordinary contacts with the resultant blunting and vulgarization of perception, accounts largely for the sensitivity, keenness and fastidiousness of Nadine's literary eye. She remarked that the ways of seeing we acquire in our youth remain with us always.

What of cocoons to-day? *A World of Strangers* and much of *Six Feet of the Country* give me the impression of emanating from inside a social cocoon. There are very important glimpses of the faces of peasants through the chrysalis wall, but chiefly we have an exposé of the futility, narrowness and selfishness of fashionable people. Is it significant that for the setting of *The Last Kiss,* a recent story, she returned to the East Rand of her youth? Is it that she feels that for what she has to express, the aspects of contemporary Johannesburg life she has been exploiting have become effete—that the cocoon is outgrown? Are we going soon to see an even more startling emergence than we have seen so far? I believe it is likely.

But this important change which seems to be in process does not mean that Nadine Gordimer will have done with cocoons. That, I fancy, will not come yet a while, if ever. Another story in *Friday's Footprint,* called "Check Yes or No," makes a curiously direct acknowledgement of the ineluctability of the cocoon. In the striking final passage the protagonist makes a crucial identification between herself and a circus performer who walks a tight-wire completely enclosed in a bag. If I am not quite wrong to add so personal a dimension to the meaning of this symbolism, I am still unable to suggest precisely what form of limitation it is that Miss Gordimer is here, temporarily at least, resigning herself to. I only feel sure that it is not the same grave shortcoming that showed so clearly in *A World of Strangers* and *Six Feet of the Country.* For recognizing herself in the perilously enclosed artiste restores to Phoebe van der Camp her human balance, and suddenly she is able to extend sympathy to both the peasant-like stranger on one side of her, and her husband—essentially, eminently presentable, for all his having humiliatingly faltered—on the other.

I have not had space to comment on Nadine's lively interest in contemporary affairs, on her liberal views and on the other manifestations of her generosity from which I have several times benefited. It must suffice to note that a cocoon is not an ivory tower.

Withering into the Truth:
The Romantic Realism of
Nadine Gordimer
Alan Lomberg°

Nadine Gordimer has acknowledged that the two writers who have influenced her most profoundly have been Forster and Camus.[1] It is possible to see many similarities in approach and ideas between herself and her "mentors." Her description of herself as someone with "no religion, no political dogma . . ."[2] together with her obvious concern for human relationships in all of her work, bears much resemblance to Forster's statement of his position in "What I Believe."[3] The strain of skepticism is something she shares with both Forster and Camus and, like both of them, she rejects any schematic explanation of man's situation in the world. Her sense of her role as a writer, and her artistic integrity lead her to side with Camus against Sartre in the belief that one cannot put one's writing "at the service of a cause."[4]

There are even many details in the work of Nadine Gordimer which provide echoes of both Forster and Camus. Several of the attitudes of whites towards blacks in *A Guest of Honour* (Mrs. Pilchey's, those of the customers in the Fisheagle Bar) sound little different from the opinions of such people as Callendar and the Turtons in *A Passage to India*. Forster's "early novels" are referred to in *A World of Strangers*, and Toby Hood's reference to "girls . . . whose lives are changed irrevocably after being spectator to an Italian quarrel in an Italian square," relates to his own expectation of "the face or the street-fight" round "some corner, some day" that would do as his "destiny."[5] A number of ideas in Camus' *The Fall* appear in Gordimer's works: the distinction between surface and reality in Jessie Stilwell's life in *Occasion for Loving*.[6] Max's attack on the guilt-assuaging "charity" of certain whites in *The Late Bourgeois World*.[7] One even finds lines which are close to direct translations: Clamence says, "after a certain age every man is responsible for his face," and Ann sees Jessie as "a woman whose face was beginning to take on the shape of the thoughts and emotions she had lived through."[8]

But nobody, certainly no writer of genuine ability, simply borrows mechanically from other writers and thinkers; and it seems unlikely that a writer will draw for inspiration or instruction upon those with whom she does not feel herself already in sympathy; there must be some predisposition, some sense of intellectual, moral, emotional kinship which establishes the sort of personal literary tradition by which Forster and Camus become Gordimer's chief influences. Some

° From *English in Africa* 3 (March 1976):1–12. Reprinted by permission.

of the qualities which link them have already been suggested. But, whatever the similarities, and however many the received insights, she has a clear view of her own purpose and place apart from them. She expresses a common artistic fact in saying that one outgrows "influences" as one outgrows friends; and that even those writers who influence one "profoundly, for ever" disappear within one and become "something new" of one's "own."[9]

Gordimer believes that a writer's purpose is to convey to a reader "what sense" she "makes of life," and therefore to address herself to the question, "What is the life of man?"[10] But she points out that in Africa, including South Africa, a writer cannot do away with "Balzacian detail" as critics like Nathalie Sarraute demanded, because:

> In South Africa, in Africa generally, the reader knows perilously little about himself or his feelings. We have a great deal to learn about ourselves, and the novelist, along with the poet, composer and painter, must teach us.[11]

Nadine Gordimer's first four novels attempt to do just that with regard to South Africa, as *A Guest of Honour* does in a much larger setting. But, as any writer of perception comes to gain applicability beyond the confines of her own country, so Gordimer, in exploring so meticulously the quality of life in South Africa, reaches out to certain basic human concerns: how to live fully in a world in which prejudice, political pressures, and restrictive social conventions channel and constrict life. In the process of exploring this general theme, she touches upon many small qualities of life through which she suggests the range and scope of human feeling and awareness, a range and scope that are always in danger of being limited, even eroded by restrictive and repressive forces.

In her first novel, *The Lying Days*,[12] Nadine Gordimer established a pattern which all the other novels were to follow; it has particular applicability to that *Bildungsroman*, but it signifies a process inherent in her overall vision of life, and is reinforced by her style, which embraces two large principles that, in simple terms, one can call particularising and generalising. The former involves a capacity for microscopic observations of human behaviour, the latter the capacity for discerning general features and principles objectively, and from a distance. The former is allied to a remarkable sensitivity which can capture a nuance of gesture, a shade of feeling; the latter proceeds from an analytic perceptiveness which can succinctly remark the general features which characterise an individual, or descry the larger principles manifested in specific instances.

This bi-polarity of style is a reflection of a bi-polar vision. Fifteen years ago, Lionel Abrahams suggested that Nadine Gordimer's approach combined "two mutually contradictory attitudes to life: compassion and cynicism."[13] Like Machiavellianism, cynicism is a term which has acquired, exclusively, its pejorative connotation. For that reason, I prefer Gordimer's own description of herself as a "romantic-realist."[14] The hyphen unites what, properly seen, are "complementarities" (to borrow a term from I. A. Richards), not "mutually contradictory attitudes." And the effect of the interplay between these "complementarities" is to make of each of the novels an example of withering into the truth; and, while the "romantic" vision withers before the cold eye of "realist" appraisal, it becomes clear that an entirely romantic interpretation would be as false as an entirely realist vision would be brutal. This recognition of life as a continual interaction between the envisioned hope and the encountered possibilities which qualify that hope is an expression of devout agnosticism.

The bi-polarities of vision and style are applied to the constant themes of life, love and the pursuit of truth; life against the forces that seek to restrict it and to prevent one from living fully. The first restrictions come in the form of parental attitudes and values, representing those of society at large. To live, one must test those attitudes and values against one's own experience; to grow, one must be open to experience, and must extract from it the truths which will form the basis of one's own attitudes and values. What matters most in life is the living of it; personal relationships matter; and we become fully human "according to the measure in which we have loved people and have had occasion for loving."[15] Sex is part of love, and is, Liz van den Sandt claims in *The Late Bourgeois World*, "the defining need of our youth" (p. 12). There is also an "inner" life which reflects "the true graph of experience,"[16] and which may bear little relation to the exterior series of events by which other people sum up one's life. The changes which take place in people come about as the result of a process which is "a long, slow mutation of emotion," not as a result of "the conscious changes made in their lives by men and women."[17] And, in the final analysis, the "real doubters," those who look honestly at life, as opposed to the "consolation-seekers,"[18] are forced to acknowledge that the true "state of life" is that in which one can "never hope to be free of doubt, of contradictions within;"[19] to which acknowledgement is added the realisation that every life has repercussions, that what we do "goes on making . . . new combinations" even after we are dead, and that death thus becomes "an interruption."[20]

Having dealt in very sweeping terms with general aspects of theme and style, it is necessary to demonstrate their development in the novels. I propose to consider the novels chronologically in the hope of revealing not only the persistence of certain thematic concerns and stylistic devices, but their growth and adaptation. A sense of that growth and change may be gained simply by setting down a selection of the super-scriptions to the novels:[21] "Through all the lying days of my youth, / I swayed my leaves and flowers in the sun, / Now I may wither into the truth;" "I want the strong air of the most profound night / to remove flowers and letters from the arch where you sleep / and a black boy to announce to the gold-minded whites / the arrival of the reign of the ear of corn;" "We have all become people according to the measure in which we have loved people and had occasion for loving." "There are possibilities for me, certainly; but under what stone do they lie?" "An honourable man will end by not knowing where to live." There is a devolution from confidence and affirmation to uncertainty and near-despair. As that sense of assurance in the possibilities for the realisation of liberal ideals decreases, artistic assurance and control increases.

In *The Lying Days* Gordimer treats growth from adolescence to young adulthood. The stages of Helen Shaw's development are revealed through a series of personal relationships, each of which marks a stage of emotional and intellectual, cultural and political growth, a growth by which the heroine moves from complete dependence on her parents, through increasing conflict with them, to complete independence. The seeds of all of this are contained in the first chapter of the novel; and, significantly, the first incident in the novel is an act of rebellion on Helen's part. Equally important is the fact that, after her parents have gone off to their tennis match, Helen embarks on an exploration of her physical surroundings, an exploration that is later paralleled by her first gropings into the world of love with Ludi, her subsequent venture into the world of books and ideas with Joel, and finally by her relationship with Paul, which involves her in life more fully than any of the other explorations.

If the walk to the tennis courts may be seen to prefigure Helen's growth to independence of attitude—a determination to look at the world herself and make her own judgements about it—the walk also reveals her extraordinary sensitivity to the world around her. It is as a result of that kind of sensitivity and alertness, and as a result of fidelity to the teachings of experience thus gained that one comes to rebel against a world which substitutes "rules for the pull and stress of human conflict which are the true conditions of life" (p. 218). Helen's distance from the world of her parents—the world of the Mine—is first suggested by her inability to find some image by which to conjure up that world. It is later expressed more explicitly:

> I understood that almost all of my life at home, on the Mine, had been like that, conducted on a surface of polite triviality that was insensitive to the real flow of life that was being experienced, underneath, all the time, by everybody. (p. 62)

The idea—adapted, expanded, refined—occurs again and again

in Nadine Gordimer's work. The barely visible metaphor in the passage is also significant. One could patly ascribe the persistent appearance of the sea in Gordimer's work to a reflection of the condition of a people who, having trekked inwards, repeatedly look back to the expansive waters from which they first came, and of course one could carry it back further still. But the significance is not only a general one, for *The Lying Days* is built upon a pattern of water imagery linked, by an underlying notion of rhythm, to music and the blood.

The choice of imagery is apt in so far as it suggests the fluidity of Helen Shaw's state of being as she moves from early adolescence to early adulthood. And the pattern of imagery is developed in the first chapter of the novel in much the same way as are the thematic concerns. During the course of her walk, Helen trails her fingers along a fence and they rise and fall over the corrugations "in an arpeggio of movement." Immediately after this, she thinks "of water" and the paragraph goes on to establish a rhythmic association between music, water and blood (p. 6). Blood and water are again connected in Helen's reflection on qualities inherited from her mother: the blood from her mother "ran narrowly" and drained off the "real torrents" into "neat ditches" (p. 272). Here we have again the opposition between a view of life which responds to its true flow—to the real movement of thought, feeling, experience—and an opposing one in which the true flow is drained of its energy and freshness by being constricted, and channelled into "domestic and social habit."

Water is also associated with Helen's increasing experience of love and sex, which begins to develop in her relationship with Ludi. The two of them swim almost incessantly, and she goes into the sea as if plunging repeatedly into the new world of emotions which is washing over her. There are many later references, as well, to the sea and water. Helen speaks of herself as "one of those women . . . who drown in sleep" (p. 190). More significantly, the way in which she describes her first reaction to Paul, with whom she has her fullest and most passionate love affair, is also in terms of water:

> It gave me a kind of simple sensual pride to understand out of experience the flow of this current. To wait till it should take me up again; till I should lay myself down Ophelia-like, and be carried by it. (p. 199)

This passage, together with a later one in which she speaks of the inability of Paul and herself to resist a sudden desire for sex as being like the inability of a salmon to resist its "death leap upstream" (p. 215), introduces a new element: a trinity of sea, sex and death is established; and, as the sea suggested a certain kind of life, and has become linked with sex and the flow of emotion, so also sex and death have become linked through the sea. In this particular instance the point is clear enough: the flow and movement of emotion is not only spontaneous, like the flow of water in its natural state, but there is an elemental force to it which drives to a conclusion as inevitable as death, a force so powerful that it renders one oblivious to the conclusion, however final that may be.

Something of the same instinctiveness, the suggestion that instinctive impulses still play a considerable part in the lives of people, is found in the animal imagery of *A World of Strangers*. But the use of such imagery also serves as a comment on that novel's narrator, Toby Hood. This is made clear through the repulsive tick-bird metaphor which he uses to characterise the relationship between "victims" of injustice and their "champions" (p. 32). His attempt to appear ingenuous—"Do I sound sneering? I don't mean to be"—at the end of his snide exposition is an instance of the author's distancing of herself from her narrators. The passage as a whole helps to fix the nature of this particular narrator. It is reflected in his repeated use of similes involving animals: a man moving out onto a balcony is spoken of as "looking out into the evening like a horse put out to grass after a day's carting" (p. 80); and the fondling of a girl by a young man is likened to "the impersonal, momentary, instinctive recall to sex with which a dog will briefly lick, once or twice, another dog" (p. 56). One culmination of this imagery is the hunt which takes place towards the end of the novel; but a careful reading of the imagery also indicates the varying degree of approval or disapproval with which Toby looks at the other characters. Anna Louw has the "neat head of a tiny bird" (p. 70), while Kit Baxter's homemaking is spoken of in terms of a nesting instinct (p. 59), and the Alexanders' pool is as lively as "the seal enclosure at the zoo" (p. 189)—a comparison which seems purely frolicsome at first, but, on reflection, appears less than kind. By contrast, Helen Shaw in *The Lying Days* would liken a series of "movements and gasps of laughter" to the "commotion of swimmers rubbing themselves down" (p. 17), or her dabbling in books to the sort of interest displayed by "a child playing in the ripples at the water's edge" (p. 89). The imagery is different, the use of similes is persistent.

The simile is one of the distinctive features of Gordimer's style, particularly in the first two novels. It is used to convey attitude, capture a particular flavour, suggest a nuance of meaning, a shade of feeling; it is also used to pin things down precisely. Indeed, there is a tendency to define, to "fix in a formulating phrase" in both of these novels. There is also a tendency to capture more complex things—the atmosphere of a place, the distinguishing characteristics of a group of people, or the association of a series of ideas—by employing the burgeoning Jamesian sentence, with its multiple clauses and qualifiers, such as the one defining the situation of liberals in South Africa.

Structurally, both *The Lying Days* and *A World of Strangers* follow a movement from passages of action and experience to ones of reflection and analysis. This aspect of the structure underlines the concern to extract truths from experience. It is most noticeable in the second novel which is built around a series of social gatherings, with Toby Hood moving as an observer from group to group, and eventually finding himself becoming increasingly attached to a representative of each of the groups until he is forced to realise that he can no longer enjoy the "private liver's" freedom of movement, and must give up the "safe conduct of the open mind" (pp. 122–23)— the mental passport which allows the "private liver" to form his friendships without regard to social "right" or "wrong" and to treat people simply as people.

After the experience of any one of the parties, Toby withdraws into contemplation and analysis. This overall pattern—the movement from particular experiences to generalised judgements—is a reflection of the bi-polar treatment and vision: minutely detailed observation is balanced by analytic generalisation. A good example of this, in *The Lying Days*, is provided by the description of Helen's transferring all her consciousness into her dangling hand as she walks with Ludi on the beach:

> All my being was concentrated in my left hand, which hung beside him as he walked. My whole body was poured into that hand as I waited for him to take it. It seemed to me that he must take it. . . .
> (p. 50)

The particular incident related here, with its passionate expectation, the disproportionate importance placed on that dangling hand, is later gathered into a generalisation:

> Nothing is more serious than this apparently laughable lack of the sense of proportion in the young. With the command of emotions like a stock of dangerous drugs suddenly to hand, there is no knowing from experience how little or how much will do; one will pitifully scald one's heart over nothing. The nothing may be laughable, but the pain is not. (p. 60)

Several particular incidents, several moments of disproportionate ascription of importance to things, have been drawn together, and a general truth about them has been formed.

The acuteness of sensitivity and the capacity for forming general judgements come together in those observations which attempt to capture something frequently and unconsciously noted, but never before articulated, such as "the knowledgeable eagerness with which people love to impart information of which they themselves were ignorant until a few moments before."[22] The nature and frequency of such observations in Gordimer's work suggests the importance of daily life, of the life of the emotions and human relationships, the range and subtlety of which the observations reflect and measure. The same tendency, however, when it is operating through detailed descriptions, is often in danger of a wordiness which smothers the content, as an early reviewer pointed out, citing an especially congealed passage in *A World of Strangers*.[23] Similarly, the drive to define, to order, to capture precisely, tends at times to undermine the vision of life which is opposed to its constriction and limitation.

In the third and fourth novels there is less tendency to make definitive pronouncements. Rather, the style is made to suggest, to create more blurred emotional settings. This is chiefly notable in the use of symbols and allusive imagery, which are necessary for the treatment of life in those novels. Where *The Lying Days* can be used to illustrate life as rebellion against one's parents, and the stages by which a young person comes to discover and establish a way of life for herself; and where *A World of Strangers* provides an illustration of the frustrations of a "private liver" attempting to maintain the "safe conduct of the open mind" in a world which demands commitment, *Occasion for Loving* gives us an insight into the "inner" world in which the "true graph of experience" is plotted.

In order to convey that "inner" world, to cope with the musings and reminiscences of Jessie Stilwell, the more allusive style is obviously essential. The very opening pages of *Occasion for Loving* indicate the change in style. Jessie's "inner hum of empathy with the plants," the fact that she "had never been out of the garden" (p. 3), and the whole way in which the garden is related to her, establish a symbolic significance. In addition, levels of "consciousness" are referred to, Jessie and her husband Tom are figured as "two boats, rocking gently on the same evening water" (p. 5), and the narrative slides, without warning, from the inner world of Jessie's thoughts to the actual world of events. Lines of dialogue break into Jessie's musings, but are only slowly allowed to assert the present and external world of the conversation she is having with her husband, eventually made clear in, "All at once, she spoke up out of herself" (p. 6).

Jessie's movement from one "level of consciousness" to another, or from one "world" to another, is not only revealed in embodied reconstructions, but through the generalised statement—"She scrambled back to the level of half-truths on which daily life is conducted" (p. 6), or "it restored her to the surface facts of life" (p. 34). These more generalized statements, as distinct from the specific instances, indicate the continued operation of the double approach. And there are still generalisations of the type found in the first two novels—

"Like all statements of a stand, reiteration tended to make it smug and rhetorical" (p. 8)—but they are fewer, and less indicative of the style of the novel than the association of symbols with characters; with Jessie we associate the garden, with Ann Davis, birds.

There are generalised comments about Jessie and the garden—such as the distinction drawn between her apprehension of it and the way in which Tom "showed her the garden"—but the most potent connections are those which suggest a response, but do not pin it down in abstract terms:

> She stared down at the dark and forgot herself. Under the plastered, hammered earth there was a fecund stirring in the old garden. Under stones, out of decay, sticky wings, moving jaws, feeble millipede wavings—they were all coming back to hunger and re-production. . . . (p. 17)

The "stirring" in the garden is an analogy for the restless move-ments troubling that other "garden" which is the milieu of Jessie's inner life. And the half-conscious sense of identity with the primal forces of life which is intimated here, recurs when, at the sea, Jessie feels a sense of communication with the porpoises, an instinctive knowledge of their presence (p. 199).

Although the creature is never mentioned, Jessie's burrowing into her past is aptly figured in terms of a mole: she moves "down there . . . in the dark" (p. 67). Ann Davis, by contrast, always concerned with the present, is a creature of the air: her "questions and comments darted like swallows" (p. 31); she responds to Gideon with a "laugh that is as female as the special note that birds find when they call to their young" (p. 103); and her brief pauses between periods of frenetic activity are like the action of a "bird balancing a moment on a telephone wire" (p. 107). This figuring of Ann in terms of birds finds its culmination in the "bat" metaphor, which she herself uses, and which is used by Tom about her (pp. 169, 301). The impulsiveness of the creature, and its blindness (in terms of normal human vision) convey perfectly the essence of Ann's nature.

The structure of *Occasion for Loving* serves to emphasise one of the themes of the novel—that there is an inner life to which not even the closest friends or relatives might be privy. Several different perspectives are provided—Jessie's, Ann's, that of the independent narrator—and the juxtaposition of certain chapters strikingly em-phasizes the importance of those perspectives. Chapters 6 and 7, and 16 and 17, for example retrace in the second chapter of each pair the time span covered in the first. The former pair provides the better illustration since Jessie's startled realisation at the end of Chapter 6 that Ann and Gideon are "lovers" comes against the background of Ann and Jessie's having lived together all the time.

Jessie's shock at the discovery is indicative of the extent to which something major has been developing of which she, preoccupied with her own affairs, has been quite unaware. Chapter 7 makes this clear by covering the same period from Ann's point of view. The contrast between the events selected in the two chapters demonstrates the extent to which two lives, lived largely together, can still be so much apart; it is also indicative of the differences between Jessie's approach to life and Ann's.

The retracing, and the shifting perspectives also allow for a slower and fuller development of a few characters, by contrast with the first two novels in which there was a fuller treatment of social portraits and a large number of characters who, like Toby Hood's secretary, Miss McCann, were quickly and briefly depicted. In *Occasion for Loving* even a relatively minor character like Jessie's son Morgan is gradually revealed and grows to a fullness of identity through a progressive unfolding of character, rather than being revealed in a definitive summary which is subsequently exemplified in a few periods of action.

The gradual revelation of character is paralleled by a similar revelation of the meaning of certain recollections or reactions, a meaning which emerges only when the original incident or response has become little more than a dim memory. One example of this is Jessie's eventual explanation of the fear of someone coming up behind her; that explanation comes two hundred pages after the fear is first mentioned (pp. 70, 276). Another example is Tom's flinching reaction to a bright, cheerful reply of Ann's. The reaction, which seems slightly odd at the time, only comes to full articulation at the end of the book when he gives his final judgement about Ann and about Jessie's influence on her relationship with Gideon (pp. 300–301). That judgement is the product of a series of glimpses of Tom's feelings about Ann, which work by implication, and develop by accretion, suggesting a similarity to the process of the "long, slow mutation of emotion" by which people's lives change.

In *The Late Bourgeois World*, there is again gradual revelation of character, a reappearance of the notion that whole areas of people's lives may be hidden even from those close to them, and the use again of more than one perspective on events. In this fourth novel, however, we have the shifting perspective of a single consciousness, viewing the same people and events from different starting points. Liz van den Sandt reveals her former husband, Max, to us in a narrative which largely retraces the same ground several times, defending Max, attacking Max, and revealing the narrator at the same time. The allusive technique developed in the previous novel is again at work here, but tone is far more important and intimations which might have been conveyed through image or symbol in *Occasion for*

Loving must here be sought in the very language, in the meticulous phrasing by which the author is able to depict the narrator through her own narration.

Perhaps the most distinctive feature of the narrative is the defensive tone in which so many of Liz van den Sandt's statements are couched. She declines having dinner with her lover, Graham Mill, on the grounds that "there's some damned dinner party," and then gives us his reaction:

> He's not a child, he's forty-six, and he took up his cigarettes and car keys without pique. But as he was leaving the flat I was the one who said. . . . (p. 8)

Clearly, the significance of the passage lies, not in the ostensible description of the man's reaction, but the implied feelings of the woman: guilt at the half-truth with which she has fobbed him off, and which necessitates some gesture to attempt to restore faith between them; hence the "but" and the emphasis thrown onto "I". And this type of statement, with its obliqueness and hidden implications, is indicative of the aura of frayed nerve-endings which pervades *The Late Bourgeois World.* It is revealed in Liz's defensive tone, in her tendency to rhetoric, a tendency to throw questions at the invisible listener of her conversations. "Max wasn't anybody's hero," she says at one point, but immediately after that comes the rhetorical question which develops into an accusation: "and yet, who knows?" And the end of the paragraph, despite the ostensibly speculative quality given to it by the use of the subjunctive, is in fact a bitter taunt: "He may have been just the sort of hero we should expect" (p. 21). The rhetorical question, with its implied defensiveness, appears again and again to cover up the contradiction of Graham's being a committed liberal but "living white," to challenge the "listener" to say why certain types of relationships shouldn't be considered forms of "love," to indicate her unwillingness to inspect her feelings too closely, as in her "toing-and-froing" about her real feelings for Luke Fokase.

The counterpoint to the rhetorical questions—sometimes lurking beneath their sarcasm and near-hysteria—is the genuine probing after the meaning of life and love, the former expressed through the active rebellion which carries Max eventually to the bottom of the sea, by the sort of ambition and aspiration which has placed men on the moon, and by the assumptions that lie beneath the preservation of Liz's grandmother in a nursing home; while love can be presented as any one of several "definitions" that are "neither more nor less acceptable" than Max's desire for approval (p. 60). A parallel counterpointing exists in the progression of activities which comprise the actual content of Liz's life and the brief span of actual time in the novel, set against the circling motion of recollections which traverse remembered time. The combination produces an effect of spiralling which slowly narrows to the conclusive alternatives represented by the tick-tock of Liz's heart beats: "afraid, alive, afraid, alive" (p. 120)—evasion or participation; to be or not to be; to act or not to act. All the questioning and probing has been reduced to this.

The flow of life over the course of the first four novels slowly narrows until it contracts almost to the throttling point; from the relatively hopeful exploration of life in the first novels there has eventually emerged the bleak, bitter, agonized "mindscape" of *The Late Bourgeois World. A Guest of Honour* opens up the possibilities again in the context of the joyful sense of freedom which the achievement of independence brings to an African state. The sense of constriction, of uncertainty, hesitation, fearfulness which characterised its predecessor is swept away at the beginning of the fifth novel by scenes of celebration and a sense of variety which foreshadows the vast portrait upon which the novel is embarking.

Far larger in scope, and much more complex in its interwoven plot and subplots than all its predecessors, *A Guest of Honour* addresses itself to the educational, economic, legal and moral questions involved in the formation of a policy by which the newly independent state is to be developed. The scope of the novel is evident not only in the treatment of these issues on the level of debate as well as through exemplification in individual lives, but also through the immense range of characters, reflecting the international hodge-podge of advisors and assistants frequently found in newly-independent African countries, and, in addition, the many levels of African society as well. The effect of these latter portraits is to create a more balanced picture than the one provided of South African society in the earlier novels; the numerous characters also give the novel some of its epic quality, the feeling of a vast span of life being inspected.

Richer in the feeling of life created, and more wide-ranging in its treatment of political theory, *A Guest of Honour* yet retains many of the qualities and techniques of the earlier novels. The creation of place through a series of evocative and definitive images—whether features of vegetation, some conglomeration of manufactured objects, or characteristic actions and gestures on the part of people—is particularly well illustrated by Bray's picture of the teeming life of the capital, and into that picture Nadine Gordimer deftly introduces a bit of foreshadowing, so unobtrusive that it almost passes unnoticed. After recording a vibrant bustle of laughing, calling, arguing people, we have:

An advertising jingle from a transistor radio held intimately to a young man's ear as he walked, rose and tailed off through the people. (p. 39)

It is an intimation of coming change—interest not in people and what they are doing, but in the radio with its commercial message. This illustration may serve both as an example of the density of texture of the novel, and also as an indication of the persistent Gordimer concern with those changes in the quality of daily life which tend to pass unnoticed in the midst of the large ideas and slogans which we usually take as the definitions of social change.

A *Guest of Honour* affirms again, through the relationship between its hero, Bray, and his lover Rebecca Edwards, the importance of the private life made up of personal relationships; and the central conflict of the novel touches upon that as well, for Bray is beleaguered precisely because of his close friendship with the opposing figures of Mweta, the president, and Shinza, the old fighter for independence. In his choice of sexual freedom with Rebecca rather than fidelity to his distant wife Olivia, as in his choice of political freedom in his support of Shinza, Bray draws together ideas which have been developing all through the novels and which came together in Jessie Stilwell's reflections on de Chardin in *Occasion for Loving*. Though lengthy, the passage is worth quoting in full. Its affirmation of fidelity to one's experience, and of intellectual integrity and moral responsibility is central to Gordimer's ideas. Speaking of *The Phenomenon of Man*, Jessie says it was:

> A book that, that year, people were reading who, without distinctions of worth, had last year read interpretations of Buddhism, and the year before Simone Weil, or Ouspensky. They were read, quite often, in the same half-secret, deprecating way in which the same people, when they were twenty, had read treatises on sex *(The Function of the Orgasm)*, for people between thirty and forty tend to have towards the meaning of their existence the anxious, suppressed urgency which at twenty they felt about sex. The real doubters and the mere consolation-seekers often go to the same sources; and it is the consolation-seekers who usually find something that will serve them—and if they do not, go on to another and yet another source, finding consolation in the activity of the search if nothing else. The real doubters include those for whom politics has gone as deep as sex, but the consolation-seekers are not intelligent enough to have sought any kind of discipline outside themselves; they have never wanted to change the world: only to get their sweet lick. (p. 205)

The passage clearly equates "real doubter" with "genuine seeker after truth." It is not enough to seek knowledge and experience; one must approach life with a healthy skepticism which will prevent one from becoming satisfied with the first "scrap" that suits one's needs.

The person who is deeply committed to social reform will be found among the "real doubters" because, presumably, such people have found a "discipline" in middle age which involves a passionate commitment and belief that touches their lives as profoundly as sexual passion did in youth. One may reach back from that passage to Helen Shaw and her relationship with Paul, and to Liz van den Sandt and her confusion of sexual desire for Luke Fokase with the desire to give him political assistance, and one may draw in as well the persistent strain of the pull of ideals and hopes against the possibilities encountered, the possibilities which, realistically appraised, qualify the ideals and hopes. Finally, one may set against that passage James Bray's expression of the same ideas:

> it seemed to him . . . that one could never hope to be free of doubt, of contradictions within, that this was the state in which one lived—the state of life itself—and no action could be free of it. (pp. 464–65)

That statement is free of the irritated tone which characterises Jessie's one, and the calmness is a mark of a more mature "doubter" but also of the more mature and sober vision which informs the fifth novel.

Like the protagonists of all Gordimer's novels, Bray discovers that the fullness of the dream is always reduced by the operation of political and social restrictions. Although he comes to believe that an individual's life goes on producing reverberations (and the publication of the Bray report at the end of the novel demonstrates that), the essentially bi-polar vision is still operative. It is a vision for which I should like to offer the image of Michelangelo's last pieta, where, from the sumptuous and polished base, the rough gaunt figures are seen to emerge as though the artist, reaching beyond the fullness, has honed and pared his way to a gaunt but terribly strong and hauntingly beautiful core of truth within.

Notes

1. Nadine Gordimer, "A Writer in South Africa," compiled by Alan Ross from interviews with the author, *The London Magazine* (May, 1965), pp. 21–28.

2. *Ibid.*

3. E. M. Forster, "What I Believe," in *Two Cheers for Democracy* (New York, 1951).

4. Nadine Gordimer, "A Writer in South Africa." See also Germaine Bree, *Albert Camus* (New York, 1966), p. 39.

5. Nadine Gordimer, *A World of Strangers* (Harmondsworth: Penguin, 1962), pp. 15, 81. All references are to this edition.

6. Compare Clamence's remark in *The Fall*. Albert Camus, *The Fall*, translated

by Justin O'Brien (London: Hamish Hamilton, 1957), p. 38. All references are to this edition.

7. Camus, *The Fall*, p. 85. Nadine Gordimer, *The Late Bourgeois World* (New York: Viking, 1966), p. 36. All references are to this edition.

8. Camus, *The Fall*, p. 43. Nadine Gordimer, *Occasion For Loving* (New York: Viking, 1963), p. 13. All references are to this edition.

9. "A Writer in South Africa," *loc. cit.*

10. *Ibid.*

11. Nadine Gordimer, "The Novel and the Nation in South Africa," *The Times Literary Supplement* (August 11, 1961), pp. 520–23.

12. All references are to the Simon & Schuster edition, 1953.

13. Lionel Abrahams, "Nadine Gordimer: The Transparent Ego," *English Studies in Africa* (September, 1960), pp. 146–51.

14. "A Writer in South Africa," *loc. cit.*

15. The quotation from Pasternak is one of the epigraphs to *Occasion for Loving*.

16. *Occasion for Loving*, p. 21.

17. *The Lying Days*, p. 222.

18. *Occasion for Loving*, p. 205.

19. *A Guest of Honour*, pp. 464–5. All references are to the Jonathan Cape edition, 1971.

20. *Ibid.*, pp. 385, 465.

21. The epigraphs have been selected from the novels, in chronological order, from *The Lying Days* to *A Guest of Honour*.

22. *A World of Strangers*, p. 9.

23. *The New Yorker* (November 29, 1958), pp. 223–24.

Cutting the Jewel:
Facets of Art in
Nadine Gordimer's Short Stories   Kevin Magarey*

With *A Guest of Honour* (London: Jonathan Cape, 1971: James Tait Black Memorial Prize, 1971, and nominated "the best novel of 1971" by the *The Sunday Telegraph* and *The Observer*) Nadine Gordimer[1] has brought it off, or so I think many of her readers will feel: she has written a major novel, her first to belong clearly in that category. It is indeed, as the reviewers have noted, her most ambitious work, to date. And though the earlier novels are all artistic successes in their way, they are not so easily seen as such, nor are they so

° From *Southern Review* 7 (1974):3–28. Reprinted by permission.

I acknowledge with pleasure and gratitude the substantial help I received in the writing of this article from my colleague and former co-editor, Dr. Ian Reid, and from Ms. Sue Higgins.

substantial: a lack of cohesion or pressure seems to result from a deliberately cool technique and style and an unemphatic, apparently directionless ethos which this article will discuss. Even in *A Guest of Honour* it may not be at first sight wholly clear which of two is the unifying preoccupation—the vivid fictional analysis of politics in a post-colonial African state, or the tragic dilemma of the very intimately realized neo-liberal English hero, Colonel Bray, whose commitment to Africa remains far from inevitable, one feels: uncertain and even— but this is the point of the novel—slightly arbitrary. The gap, if there is one, is in the reality portrayed: it is symbolized in the novel by Bray's English-country-house-bound wife with the Shakespearian name, Olivia, who never appears, so to speak, on stage. The novel's achievement is thus the one assigned to epic, to portray a historical movement or moment in personal terms: if this sounds pompous, still it is hard to think of a novel in English that combines with such astonishing range, hard-headed but progressive grasp of what must be called contemporary history with profound, intense and delicate personal observation and intuition. Range of response is perhaps Nadine Gordimer's special contribution to the English novel. *A Guest of Honour* is an exciting and intensely serious novel, a great novel—its density of feeling, creative span, thematic coherence and narrative assurance justify the word.

Until *A Guest of Honour*, one would have regarded Nadine Gordimer as primarily a short story writer; it was her stories that left one confident that she is a major writer. *Livingstone's Companions* (Cape, 1972) has revived one's sense of her commitment to the genre, and her distinction in it. I propose to study her stories here. The short story, as any publisher will verify, is not a popular form, though it may give more purely artistic pleasure than the novel. With a few masters—Chekhov, Kipling, sometimes De Maupassant—one hardly notices that one is not reading short novels: but, since Katherine Mansfield, one is more likely to feel deprived of the pleasures of mere illusion that reading a novel provides, the mysterious pleasure of immersion in a fantasy world, the heady sense of being absorbed in a narrative sweep of realized myth. It is as though one were confined, by a volume of short stories, to reading the first twenty pages of a succession of novels—the openings of the novels, with which it is notoriously most difficult for both writers and readers to engage. Characters can be established but they cannot become recognized, familiar; identification or projection is curtailed; situations can be developed but hardly explored. Katherine Mansfield's slices of life did much to establish the short story as a genre of its own, but they simultaneously deprived it of much narrative momentum, and moved it into a world of sensitive and poetic description. (Professor Ian Maxwell used to define description as "narrative's original sin.") A Gordimer story is often best regarded as a poem or an essay as much as a story, even when the technique is narrative and covers the span of a life (e.g. "A Commonplace Story," SVS 19,[2] "Clowns in Clover," SFC 2, "Through Time and Distance," NFP 4).

But this state of affairs has its compensations. Poetry, for those lucky enough to have acquired the ability to read it, affords a pleasure of quite a different order of intensity from that generated by novels; and to the extent that the modern short story really approximates to the conditions of poetry, the same is true of it. Art, like any other form of being, thrives on limitations. The best of Nadine Gordimer's stories have a unity and relevance ("decorum" was the old word), a concentration and a coherence of experience as recorded, as selected and as significant, that is hardly possible in the novel. The novel is a baggy monster of an art form: it inevitably contains more detail than my (for example) rather average memory can assemble in one inward look. The short story is the right length to light up in the mind: it can produce an undiluted beauty and power that the novel cannot. And some of Gordimer's stories do approximate to the condition of poetry in their intricate relating of event, meaning and symbol.

The purpose of this article is to establish through some examples this poetic structure of some of Ms. Gordimer's stories. It seems, as far as I can discover, pretty much *sui generis*. It is her replacement for the satisfactions older story tellers offered: of identifying with the sahib-type in Kipling, of the cut of De Maupassant's Gallic black humour or the thrill of his macabre, or the hallucinatory vision of Ambrose Bierce, or the moment of strange half-animal intuition in Lawrence. In my judgement it makes Nadine Gordimer rank with these I have mentioned and with others, Frank O'Connor and Lawson and Katherine Mansfield, that is, in (however loosely defined) the first rank. This habit of poetic structure is all the more remarkable in that what strikes one first about Gordimer's writing, and what struck her critics first, is her intensely sensitive detailed recording of experience itself. It was this, rather than the metaphoric structure of her stories as a whole, that her early reviewers found "poetic"— and indeed she does record with a minutely accurate eye, and respond with a delicate and intuitive empathy.

> The veld is flat round about there, it was the end of winter, so the grass was dry. Quite far away and very far apart there was a hill and then another, sticking up in the middle of nothing, pink colour, and with its point cut off like the neck of a bottle. Ride and ride, these hills never got any nearer and there were none beside the road. It all looked empty but there were some people there. It's funny you don't notice them like you do in town. All our people, of course; there were barbed wire fences, so it must have been

white farmers' land, but they've got the water and their houses are far off the road and you can usually see them only by the big dark trees that hide them. Our people had mud houses and there would be three or four in the same place made hard by goats and people's feet. Often the huts were near a kind of crack in the ground, where the little kids played and where, I suppose, in summer, there was water. Even now the women were managing to do washing in some places. I saw children run to the road to jig about and stamp when cars passed, but the men and women took no interest in what was up there. It was funny to think that I was just like them, now, men and women who are always busy inside themselves with jobs, plans, thinking about how to get money or how to talk to someone about something important, instead of like the children, as I used to be only a few years ago, taking in each small thing around them as it happens. ("Some Monday for Sure," NFP 15, p. 199)

This is mature Gordimer: the verbal "poetry" is well under control; moreover it is dramatic: the first person narrator is a young South African saboteur riding a bicycle to survey the site of an explosives lorry hold-up, whose use of the present and past tenses might be thought improbably precise. I don't find it so myself. The necessary merger of writer and character seems effortlessly, beautifully right, in diction and image (the bottles). I chose this passage very much at random, in the first instance, but it would be hard to find a piece of writing that conveys the South African veld with such economy. The implicit social comment is not too obtrusive, unless to an over-refined taste—the social situation commented on is not over-refined. What is specially typical in the passage is the concluding reflections. They are perfectly in character, and neatly reflect on the passage they conclude. They are beautifully under control: but one could imagine a danger that such comments would seem faintly arch, displaying sensitivity with a hint of indulgence. And what is typical is that such a passage is a key one. Symbolically, in microcosm, it conveys the whole point of the story, what its title suggests, the profoundly serious, concrete observation that the story is written for: the South African African liberation movement is at this point of growth, too young but "busy inside [itself] with jobs and plans, etc."; some Monday, for sure, it will go to work. Gordimer's use of the data of her own stories as metaphor seems to involve, in the end, a metaphysical observation: it is reality itself, history itself (reality is peculiarly history in Gordimer), which, harsh as it is, contains these parallel facets, these harmonies.

In the next three sections I want to examine some examples of this particular kind of structure in Gordimer's stories. For reasons I shall mention later, I draw the examples from the first four collections. For a full treatment one would have to pay some special attention to the theme of race, both because this is of particular interest and because the stories which treat it are some of her best. There will not be room for this here (I hope to write a further article on it): it seems in any case important to know how to read Gordimer's stories, before looking for the light she throws on this or any subject.

2

Ms. Gordimer seems to announce her method, as well as one of her central themes, in the first story of her first collection of stories, "The Soft Voice of the Serpent."

The nameless protagonist of this short short story is recovering from the amputation of a leg, from unspecified causes.[3] The material point of the story is the hero's unreadiness to accept the full consciousness of his loss—in other words, in Gordimer's world, to become mature, "to live like a grown man, with the conditional instead of the absolute" ("A Thing of the Past," FF 11, p. 159). For Gordimer maturity consists in the full acceptance of both sex and death—the fact of death and the inevitability of it: the amputation of a leg is a partial or premonitory death. The hero is recuperating in the garden of his home; the garden is associated, in the first paragraph of the story, with Eden. He has a "system":

> He felt that he had no leg. After a few minutes he went back to his book. He never let the realisation quite reach him; he let himself realise it physically but he never quite let it get at *him*. He felt it pressing up, coming, coming, dark, crushing, ready to burst—but he always turned away, just in time, back to his book. That was his system; that was the way he was going to do it. He would let it come near, irresistibly near again and again, ready to catch him alone in the garden. And again and again he would turn it back, just in time. Slowly it would become a habit. . . . (SVS 1, p. 8)

The hero and his wife one day notice a locust, in the garden, which has also lost a leg. Through watching it, the hero seems to be in hopes of coming to terms with his limitation. His wife, who understands his psychological condition, encourages his attention to the locust; but when she prods the locust very gently with a thin stick it flies away—"She . . . appealed, unnerved as a child, 'What happened? What happened?' There was a moment of silence. 'Don't be a fool,' he said irritably. They had forgotten that locusts can fly." (p. 12) The formal point of this story seems to be what the title suggests, the ironic inversion of the story of the Fall. The locust is a variant of the serpent in the garden—"he became aware of a curious old-mannish little face, fixed upon him in a kind of hypnotic dread": it is "tempting" the hero to move out of his false paradise, his "system," to accept the dark, crushing realization of the loss of his leg: tempting him as the death consciousness, of which it is a sort of emissary, had been tempting him. It is tempting him to true wisdom, which might be defined for Gordimer as the acceptance of disillusion or angst. The nub of the story is the cruel twist or joke, a kind of double disillusionment, that the temptation to disillusionment turns out to contain an illusion itself. I remain unclear just how far the logic of this dénouement is meant to be pursued: it feels primarily reinforcive—life is simply, or rather doubly, tough.

"The Soft Voice of the Serpent" is interestingly placed at the head of all Gordimer's work just because its impact is so evenly balanced between content and symbol—or rather, tipped towards the symbolic structure of the ironic Genesis parallel. This poetic image—one wants to call it almost a conceit, in the Elizabethan sense—is more than half the point of the story. The matter of the story, meaning by that the special contingency of its plot, the loss of a leg, seems of no particular interest in the story—it is just a loss, an occasion for death consciousness. The symbolic structure is, of course, meaningful—this is Gordimer's post-Freudian, post-Hitlerian, post-her-own-South-African-"lying-days" version of the biblical myth. Still the balance of emphasis is important. Many readers go to Gordimer's fiction, I believe, for its material interest—for her admittedly vivid record of life in a controversial country, for her record of feminine experience, for her judgement on the key twentieth century question of race. Gordimer is most vividly a South African, a woman, and an anti-racist; but she insists—so this positioning would suggest—that she is first a human and an artist.

There is thus a piquant fitness in the appositioning of the second story in this first volume,[4] whose title may and should be seen as a variant expression of the ironic point of the first story about "the fall"—"The Catch" (SVS 2). For it, by contrast with the first, locates us, with Gordimer's characteristic and brilliant particularity, in the South African scene.

The, also nameless, tenants of the point of view[5] in "The Catch" are a young white couple holidaying at a small coast resort not far from Durban—in, one would imagine, the early 1950s. The substance of this story is a tentative inter-racial acquaintance—friendship would be too strong a word—they establish with an Indian, also on holiday, as it emerges, from a sugar refinery, who fishes from the beach. To portray the tenuous and fragile progress of their communication across the South African consciousness of race is Ms. Gordimer's forte, and I make no attempt to paraphrase it.

> The tendrils of their friendship were drawn in sharply for a moment when, putting his catch into a sack, he inquired naturally, "Would

you like to buy one for lunch, sir?'' Down on his haunches with a springy strand of hair blowing back and forth over his ear, he could not know what a swift recoil closed back through the air over his head. He wanted to sell something. Disappointment as much as a satisfied dig in the ribs from opportunist prejudice stiffened them momentarily. Of course, he was not in quite the same position as themselves, after all. They shifted their attitude slightly.

"Well, we live at the hotel, you see," said the girl.

He tied the mouth of the sack and looked up with a laugh.

"Of course!" he smiled, shaking his head. "You couldn't cook it." His lack of embarrassment immediately made things easy.

"Do you ever sell fish to the hotel?" asked the young man. "We must keep a lookout for it." (SVS 2, p. 15)

The Indian in due course catches an eighty pound salmon, which they admire and photograph for him; what will he do with it?—try to sell it at a boarding-house about a mile away. At lunch-time the couple is visited by three friends "from home up country": the five decide to drive into Durban for dinner. On their way they pass the Indian at the side of the road with his fish: "he couldn't sell the damn thing, and now he can't carry it home," the husband discovers. In some confusion, while the three newcomers in the back sit in chilly silence, the couple decide to offer the Indian a lift, putting the salmon in the boot: the Indian sits in the front next to the wife. " 'So your big catch is more trouble than it's worth' she said brightly." He repeats her words as they drive. They leave him at his turn-off, and drive on. The story ends:

"The things we get ourselves into!" she said, spreading her skirt on the seat. She shook her head and laughed a high laugh. "Shame! The poor thing! What on earth can he do with the great smelly fish now?" And as if her words had touched some chord of hysteria in them all, they began to laugh, and she laughed with them, laughed till she cried, gasping all the while, "But what have I said? Why are you laughing at me? What have I said?" (SVS 2, p. 27)

This story is representative of Gordimer's short story method in a number of ways. One of these is the way in which the story is focussed in the title, which is at least a triple pun; the "catch" is the salmon, the Indian, and the catches about these catches—parallel, in the suggestive way subconsciously sensed by the laughing five in the car at the end: as the "great smelly fish" is to the Indian, so the Indian has become to the whites—" 'more trouble than [he's] worth.' " The whites are laughing at this parallel without quite knowing it: " 'What have I said?' " That is, in another way again, the catch.

The title of a Gordimer story is like the centre of a jewel brooch. It may be left unmarked, simply filled by the substance of the story itself—"Ah, Woe is Me" (SVS 13), "The Last Kiss" (FF 2), "The

African Magician" (NFP 9). Most typically, perhaps, it is a simple overlay. "The Kindest Thing To Do" (SVS 3, the next story after "The Catch") is both what the girl must do: kill the bird that has been savaged by the dog—and what the mother does: refuse to do this for the girl, who is old enough to need to experience death in this vicarious way. But this central condition, so to speak, of the centre is itself faceted in a different way in each story. A glance at the title "The Amateurs" (it refers to a group of amateur actors that has done a performance for Africans in a location) as one reads the conclusion of that story—" 'But what could we *do?* ' "—lights up the helplessness of well-disposed half-committed whites, even all whites, facing the whole South African racial dilemma, in a poignant tragicomic flash (SVS 10). "My First Two Women" projects the story of the child of a divorced couple into the future-present of the story or its telling. (SFC 7). "The Cicatrice" simply points at the symbol of the divorcee's failure, well-established as such in the story itself (SFC 9). "The Night the Favourite Came Home" (FF 3) is a deliciously temperate account of a progressive university woman finding herself by accident in the house of some very average South African mineworker whites on a day when the hostess has won eighty pounds on a race. The title seems at first sight a rather ill-assorted pun on the horse and the heroine, one quite unrelated to the closing image of her pathetically creating a context of comfort for herself in her lonely bed, with her memo-pad reminder as a surrogate for a doll for a mother—"My Books." But the connection, once established, seems to accrete decorum like a grain of sand in an oyster, a process that familiarity with Nadine Gordimer's stories familiarizes. That it was the favourite that won stamps the celebrations at the Ardendycks' with a special stamp of the expected, the utterly—but spontaneously, vitally—commonplace, that is suggestively the opposite of Vera Grant's affectivities. Liking this story is a good test of addiction to Gordimer— there is so little orientation provided in it by tone or overt indicators of value. (Indeed, there is possibly no evaluation in it: it simply records a syndrome. It is with something of a shock that one sees it might be funny.)

A variant of these punning titles is the presence of a variously radiating irony: "A Present for a Good Girl" (SVS 11), "Happy Event" (SFC 3). The title is usually echoed in (or echoes) a passage of the story. Sometimes the passage occurs quite naturally ("The Defeated," SVS 18, "Enemies," SFC 11), sometimes it enunciates what is itself an image ("Another Part of the Sky," SVS 14, "Friday's Footprint," FF1). Sometimes, as in "The Catch," the pun is multiple. "A Thing of the Past" (FF 11) stands for almost every entity in that extraordinarily suggestive story, the heroine's house, her society, her first husband (an archaeologist) and her love for him, the heroine herself, and finally, with a trenchant shift of meaning, her husband's love for her. The story is set, with Nadine Gordimer's unique capacity to make wholly realistic settings, plots and significances mutually irradiate, in post-revolution Egypt. But the hero—it is so coolly done, and totally plausible, of course—is a South African; and at certain moments when one reviews the story the main impact of it, as sometimes with Gordimer, seems political: it is, obliquely but with a central light that dawns in the reader (as it has, we realise, in the hero), the South African set-up that is the real "thing of the past." In other stories the title is a voice from outside commenting— Gordimer has no qualms about authorial comment, her art is assured enough for such liberties, and indeed one hardly notices them: "Is There Nowhere Else We Can Meet?" is a generous laconic comment on an account of that everyday South African occurrence, a bag-snatch by an African (SVS 9); "Out of Season," the title of a deliciously catty story, somehow prudishly suggests "heat" (or the lack of it) and "bitch" (SFC 13).

A second way in which "The Catch" is representative is the subliminal level of the revelation, at least for those inside the story. As we have seen "The Soft Voice of the Serpent" seeming to suggest: if Nadine Gordimer had a Bible other than life itself, one would have to assume, I think, that it was the works of Freud. (The proviso is important, and readers should feel reassured: I do not think that to understand her stories one needs to read the works of Freud.) In one out of every two stories the reader, like the psychoanalyst, sees more than the actors or narrator, and in the great majority of these cases what the reader sees is, as in "The Catch," in the consciousness of actors or narrator, but subliminally. In the stories where the narrator or actor participates in the revelation this may occur through long reflection, though sometimes, as in "The End of the Tunnel" (SVS 17) or "A Chip of Glass Ruby" (NFP 8), the realisation is the happy ending of the events narrated. A characteristic motif is for the realization to occur when the protagonist is on the brink of sleep; another is for it to occur as a result of a parallel incident involving a comparable realization, but one to which there is less resistance; both these motifs occur in "Another Part of the Sky" (SVS 14)—the realization is that the philanthropic hero has been overlooking his wife. A number of stories are, like "The Night the Favourite Came Home," the portrayal of an unconscious syndrome, interesting to the reader as either deeply typical of the human condition, or faintly comic or grotesque, or both. An example predominantly of the first of these types is "The Umbilical Cord" (SVS 15), in which an adolescent on the brink of the passage into maturity, which involves rejecting his parents' ambience and values, is frightened into intense regression and re-enacts with his mother a gesture typical of early childhood. An example of the second is "Enemies" (SFC 11), where an old lady of habitual self-control travels on a Cape Town-Johannesburg train with an embodiment of her self-indulgent alter ego, a fat lady who dies during the journey; on arrival the heroine sends a telegram to her Malay chauffeur in Cape Town, "It was not me—Clara Hansen." It is a dryly macabre story, amusing and a little puzzling. Its point seems to be Mrs. Hansen's prudent, inhuman and faintly grotesque overreaction, rather than any reference to Donne's well-known injunction not to ask for whom the bell tolls. Subliminal material treated with decorum is likely to emerge as nuance, and the point of a number of Gordimer's stories seems to be a matter of nuance. Clara Hansen will be discussed at greater length in the next section: she has the distinction of being the only character in a Gordimer story to reappear in a subsequent one.

A third way in which "The Catch" is a typical Gordimer story is the unobtrusive but effective way in which all the details of the story are relevant, and some metaphorically so. The couple see the Indian at first upside down, in effect (I have quoted the opening sentence in footnote 5), as one does a fish. They are themselves "washed up thankfully out of the swirl and buffet of the city": they are pictured again later in terms of water—"As though the dam of their quiet withdrawal had been fuller than they thought, fuller than they could withstand, they found themselves toppling over into their old stream again, that might run on pointlessly and busy as the brook forever and ever" (SVS 2, p. 23). The sea is a potent symbol in Gordimer, as one might expect in such an instinctively Freudian writer as she seems to be: it signifies much what it does in Shakespeare—death, universality, other dimensions of life, the unconscious. "The Indian knew the sea." When he has caught his salmon "interest spread like a net, drawing in the few, queer fish of the tiny resort. . . ." When they pick up the Indian, "His presence in the car was as immediate as if he had been drawn upon the air. The sea-starched folds of his trousers made a slight harsh rubbing noise against the leather of the seat, his damp old tweed jacket smelled of warm wool, showed fuzzy against the edge of light. He breathed deeply and slowly beside her" (p. 26).

That passage is typical of Gordimer's minutely sensuous and realistic perceptions, and the first sentence is also a typical, gentle and oblique, uncertain reminder of the story's image-motif. It seems fair to call it poetry.

A fourth way in which "The Catch" is typical of Nadine Gordimer is implicit in the third: it is that the material for all the analogies in the story is to be found, in principle, within the story itself. A discussion of this point will be the focus of the next section.

3

This method of constructing a story around analogies or metaphors found within the material of the story itself might be held, as I have already suggested, to have metaphysical implications: it is sometimes almost as though reality were found to be a symbol for itself. I do not propose to pursue these speculations here (though I am far from sure that they would be fruitless as a subject for research, and I certainly think Nadine Gordimer's work warrants research). I shall suggest instead an image for Gordimer's method drawn from Gordimer's work itself.

In this section I want to take three stories that are in one respect or another in what one might call limiting positions of her method. It happens that each of these stories has also some possible reference to literary methods and perhaps to Gordimer's own method, though this is in each case not overt enough for the reader to be quite sure it is intended to be read as such. The first of these stories seems to me wholly successful, the second only partially—interestingly partially—so, and the third seems to depend—deliberately to depend.

The peculiarity of "Check Yes or No" (FF 7) in the Gordimer canon, over and above its brilliant success, is that whereas in other stories one image or more drawn from life is used to express or reinforce an observation about life, the upshot of "Check Yes or No" is an image itself—an image for life, or rather for living.

The action of the story is essentially that the heroine's second husband, of whom "strength and nervous determination are the overt qualities with their implication of the private covert ones of tenderness and self-confidence," for once lets the heroine down and makes a fool of himself in front of no less an audience than that of a circus: and in particular of a family, the Dunns, who "had lived in the flat next door to her, three years ago, before she had remarried," had witnessed her style of life then and helped her, and are thus people she is particularly eager should see that she had "made it, and with ease, and with nearly all of [her]self to spare." Victor Seeker is trying to claim his family's reserved seats in the circus auditorium; he loses his temper with the assistant ring manager, and gets knocked down into the sawdust of the lane opening into the ring. The situation is saved in the first instance by a fat old Lithuanian Jewess[6] who makes room for the Seckers on "the tiered planks above Block F"; and then, while Phoebe, stunned, is telling herself she will go and sit in the car, by a circus act that gradually gains her attention—a tight-rope walker who is "slowly getting himself into a great brown sack," which covers him head and feet. "The man in the brown sack, looking, apparently, nowhere, because he had no face, poked out the bottom of the sack with the tentative, nervous, hesitant movement of some delicate animals' paw and took the wire." "As he balanced up there, pausing in an immense crisis of decision each time before he put his groping foot down, his figure became for Phoebe the focus of a strange and suffocating recognition. She *knew* him, not in the usual sense, but as if she had come face to face with the embodiment of some part of the vast, common human state" (FF 7, p. 103).

I draw attention to this story not only because it represents one apotheosis of Nadine Gordimer's method but also because it seems to me a very fine story, peculiarly appropriate to the second half of the twentieth century—not that its message is one thing or another, existentialist or neoevolutionary, but just because (among other things) it is merely human. The beautiful ending has the Gordimer ambiguity of which I speak. ". . . on an impulse, she smiled and said to the old woman beside her: 'It's all right. He does it everyday' " (p. 103). What does he do—his act, or any act of which his act is the symbol?

"Check Yes or No" does not quite fit the metaphysical description of a Gordimer story I gave at the beginning of this section, because the image of the story is not quite simply part of life—though one has no doubt, of course, that this particular circus act does exist, somewhere in the world. It is "an act"—that is part of the beauty of this particular story. I do not, in any case, want to give the impression that construction round an image or analogy is a standard procedure in Gordimer's stories. It is used in only a minority and even in those it is varied in each story to fit the material: this last principle, the old-fashioned name for which I have already suggested to be "decorum," is the only *formula* I would claim to find for the principle of construction of all the stories. One other formula that has been suggested[7] is that the stories contain a revelation: but this would be either so general as to be meaningless, or not general enough. Many of her stories are essentially nothing more than a description of someone's emotional, psychological or circumstantial condition (e.g. "The Defeated," SVS 18, "Charmed Lives," SFC 10). One moving story consists simply of an account of a certain Sunday's work by the African "cook-general" of a white family living in a South African flat ("Monday is Better than Sunday," SVS 20). Others narrate some exciting incident or crisis—a woman's realization through a macabre intuition that she is dying, an indecent assault, a riot, a murder avoided (SVS 16, FF 2, NFP 4, 11), though certainly not in the tradition of the adventure story. Brief biographies constitute some (SVS 8, 19, SFC 2, FF 10, NFP 12). "The overlooked element" is a formula that would apply to some, including a number where the element concerned is the woman's point of view. (An interesting study could be made of the occurrence in Olive Schreiner and in Nadine Gordimer also of the sort of material that has made a third woman writer of South or Central African origin, Doris Lessing, be taken up by Women's Liberation.) The race stories—which are some of her best—sometimes make use of analogies or parallels often with an ironic twist, but some are simply tales of white blindness or cruel absurdity.

Gordimer's method of metaphoric structure probably seems her characteristic method simply because it occurs in the largest minority of stories; but one story, not as successful as "Check Yes or No" but still interesting, suggests a possible context for it. It is one of the small minority of stories whose title is not echoed verbatim in a passage of the story itself, and it is only the title, "A Style of Her Own," that suggests a reflective reference to Gordimer's oeuvre (FF 5). The story has been foreshadowed already: it is the second about Clara Hansen, the only one in the canon to re-introduce a character: this and the Clara Hansen characteristic of having alter egos[8] both perhaps suggest a special significance for it. The matter of the story is an elaboration of a phrase in the opening paragraph of the previous Clara Hansen story, "Enemies" (see above p. 10), viz. that Clara Hansen had "survived dramatic suffering." "When Mrs. Clara Hansen travels, she keeps herself to herself. This is usually easy, for she has money, has been a baroness and a beauty, and has survived dramatic suffering. The crushing presence of these states in her face and bearing is nearly always enough to stop the loose mouths of people who find themselves in her company" (SFC 11, p. 162).

The second story operates by a flash-back to Clara Hansen aetatis 43, after an introduction. The old ladies (the story begins) in a private hotel in Johannesburg, where Mrs. Hansen has been booked in by a perhaps subconsciously intentional mistake, remark on her dignity. These old ladies are Mrs. Hansen's alter egos in this story, and she relaxes so far as to tell one of them that dignity does not grow on trees. The flashback is introduced:

> No, not on trees. No, no. She knew very well where it had come from, that look on her face, that tone in her voice, that presence. She knew where and when it had been bought, as one is always able to find again, in one's mind, the exact circumlocution of back streets by which chance led to the little shop in a foreign town where, on a certain day, a particular piece of jewellery was discovered. (FF 5, p. 72)

This striking and just image, with its strange particularity, is a Gordimer image: that is to say, it is an image of and from the story it tells. As well as echoing the Barret-Tromp Residential Hotel, that "complex of old houses joined by passages where the electric lights had to burn all day," it is a proleptic image of the dénouement, where Clara Hansen discovers her husband to be committing adultery with "the only woman who came to" their flat, "a plain, timid middle-aged spinster who spent a day there once in two weeks, sitting at the sewing machine," in a house in a back street in the dock area of Durban.

The dearth of female company in the Hansens' comfortable flat is a measure Mrs. Hansen has taken in the ten-years' marital warfare induced by the omnivorous sexual appetite of her handsome, wealthy Danish husband. Mrs. Hansen has come, half-incredulously, to suspect the sewing-woman; the story relates how she takes a taxi to her address to confirm her suspicions; finds nothing there, and, relieved, walks round the block; and comes on her husband's car in a side-street, with the lights left on. She returns to "7a Beryl Gardens" and rings the bell; after a time the dressmaker comes to the door— "the pale, plain old maid." "Mrs. Hansen took her in, from head to foot, a licking flame of a glance, and then it was out, and cold. She said, 'Tell my husband he has left the lights of his car burning.' And jeering, mourning, she turned and walked out into the street before the eyes of the dress-maker, like a queen" (p. 81).

The significance of this story for Nadine Gordimer's style seems to lie in the area of alter egos. This is speculation, but there is one respect in which Clara Hansen is very much the opposite to everything one knows or guesses of Gordimer through her writing. Clara Hansen is a volitionalist:[9] she imposes her will on herself and, where she can, the world. She is a woman of—in Gordimer's view, it seems— grotesquely excessive self-organization and self-control, sometimes for its own sake ("Enemies," SVS 11, p. 164, last paragraph), who will fight for her rights or desires, or fight for fighting's sake: "At first she fought him because she wanted him, and later she fought him because she didn't see why she should let go anyway; he was the torn and bloody rag of something whose original form and identify had been forgotten, but which was guarded, in that name, even more savagely than it itself had been" (p. 74).[10] The last image there, of a banner in a battle, evokes a Clara Hansen who is the very spirit of militarism. She is also, clearly, a woman of limited sympathies: the spinsterish sewing woman, for example, is someone the possibility of whose sexual life existing is a revelation to her—or rather would be, if she ever took it in.

These two characteristics would seem to go together, and together their contraries go some way perhaps to define the style of Gordimer's stories. I have already attempted to describe this style elsewhere. Based on a policy of passivity, itself evident in a kind of stillness in the style—the silence in which her sense impressions are registered— it involves a self-abandonment to everything that happens and so, above all, a wholeness, a relaxed and undivided acceptance of all aspects of human experience, and a refusal to judge, a nonethical approach, "discriminating without evaluating."[11] Verbally it means that Nadine Gordimer, of set policy, has very little verbal "style of her own"—the sort of thing that makes a page of Henry James or Patrick White unmistakable. Tonally it means that her writing is flat and cool, casual, not monotonous because it is so responsive but rarely excited and emphatic. Structurally—the concern of this article—it means that she will not impose a shape or an analogy from outside on her material—rather she will look for her symbols, analogies or parallels in the material itself. Though "A Style of Her Own" may mean that Gordimer disclaims a style of her own, there is still a distinctive quality to her art (she is often oblique, like Clara Hansen's last remark), and the story may also be taken to provide the ambience of an image for this general style (I have called it a "method," which is too programmatic a word), namely, jewellery. The art of cutting jewels is, I am informed,[12] not to impose, but to find and follow the shape *in* the jewel, the planes or lines of growth that are already there, the parallel or echo of an angle that is not imported or imposed from outside. This is Gordimer's way with her material.[13]

I include the third example in this section to illustrate a quality which it may involve some embarrassment to touch on. It is this. Because of the characteristics I have described, the unobtrusive wit, the importance of nuance, the flat, cool, unemphatic tone and style and so on, some of Nadine Gordimer's stories are not easy to get the point of. One would welcome more discussion, even some controversy, over their interpretation. I am still uncertain about the exact interpretation of a good quarter of them, and in greater confusion over eight or nine. "Still," because time can help. With T. S. Eliot, the eventuality promised us by progressive critics in the 1930's has come to pass, and much of what was baffling then has ceased to be baffling now by becoming, not more intelligible, but simply familiar: one no longer asks with such urgent puzzlement, why *lilacs*? why *St. Mary Woolnoth*?—that is just the way the poem is, and the broad outlines of the sense shake themselves free a little. The same thing happens with Nadine Gordimer, and the other predictable thing happens too, namely that long reflection reveals the often subliminal point of stories in which, often, long reflection is precisely shown to be thus revealing. It is for this reason that I use no example from *Livingstone's Companions* in this article.[14]

It is in this context that the fact that some of the stories demonstrably possess a highly intelligible structure (however nuanced) is important. In an age when unintelligibility passes without comment and even seems often de rigueur, it is comforting to find some authors who can look modern but still have a rational coherence of a renaissance degree of lucidity. Hopkins may seem an improbable comparison for Nadine Gordimer, but he has, for me, this quality: difficult perhaps, but always finally quite clear in meaning, just as his metre reaches the limits of freedom without becoming free verse. That some of the stories can be seen to be totally meaningful suggests that all are so. My last example, "Message in a Bottle" (NFP 13), may throw some light on this possibility.

"Message in a Bottle" was mentioned and quoted on a dust-jacket of its volume—I assume authorial authority for blurbs—as being about the problem of communication.

> The problem of communication, of how human beings can break through the barriers—often "merely" emotional—that divide them, is presented with truly classic directness in the story fittingly called *Message in a Bottle*, which ends in the enigma of the suicide in the car boot: "It's like a message picked up on the beach, that may be a joke, a hoax, or a genuine call of distress—one can't tell, and ends by throwing the bottle back into the sea."
>
> *(Not for Publication*, last page of dust-jacket)

"Truly classic directness" may be a sort of joke. "Message in a Bottle" is certainly very short, and has a terse, quick, slightly telegraphic style with a hint of impatience or suspension in the tone, as do some of the other stories in *Not for Publication*. The impression of irritability is partly dramatic, attributable to the first person narrator, a married woman with a child of seven or eight who has had a painful infection on the inside of her eyelids for some months which various treatments have failed to cure. The narrator uses the present tense, and the technique is as near to stream of consciousness as Nadine Gordimer ever comes; the incidents in the story are on the face of them arbitrary and inchoate, but also curiously thematic for the chance observations of a morning and an evening. The woman and her daughter have coffee in a café where a beautiful blonde girl is weeping continuously as she talks inaudibly to an oldish, well-to-do-man, to whom the narrator unexpectedly relates as their eyes meet. The man is long-sighted, and watches people in the street, "on the other side of the glass barrier"; the couple drive off in a big black car. The mother and daughter drive to a pathology clinic where a culture of the bacteria from the infection will be made: they see in cages the animals in which the cultures are nurtured, and the child feels guilty at the thought.

> "Now we're going to try and grow these nasty goggas from your eye, dear, and we're going to grow them in an egg and see whether we can make you well."
>
> The woman in the white coat talks soothingly as she works on the eye. While she is out of the laboratory for a moment we listen to a kettle that is singing up to the boil and I say, "Don't rub it." The child says after a silence, "I wish I could be the one who sits and watches." Pain is taking her innocence, she is getting to know

me. But if she indicts, she begins at the same time to take on some
of the guilt: "They will grow mine in an egg? Only in an egg?"
(NFP 13, p. 179)

Gordimer habitués (readers of this article may I hope be regarded
as induced members of this class) will recognise the multi-faceted,
uncertain, open images of a Gordimer story—except that the images
of this are of, precisely, mutual containment or enclosures, glass
windows and closed cars and cages and infected eggs and singing
boiling kettles, separation, ignorance, non-communication at various
levels, from the physical to the intimate (the mother and child know
each other well: it is the experience of pain that divides them).

The end of the story is already too economical to shorten (an
objection that applies to all my synopses), but it must be attempted.

> My husband has a story to tell when he comes home in the evening.
> An acquaintance, who took him out shooting last weekend, has
> committed suicide. . . . "He asked when I was going to bring you
> on a shoot again . . . he remembered that time last year when we
> had such a good time in the camp". . . . "Shut himself in the boot
> of the car and shot himself through the head." I scarcely knew the
> man, met him only that once at the camp, but at this detail of the
> manner of his death, I suddenly think of something: "But don't you
> remember, he used to shut his hunting dogs in the boot? He did
> it that day, and when I picked him up about it he said it wasn't
> cruel and they didn't mind being shut in there!"
>
> Nobody knows why he killed himself, he has gone without a
> word to anyone—except this. The stranger who cannot remember
> what he looked like is the one into whose hands his last message
> has fallen. What can I do with it? It's like a message picked up on
> the beach. . . . (pp. 179–180)

There follow some reflections and two snatches of dialogue, one
imaginary and one real.

Perhaps the narrator "knew" the textile-factory owner in the
café that morning ("you don't always choose the ones you know")
because they were both more loved than loving? The narrator scarcely
remembers the suicide, but the suicide seems to have remembered
her, and may even have wanted or hoped to see her again. The
"message" conveyed by the place of suicide is a strange negation of
itself, as though the sender was admitting the mistake in his self-
defence about the hunting dogs: but at least it sounds a little as
though the suicide knew whom he was leaving his message for. Love,
or more specifically sex, is always the only hope for communication
in Nadine Gordimer: the next story in *Not for Publication*, "Native
Country," a polished and moving one, is about a South African girl
whose only, but sufficient, communication with her sophisticated and
cosmopolitan European collector husband is through (what is sug-

gested to be) the speciality of her "native country"—sex. (The symbol in this story is an "alexandrite," a kind of beryl.) It is possible that I understand "Message in a Bottle," but I can't be sure. When I first thought of discussing it here, I envisaged suggesting that it was a sort of paradox, a story which communicated just as well if its meaning was not understood. I am not sure now whether that is a valid suggestion. The story remains one of those of which, for me, the interpretation is uncertain. Certainly, though, the image the story creates is in its own strange way beautiful: pregnant, precise, and very nearly if not quite transparent.

4

In this section I want to show Nadine Gordimer's style of structure operating normally, so to speak, by briefly examining a very successful mature story that is not one in which the meaning is confined to an image, nor one in possible relation of contrast to the author's view, nor one concerned with the limits of communication, but one displaying through a narrative a normal Gordimer subject (if there is such a thing)—in this case, repression.

"Friday's Footprint" is the title story of Ms. Gordimer's third collection. A certain development is visible from one collection to another, though it is not very marked—the style seems to be established in all its essential features in her first volume. But its stories are shorter and the verbal style rather looser, more productive of a sense of possible alternatives, than in the later volumes. The stories in *Six Feet of the Country* have more comfortable milieus, and seem the most elaborate and highly wrought, especially the five stories about race. In *Not for Publication* the style is plainer and terser, as I have suggested above; its sense of tragic tautness seems absent from *Livingstone's Companions*, though there are passages of near-ellipsis (and wrenching tragedy). *Friday's Footprint* is somewhere between SFC and NFP: spare, but full and mature, it is perhaps her finest collection to date.

"Friday's Footprint" is the twenty-page story of Rita Cunningham, the wife of a hotel proprietor in a nameless "territory" in Central Africa, Zambia (as Northern Rhodesia) or Botswana or South-West Africa. The physical environment is important, though it is established through a mere handful of brief images, and not all at once: and it is as though there is some sort of interlocking parallel between the rhythm of the successive stages of this allusive description and that of those of the explanatory narrative, in intermittent sections, of the heroine's life, the geography of her mind. The hotel is an outpost in the desert, at an African village (Olongwe) on a tropical river; people arriving there had travelled two days from the last village over desert and dried out salt-pans; they had slept out under the crushing silence of a night sky that ignored them and held no human sound other than their own small rustlings. They were inclined to emerge from their jeeps feeling unreal. The sight of Mrs. Cunningham, in her flowered print dress, with a brooch on her big bosom, and her big, bright-skinned face, looking clerically dazed beneath her thick permanent, was the known world, to them; Friday's footprint in the sand. (FF 1, p. 12)

This is the longest passage devoted to the setting. The writing is excellent, its pace and proportions perfectly calculated. In this synopsis I will follow as well as I can Gordimer's arrangement, but I hope the reader will be persuaded to seek out and read the story, surely one of the half dozen greatest short stories in English.

Mrs. Cunningham has been married twice; her first husband, Arthur, is dead, drowned bringing a boat-load of goods over the flooded river. Her inner life is introduced in the story as she looks at the river, sometimes not even seeing the water, sometimes imaginatively recreating a picture of her first husband's death. Her second husband, Johnny, was her first husband's step-brother—he is small and slender, young-looking for thirty-nine (she is forty). The news of her first husband's death is brought to her while she is on holiday in Johannesburg, watching cricket, which she loves (the description of that scene at the Wanderers' is a small masterpiece too). She returns to the hotel and gradually gets the whole picture of her husband's death: a boat overloaded at Arthur's own insistence, the load crowned by an iron bedstead "for the Chief's new wife," had overturned, the bedstead trapping Arthur and some Africans as it sank. (The Freudian symbolism of this detail is perhaps made too obtrusive by synopsis: in the story it is a realistic, plausible scene.) Arthur was a male Clara Hansen, "the sort of man who got things done himself"; he bullied the white assistants and the African workers.

"Come on, Harris," he said, as if he were taking charge of a child. "Come on now, and no damn nonsense. Take hold here." And he sent the man, tottering under the weight of the foot of the bed while he himself carried the head, down to the boat.

Rita had married him when she was twenty-three, and he was sixteen or seventeen years older than she was. He had looked almost exactly the same when she married him as he did the last time ever that she saw him, when he stood in the road with his hands on the sides of his belly and watched the car leave for Johannesburg. She was a virgin, she had never been in love, when she married him; he had met her on one of his trips down South, taken a fancy to her, and that was that. He always did whatever he liked and got whatever he wanted. Since she had never been made love to by a young man, she accepted his command of her in bed as the sum of love; his tastes in love-making, like everything else about him, were formed before she knew him, and he was as set in this way as he was in others. She never knew him, of course, because she had nothing of the deep need to possess his thoughts and plumb his feelings that comes of love.

. . . .

His step-mother had been an enemy of his, in that far-off childhood that he had overcome long ago, but he had had no grudge against his young step-brother, her son. . . . (pp. 18–19)

Johnny is a self-contained rolling stone, who comes alive at the Saturday night dances, after which he often sleeps with one of the guests. After Arthur's death Rita plans to sell the hotel, but she finds that she and Johnny can do the work Arthur formerly did.

Johnny . . . said, "What'll you do with yourself in Johannesburg, anyway, Rita? You'll have money and you won't need a job."

She put down her pen and turned round, clutching at the straw of any comment on her position that would help her feel less adrift. . . .

"But I always wanted to go. The summer . . . it's so hot. We always said, one day, when the children. . . ." All her appeals to herself failed. She said, "But a woman . . . it's silly—how can I carry on?"

He watched her with interest, but would not save her with an interruption. He smoked and held his half-smoked cigarette between thumb and first finger, turned inward toward his palm. He laughed. "You are carrying on," he said. He made a pantomime gesture of magnificence, raising his eyebrows, waggling his head slowly and pulling down the corners of his mouth. "All going strong. The whole caboodle. What you got to worry about?"

She found herself laughing, the way children laugh when they are teased out of tears. (pp. 23–24)

She grows in self-confidence as a business woman. One day Johnny, with three casual words, admits to her an overnight affair with a guest: this establishes an intimacy with her, that leads to their getting married. "They were alone together. They had an existence together apart from the hotel and the stores. . . ." He awakens her sexually as Arthur did not:

She lay on the bed alone in the afternoon dark behind the curtains that glowed red with the light and heat that beat upon them from the outside, and she looked at his empty bed. She would stare at the place where he lay, not a foot away, every night. She had for him a hundred small feelings more tender than any she had ever known, and yet included in them were what she had felt at other rare moments in her life: when she had seen a bird, winged by a shot, fall out of flight formation over the river; when she had first seen one of her own children, ugly, and crying at being born. (p. 27)

But, pathetically, their love-making becomes less frequent. Her power to recall the details of their love-making seems to increase her power of recall in general. She begins repeatedly to recapitulate scenes from the past: "guilt came slowly through them, a stain from deep down."

> She began to think about Arthur's drowning; she felt crazily that she and Johnny *knew* Arthur was drowning. They sat in the Wanderers' stand while they knew Arthur was drowning. While there, over there, right in front of the hotel, where she was looking, through the office window (not having to get up from the desk, simply turning her head) the boat with the eight sewing machines and the black-japanned double bed was coming over the water . . . The boat was turning over . . . The arms of the men (who was it who had taken care not to spare her that detail?) came through the iron bedhead; it took the men down with it—Arthur with his mouth suddenly stopped for ever with water. (p. 28)

She loses this power to recreate the past, except this vision. One day at breakfast some guests bring a Sunday paper from South Africa which contains a psychological quiz on marriage: in a marvellously realized scene, Johnny and Rita teasingly both mark their answers and Johnny tots up the score, turns to another page to see the verdict: " 'There is clearly something gravely wrong with your marriage. You should see a doctor, or, better still, a psychiatrist,' " he paused for effect, and the laugh " 'and seek help, as soon as possible' " (p. 32). Rita turns it off as a joke, "and with great skill went easily, comfortably sloppily, out of the dining room," into the office.

> She clenched her hand over the sharp point of a spike that held invoices and felt it press pain into her palm. Tears were burning hot on her face and hands, the rolling lava of shame from the same source as the blush. And at last, Arthur! she called in a clenched, whimpering whisper, Arthur! grinding his name between her teeth, and she turned desperately to the water, to the middle of the river where the lilies were. She tried with all her being to conjure up once again out of the water *something;* the ghost of comfort, of support. But that boat, silent and unbidden, that she had so often seen before, would not come again. (p. 33)

The story has the dead-pan tone and the flexible technique which can make a hasty reader find it difficult fully to grasp, or quite to credit, what is going on. The first signs of guilt in Rita, for example, are presented to the reader not as the calamity they appear by the end of the story but unobtrusively—in the narrator's voice, but from Rita's point of view at the time: "And, oddly, when he did come to her again, next day she would feel ashamed." The birth and growth of love and guilt in Rita are presented in lucid, spare and almost miraculously convincing detail: the whole story has a vatic assurance, a total and intimate verisimilitude. There is no question of psychiatric technicalities: simply of two husbands, one who communicates sexually and one who did not. Rita's tragedy is simply that she is not *used* to the possibility of sexual communication—she is not used to anything so real: that is the *un*known world to her.

The cricket offers an opening into the symbolism. Sport is a-sexual, Diana's ground, and cricket is a symbol, white togs and green lawn, of suburban order and calm. Events on the wicket and in the grandstand follow a well-regulated pattern. It is curiously plausible that Rita should love cricket, as some Australian women become enthusiasts for Aussie Rules. The pitch in its surround of green is a schematic echo of the titular image, "Friday's footprint in the sand"— the oasis of the familiar in the void. So is the hotel in the desert, and the images recede: as the pitch is to the oval and the grandstand, as the hotel is to the desert and the suburbs of Johannesburg, so Johannesburg is to Africa and England, so the white man, Robinson Crusoe, is to the world, dinner jackets and cricket in the jungle and the veldt, entrenchment against the unknown beyond the pale. And so Arthur is, for Rita, to the void: the familiar, the known world to her: so he has left his impression on her, his footprint in her sand.

But Friday's footprint is a stranger's: the meaning of the story depends on a fundamental reversibility of its central symbol. "She never knew him, of course." But in her second marriage the hotel in the desert becomes the very particular, precise place (it is place and symbol) of Rita's only experience of living communication, with Johnny, and the emptiness around it: "He always went through the business of love-making in silence: but to her, in whom a thousand piercing cries were deafening without a sound, it was accepted as part of the extraordinary clamour of her own silence" (p. 27). Johnny too, outside his warm relation with his mother and his Saturday night affairs, is partly trapped in the meaningless of bourgeois routine, "the hotel and the stores": but he accepts it, he stands alone in the void, the nothingness of death.

The naturalness of this imagery of the setting—its total func-tionality in the story, on the one hand, its starkly visionary symbolic effect on the other, and the glints of parallel or mirror image in the merging identity between the two—is almost unbelievable, even as one reads. One has the impression of a kind of imaginative optical illusion: it just cannot be true that pictures so utterly real, so much an assemblage, like a collage of newspaper cuttings, of scenes from the very stuff of the world around us, cars and amplified announce-ments and Sunday magazines, hotel dining rooms and frocks and curtains and slippers and sharply, laconically realized country, should not only be the setting for a story of intense and powerful pathos but should also be so symbolically meaningful for the condition of western bourgeois man; and that this meaning should so go to the psychological heart of the story, the narrative movement doubly binding together photo image and Blakean symbol.

Yet there are evidences, like the lines of a signature on a painting, quizzically frank admissions of art, in the story. The bedstead—is it a sort of pollution in the old Chief's kraal?—is one, despite my disclaimer above. Another is the lilies: Miss Gordimer has an occasional rather charming, classical-feeling, biblical reference among her Freudian symbols. The lilies in the river are balanced by the watchers at the cricket-ground, "people who are well-enough off to take a day's holiday from the office and spend it drinking beer, idly watching a game, and getting a red, warm look, so that they appear more like a bed of coarse, easy-growing flowers than a crowd of human faces": it is the sexual symbols that are white for purity. But the main artistic signature is the title and its bedding context, quoted above; perfectly natural and artificial at once, it integrates all the images and their meanings, Freudian and ecological.

It is illuminating to compare this story with the first story of Patrick White's collection *The Burnt Ones* (London: Eyre and Spottiswoode, 1964), "Dead Roses." In this a respectable upper-middle-class Adelaide girl, on holiday with a party at a house very like Geoffrey Dutton's at Kangaroo Island, refuses a somewhat peremptory[15] attempt at seduction by one of the party, a university scientist of some sort. On her return to Adelaide she marries a wealthy, aged, impotent Sarsaparilla widower, and they later separate, and he dies, and she travels. In the ending of the story she chances to come on her former would-be seducer, now married with four children, camping along the coast near Athens: the shock of the encounter causes her to undergo a psychotic hallucination of attempted rape by a Greek boy. The title of the story refers to interpolated symbolic incidents— the widower's house is full of dead roses when the couple arrive there after their wedding, and in Greece the scientist has bought his wife a bunch of roses and they give Mrs. Mortlock one.

Both stories deal with repression, a quasi-psychiatric subject, in a nonpsychiatric mode. Both are in settings of sand and water and bourgeois suburbia in hot southern countries. There is even possibly a comparison to be made between the tones and atmosphere of the two stories. The characteristic sensitive or tragic flippancy of tone and apparent arbitrariness of individualizing detail in the White ("As she held her husband in her opulent arms, she could feel his stomach stirring, rumbling against her, but distant. . . . On Sundays he was particularly jolly. In one of his moulded shirts" pp. 46, 47) have nothing corresponding in the Gordimer, though her style too is relaxed: but the aura of the White characters, the familiar defeated, depleted spiritual atmosphere, has some possible relation to the hot, dry, still air of the Gordimer locale and its spiritual dimension. The White is a powerful story, satirical and compassionate, with clear unsentimental lines of social sympathy and an ending of lurid, psychotic intensity (it is as though all the overt intensity in the story were reserved for the last two of its sixty-five pages). It has none of the invisible polish and non-polluting art of the Gordimer, its intense realism and decorum—the White symbolism is obtrusive, the motivation is established with powerful, sweeping off-hand brush-strokes, the four locales offer a pleasing but arbitrary balance in their parallels. It is like comparing a cartoon by Rembrandt to a finished portrait by da Vinci or Piero di Cosimo.

As a study of Rita, "Friday's Footprint" is about bourgeoisia; as a study of Arthur it is an early story about pollution, in the profoundest meaning of that word—the *imposition*, the forcible deposit of the alien on nature or man. This is one difference from the White, which uses jaded Lawrentian symbols of holidaying or camping as the natural versus the respectable suburban bourgeois: by contrast the Gordimer story was ten years ahead of its time. The hotel at Olongwe is of the sort that is representative or symbolic in real life, as an oil well or a luxury motel at Ayers Rock would or will be symbolic of Western spoliation of the world. The step-brothers are brilliant portraits from this point of view. Though Arthur disclaims "contraptions," technology, his very disclaimers, self-contradictory to the heart of them, serve a *function* like a technical device; they are impositions of the worst sort—on another human being: "I don't know what all this fuss is about water filters and what not. I've drunk water that was so filthy I've had to lean over and draw it into my mouth through a bit of rag, and been none the worse for it." What resident of Scotland, England or Australia has not met the Arthur of that speech? This stultifying assertiveness has no more essential place in a sexual relationship than the hotel has in the surrounding country. In Rita's mind ("Rita" is the name of a river) Arthur is symbolically drowned by sex, as he was really drowned by water. We have seen that in Gordimer the discovery of communion in sex and the discovery of contingency in death are complementary (cf. "Tenants of the Last Tree House," NFP 10). The awareness of another is complemented by the awareness of the void, the acceptance of the contingent self: where this does not occur it leads to immaturity and disintegration ("The Worst Thing of All" NFP 5, and "The Soft Voice of the Serpent," v. supra). In Rita's mind this necessary acceptance is sidetracked by its attachment to the dead Arthur. Thus the need for her discovery and acceptance of the void becomes instead her neurotic development of fantasy guilt. The figure of Arthur becomes a sort of super-ego of the familiar, turned to for guidance in her repression and for comfort, that sinks under the same weight as Rita's potential breakthrough into maturity, finally drowned by an excess of the very thing it needs—the sexual truth about herself. Arthur's self-imposition on Rita, his "pollution" of her, is sterile, life-depriving.

By contrast with Arthur, Johnny, who at first seems to border on being a sponger, is passive, obedient—"after the boy'd been loafing round the river and the hotel for a month Arthur suggested that he might give a hand in one of the stores. Johnny took the hint in good part—'got to stop being a bum sometime, I suppose,' he said, and turned out to be a surprisingly good worker." He is taciturn, yet with the right phrase for the moment: resigned to futility, embarrassment and non-communication except at fitful intervals through dance and sex. (It is pleasant to note that he has spent time in Australia as well as America.)

In discussing my first quotation from Nadine Gordimer I noted the possibility that her "poetic" passages could seem to have a hint of archness or ostentation. Nothing in this article has documented that claim: but the images in the passages from "The Catch" quoted on p. 7 might conceivably be called contrived. "The tendrils of their friendship": this suggests sea-creatures. "With a springy strand of hair blowing back and forth over his ear, he could not know what a swift recoil closed back through the air over his head": this is brilliantly descriptive of the situation, and it also carries suggestions of a fisherman "striking" at a non-existent bite, the fish browsing with waving fin unaware of its danger. I find this quietly witty: but a reader who found it obtrusive or contrived would find nothing to object to in "Friday's Footprint," the facets of whose art and meaning (I have hardly begun to explore their relations) are wholly natural to their material. Nothing alien is imposed—not even art: for the most important technique of Gordimer's art is also the most important thing she has to say: acceptance, obedience to reality. The reversibility of the symbol of Friday's footprint is typical; there are no villains in Gordimer; Arthur's "step-mother had been an enemy." A catholic concern is the logical result of this bias towards acceptance and passivity: it is volitional distortions that obscure wholeness of outlook and response, and wholeness is Gordimer's positive recommendation. One may, of course, be led to take sides by reality and wholeness itself. The heroine of one of Gordimer's stories is a South African *Indian* woman in whose nostril her mother had fixed, when she was a girl, an ornament that is now too "old style," even for her: "a chip of glass ruby." The story portrays her puzzled husband's chagrin when she is arrested for printing leaflets for a banned liberation movement *for Africans*. One of her daughters explains her mother to her step-father: "It's because she doesn't want anybody to be left out" ("A Chip of Glass Ruby," NFP 8, p. 105).

Appendix

A list of Nadine Gordimer's stories published in volume form, with the abbreviations for the volume used in the article above and the number of the stories in their volumes (see note 3).

Face to Face (1949) : FTF

See note 2 below, penultimate sentence. The three stories named in the list that follows were not republished in *The Soft Voice of the Serpent,* and eight stories were added, viz. SVS 2, 4, 6, 8, 14, 17 and 18. The number in brackets represents the story in SVS: 1 (1), 2 (13), 3 (15), 4 (The Battlefield at No. 29), 5 (21), 6 (19), 7 (10), 8 (11), 9 (5), 10 (12), 11 (9), 12 (3), 13 (The Last of the Old-Fashioned Girls), 14 (No Luck Tonight), 15 (16), 16 (20).

The Soft Voice of the Serpent (1953): SVS
1. The Soft Voice of the Serpent
2. The Catch
3. The Kindest Thing to Do
4. The Hour and the Years
5. The Train from Rhodesia
6. A Watcher of the Dead
7. Treasures of the Sea
8. The Prisoner
9. Is There Nowhere Else We Can Meet?
10. The Amateurs
11. A Present for a Good Girl
12. La Vie Boheme
13. Ah, Woe is Me
14. Another Part of the Sky
15. The Umbilical Cord
16. The Talisman
17. The End of the Tunnel
18. The Defeated
19. A Commonplace Story
20. Monday is Better than Sunday
21. In the Beginning

Six Feet of the Country (1958): SFC
1. Six Feet of the Country
2. Clowns in Clover
3. Happy Event
4. A Wand'ring Minstrel, I
5. Face from Atlantis
6. Which New Era Would That Be?
7. My First Two Women
8. Horn of Plenty
9. The Cicatrice
10. Charmed Lives
11. Enemies
12. A Bit of Young Life
13. Out of Season
14. The Smell of Death and Flowers

Friday's Footprint (1961): FF
1. Friday's Footprint
2. The Last Kiss
3. The Night the Favourite Came Home
4. Little Willie
5. A Style of Her Own
6. The Bridegroom
7. Check Yes or No
8. The Gentle Art
9. The Path of the Moon's Dark Fortnight
10. Our Bovary
11. A Thing of the Past
12. Harry's Presence
13. An Image of Success
14. Something for the Time Being

Not for Publication (1965): NFP
1. Not for Publication
2. Son-in-Law
3. A Company of Laughing Faces
4. Through Time and Distance
5. The Worst Thing of All
6. The Pet
7. One Whole Year and Even More
8. A Chip of Glass Ruby
9. The African Magician
10. Tenants of the Last Tree House
11. Good Climate, Friendly Inhabitants
12. Vital Statistics
13. Message in a Bottle
14. Native Country
15. Some Monday for Sure

Livingstone's Companions (1972): LC

1. Livingstone's Companions
2. A Third Presence
3. The Credibility Gap
4. Abroad
5. An Intruder
6. Inkalamu's Place
7. The Life of the Imagination
8. A Meeting in Space
9. Open House
10. Rain-Queen
11. The Bride of Christ
12. No Place Like
13. Otherwise Birds Fly In
14. A Satisfactory Settlement
15. Why Haven't You Written?
16. Africa Emergent

Gordimer has retitled a number of her stories, including six discussed at more or less length in the article above: "The Soft Voice of the Serpent" (SVS 1) was originally entitled "The Two of Us"; "Enemies" (SFC 11), "A Sense of Survival"; "My First Two Women" (SFC 7), "The Pretender"; "The Cicatrice" (SFC 9), "The Scar"; "A Style of Her Own" (FF 5), "The Lady's Past"; "Friday's Footprint"((FF 1), "A View of the River."

Notes

1. Nadine Gordimer was born in a gold-mining town near Johannesburg in 1923 and attended a convent school and, for a brief period, Witwatersrand University. She has published five novels and five volumes of stories. The novels, in order of publication, are: *The Lying Days* (1953), *A World of Strangers* (1958), *Occasion for Loving* (1960), *The Late Bourgeois World* (1966), *A Guest of Honour* (1971). A sixth novel, *The Conservationist*, will be published by Jonathan Cape this year (1974). The titles and dates of the volumes of stories are given in the "Appendix" above. The two most recent books, *A Guest of Honour* and *Livingstone's Companions*, are published at London by Cape; the remainder, all of which except *The Late Bourgeois World* are out of print, by Gollancz; but *The Soft Voice of the Serpent*, *A World of Strangers* and *A Guest of Honour* are published by Penguin, and the latest story collection, *Livingstone's Companions*, will be available in Penguin in October, 1974. Ms. Gordimer received the W. H. Smith Award for Commonwealth Literature in 1961 for her story volume *Friday's Footprint*, and the James Tait Black Memorial Prize (Britain) in 1971 for *A Guest of Honour*.

This note does not list the numerous editions in the U.S.

2. The volumes of stories will be referred to in the text by the abbreviations given in the Appendix above, and individual stories by the abbreviation for their volume and their number in it. Page references after quotations are to the Penguin edition of SVS.

3. Comment on the stories seems to make brief résumés of their plots unavoidable. The obvious disadvantages of this as an exegetical procedure can only be compensated by the value of the exegesis, whatever that will be: my intention is, naturally, to return the reader to the originals.

4. It does not appear in FTF. The order of the stories in FTF was substantially altered in SVS (see Appendix) but "The Soft Voice of the Serpent" comes first in both.

5. Ms. Gordimer is extremely flexible in her manipulation of point of view, for

example when the hero of one of her novels dies the story is continued with hardly a bump for the last thirty pages through the eyes of her heroine. In many of her later stories almost the whole narrative is implicit oratio obliqua, imagined as spoken by whatever character is, for the moment, the object of our attention. By the same token the use of the words "hero" and "heroine" should be regarded as the merest ciphers, x and y: in a high proportion of stories they are not the sympathetic characters. Technique contributes to the apparent lack of direction and the concealed precision of Ms. Gordimer's work, and the remarkable universality of sympathy that informs her very wide range of characters, all of them—as close observation discovers—individualized interiorly to an almost uncomfortable degree. Point of view is physically realised in the very opening sentence of "The Catch"—"His thin strong bony legs passed by at eye level every morning as they lay, stranded on the hard smooth sand." Namelessness, too, is exploited in the story—"They did not know his name, and now, although they might have asked the first day and got away with it, it was suddenly impossible, because he didn't ask them theirs. . . ."

6. It is perhaps worth remarking that the former Phoebe Van der Camp, the heroine of this story, is allowed to recall rather closely what one knows of Mrs. Reinhold Cassirer at about this time in real life: Phoebe's new husband's name, for example, is that of a publisher, Secker. (I don't, of course, suggest for an instant that there is any connection between the success of the story and its possibly autobiographical reference. Another of Gordimer's masterpieces is the previous story in the same collection, "The Bridegroom," which describes an Afrikaner road-maker and his relations with his African workmen.) Ms. Gordimer seems to design the references here to be recognized, perhaps as a manner of acknowledging the experience described as her own, or true to her own. Another personal reference seems to be suggested in the Lithuanian Jewess—Ms. Gordimer's parents, I believe, were Baltic Jews.

7. By Lionel Abrahams in "Nadine Gordimer: The Transparent Ego," *English Studies in Africa* III (Sept. 1960), 146–151.

8. Gordimer makes Colonel Bray comment on alter egos in *A Guest of Honour:* " 'Everybody has a private vision of what he could be at the other end of the scale, the very bottom. Nobody else recognises it, only oneself' " (p. 289).

9. In an earlier article ("The South African Novel and Race," *Southern Review* 1 [1963], 27–45) I used the word "voluntarist" (37) but this was a mistake. Voluntarism is a *belief*—that will is "the fundamental principle or dominant factor in the individual or the universe" (O.E.D.). Volitionalism is a *practice* or habit—the practice or habit of making will the dominant factor in oneself.

In my own view there is a third ism to do with will—volitionism, which is a *tendency* to make will the dominant factor—whether it is realized or not: a group characteristic. (Every man is both identical with all other humans, qua human, totally different from all other individuals, qua individual, and like some men but unlike others, qua type or member of a group.) I believe Nadine Gordimer is particularly effective as a trans-racial writer because she rejects volitionalism for herself, explicitly and deliberately, and thus becomes a potential mediator between Europeans, who are volitionists, and Africans, who are vitalists. This is a schematization of the claim that there is a basis of truth for popular stereotypes. The view of races as different but equal is replacing that obligatory among liberals when Gordimer began writing, viz. as psychologically indistinguishable. (This change could be graphed in Gordimer's theoretical references to race. Cf. the articles and books of Lorna Lippman, e.g. "Government Responsibility and Ethnic Minorities," n.d., unpublished paper.)

There is currently an extreme version of the view of races as different with which I have some sympathy but which seems to me to err by being, quite simply, extreme. It presents this difference as absolute, an insoluble mystery, an impassable barrier to communication: attempts to pass it have a quality of sacrilege, of tearing the veil. In its American version the view may be connected with the Black Power movement; in its Australian version, with its American version and a move to guard Aboriginal secret rites and rituals. This view clearly inspired what I am surely not mistaken in finding the arrogantly and aggressively a priori and misleading (though not *completely* unresponsive) review of *A Guest of Honour* by Thelma Forshaw in *The Australian*, Saturday, August 18th, 1971, p. 18.

10. I have wondered if this description of Clara Hansen's emotional condition at the time of the incident narrated is consistent with the ability attributed to her to suffer overwhelmingly through her discovery:

> I could have died, people said of certain moments, I could have died then and there, in the street. For her this became a rational statement instead of an exaggeration not really meant to be taken seriously. A hideous vertigo of the heights of emotion made her feel that she could fall dead in the street. (FF 5, p. 80)

But the moment is that of her discovery of defeat as inevitable, her coming "to live like a grown [woman], with the contingent instead of the absolute." This note is being written too late for the reservation in the text (p. 11) about the success of the story to be withdrawn: I can only record here my transition from uncertainty to understanding and admiration.

11. "The South African Novel and Race," 43.

12. By Mr. Peter Wendt.

13. Ursula Laredo, "African Mosaic: The Novels of Nadine Gordimer," *Journal of Commonwealth Literature* VIII (1973), 53, footnote 3, cites an interview article, "Diamonds are polished—So is Nadine," *Rand Daily Mail Magazine Section*, 19 August, 1972. I have been unable to inspect this article.

14. Most of the stories in it seem easy enough to interpret—"An Intruder" (but is the "something so simple that she had missed it" James's condition, or Marie's, and his reaction to that "intruder"?), "A Meeting in Space," "Open House," "No Place Like" (a disturbing fantasy, as they say), "Otherwise Birds Fly In." In some the symbolism seems complex but clear—"A Third Presence" (the real Rose); "Abroad" (Manie takes his at-home with him: his at-home shuts the rightful patrons out of theirs); "Rain Queen" (she is queen until the rain is over, but also until the fertility rite works); "The Bride of Christ" (her brief flirtation with her mystical husband is her rite of passage into maturity where she goes beyond the male parent, "a pair of outspread arms"); "Why Haven't You Written?" ("hardening metal"/mettle—an old pun—really is "his problem," to drill through the freeze of his duty-bound marriage); "Africa Emergent ("climbin' those stairs and goin' no place"). (A formula in brackets in a footnote is of course deadeningly inadequate to the real complexities of these stories.) Some seem still more oblique. "The Life of the Imagination" seems to make very strikingly the point of "the overlooked element," which is in this story the world of Africans around Barbara which she, like most South Africans, ignores, filling her imagination with her director's Chinese ceramics and her husband's Japanese architectural idiom. Livingstone's companions behave very like the people Livingstone came to Christianise. In "Inkalamu's Place" "all that" is anything but dead, and Nonny no more "free of him, and the place" than the child's hand is free. "A Satisfactory Settlement" sums up the racist mentality in ten pages: it is a brilliant, poignant study of the way whites "settle" their guilt or insecurity on their black alter egos. The full pattern of one story escapes me—"The Credibility Gap." It reminds me a little of "Message in a Bottle," but is not meant, I think, to be obscure: but how does it all fit in with the passage from Lévi-Strauss?

15. In contrast to the emotional verisimilitude of "Friday's Footprint" is the difficulty of imagining how Barry Flegg's attempt to seduce Anthea Scudamore in "Dead Roses" could have been expected to succeed. Since Mr. White portrays seduction elsewhere more convincingly, I do not quite understand his objectives in the passages concerned, but the sensuous sexual impressions of Barry in Anthea's mind certainly have the starkness, suggestions of violence and abrupt immediacy of Marlowe's narrative images in *Hero and Leander* rather than those gentle and more gradual though no less sensuous, of *The Eve of St. Agnes* (Into her dream he melted, as the rose/Blendeth its odour with the violet.)

Nadine Gordimer's *A World of Strangers:* Strains in South African Liberalism   Robert Green°

Nadine Gordimer's second novel, *A World of Strangers* (1958), provokes and perplexes. Its epigraph is the last four lines of Lorca's "Ode to Walt Whitman":

> I want the strong air of the most profound night
> To remove flowers and letters from the arch where you sleep,
> And a black boy to announce to the gold-minded whites
> The arrival of the reign of the ear of corn.

The ode was published in *Poeta en Nueva York* and composed when Lorca was in residence at Columbia University in 1929/30. "These poems," their editors remark, "reveal the shock and anguish García Lorca experienced as he, the representative of a traditional culture, was confronted with the seeming chaos of a new industrial civilization . . . these poems speak tragically and grotesquely on a prevailing desolation."[1] The "Ode to Walt Whitman" is an attack particularly on "the pansies of the cities" (*maricas de las ciudades*), more widely on a culture drowning itself "in machines and lament." The ending, on which Miss Gordimer drew, suggests the possibility of Black regeneration of America's corrupt materialist (*los blancos del oro*) civilization; it is romantic and apocalyptic.

Lorca's "Ode" has a superficial relevance to South Africa in the late-fifties, the period of *A World of Strangers*. The novel's hero, Toby Hood, a young Englishman on his first visit to South Africa, encounters something of the same desolation and alienation felt by the Spanish poet during his brief stay in New York. "The gold-minded whites," too, are plainly related to the rich materialistic Whites whose prosperity is founded on South Africa's gold. Yet Lorca's "Ode" is willed ("I *want* the strong air . . ."), visionary, non-realistic, eliding

° From *English Studies in Africa* 22 (1979):45–54. Reprinted by permission.

the period of struggle *between* the materialistic regime of the poem's present and "the arrival of the reign of the ear of corn" in the future. Such a development is, in the Spanish poem, merely "announced." Lorca's vision of political change in America as stemming from a magical transformation has very little applicability to the history of South Africa from the Union of 1910 down to 1958. The first act of Gandhian passive resistance in that country was the return of their Passes by the women of the Orange Free State in 1913, the year of Suffragette militancy in Britain. Yet in the succeeding decades the White hegemony has stubbornly and ruthlessly maintained its power, delaying and frustrating demands for change that were, until June 1961, consistently non-violent.

The record of the Blacks' struggle for fundamental human and political rights in South Africa shows, then, that the *process* of change is painful and protracted. Many have sacrificed their lives for "the ear of corn," yet *los blancos del oro* still rule in Pretoria. Gordimer's adoption of the Lorca Ode as the epigraph to *A World of Strangers* is disquieting, for it suggests that the novel too will leave unanswered questions about the mechanics of change. Fears that the novel may underestimate important aspects of South African reality are confirmed as we read. In particular the conclusion of the novel is vitiated by the gap between what the novelist has created and the reader's sense of what is demanded by the relentless logic of apartheid.

2

Nevertheless, despite the novel's indecisiveness towards the nature of political change and the personal commitment required to effect such change, *A World of Strangers* has remarkable strengths. Particularly fine is its evocation of the artificial barriers of life in Johannesburg, the existence there of two distinct, quite separate "worlds" whose isolation has been legislated and is the product of human will. It is the narrator's sense that he is living in a place whose inhabitants are strangers to each other that gives the novel its title. Here the common urban dislocations are intensely magnified. The White "world," to which the visitor is initially confined, is strikingly affluent, luxurious, and brittle. Its denizens, the English-speaking executives and businessmen represented in the novel by the Alexanders, whose wealth is based on the gold-mines, are basically lonely, with no sense of belonging to the country. They lack a common human identity and have the loneliness of any powerful minority.[2] Gordimer is excellent on the psychology of this affluent isolation, on the "unexpected desire" of some Whites "to dissociate themselves from their milieu, a wish to make it clear that they were not taken in, even by themselves" (WS, p. 64). Others, more insensitive, protect themselves by interminable social rituals—protracted parties, races, hunting trips in the veld. Lévi-Strauss has remarked in *Tristes Tropiques* that the tropics are notable for being so old-fashioned, cut off in time from metropolitan modes of thought and action. Gordimer, too, makes a similar point, that the models on which South Africa's Whites base their theatrical performances are curiously dated, as are indeed the Americanisms of Black argot. Toby, out hunting with some rich Whites, notes their limited, stilted conversation, a survival of the Messes of the Second World War: "they thought of courage in terms of gallantry, spirit in terms of gameness" (*WS*, p. 231).

Set against the stylized hermetic world of the Whites is the other half of Johannesburg, the Black "townships." Its buildings are smaller so that the people seem taller. The reality of life and death is nearer the surface here than among the rich Alexander set and Toby senses that in these streets "the whole cycle of living made a continuous and simultaneous assault on your senses" (*WS*, p. 152). The two parts of the city, Black and White, physically so close, are yet totally separate and self-contained. Contacts are maintained only in what the novelist calls the "no man's land," the few houses where people of different colors can mingle, "the space of a few rooms between the black encampment and the white" (*WS*, p. 160). Here Gordimer's metaphors are military; indeed they offer further illustration of how the language of the First World War still shapes our thinking.[3] Elsewhere the narrator draws upon an earlier historical experience, America's exploitation of the West, to describe the strain of life in these multiracial oases. Anna Louw, an Afrikaner rebel, a social worker and trade unionist, "was a real frontiersman who had left the known world behind and set up her camp in the wilderness; the skirmishes of that new place were part of the condition of life, for her" (*WS*, p. 166). Again, later, this area between the two worlds is the "frontier . . . that hard and lonely place as yet sparsely populated" (*WS*, p. 193). These descriptions of Johannesburg in terms of nineteenth-century American history or of European trench-warfare in 1914/ 1918 further indicate the backwardness of modern South Africa. Apartheid, hailed by its creators as a new experiment, is, in truth, the novelist shows us, regressive and anachronistic. *A World of Strangers* successfully recreates "the awful triumphant separateness" (*WS*, p. 193) of Johannesburg.

The novel's characters and even the rhythms of its plot—the rapid shifts from Toby's White friends to his experiences in the Black townships—reflect the deep binary divisions of South African life. (Apartheid might have been the invention of a demented *structuralist* anthropologist.) Yet we are also shown the tragic ironies inherent in these man-made divisions, for the two most compatible characters in the novel—Cecil Rowe, a self-centred divorcee and Steven Sithole,

Toby's hedonist friend—are fated never to meet. Neither had found any kind of commitment, both lived entirely for the present: "their flaring enthusiasms, their unchannelled energy, their obstinately passionate aimlessness—each would have matched, out-topped the other" (WS, p. 195). Toby is a friend of both Cecil and Steven, yet each will pass out of his life—through, respectively, marriage and death—unaware of the other's existence. These parallels between Black and White experience have been criticized as being "at times slightly contrived." Once again, the argument runs, "it appears as if Miss Gordimer is illustrating a thesis."[4] Yet the novel's appearance of contrivance and coincidence, the rigid divisions being crossed by striking parallelism, accurately mirrors the kind of society in which it is set. More so even than China, South Africa is an engineered, constructed society, one indeed built upon a racist, eugenicist "thesis." Realism demands that the novelist render this artificiality to the full.

As well as being a fine recreation of the basic human constraints of life under apartheid, A World of Strangers is remarkable for its descriptive power, for its vivid evocation of people and landscape that is a feature too of Miss Gordimer's short stories.[5] The whole of Part Four, the Whites' shooting trip in the veld, is a splendidly realized picture of the thorny "Gothic landscape" (WS, p. 212) that can sustain comparison with the shooting episode in Anna Karenina. In a quite different key there is also a fine description of the sinuous spontaneous music at a township dance:

> There was a little breeze of notes on a saxophone; it died down. A clarinet gave a brief howl. Somewhere behind the press of people, the big bass began to pant. Music grew in the room like a new form of life unfolding, like the atmosphere changing in a rising wind. Musical instruments appeared from underfoot; people who had been talking took to another tongue through the object they plucked or blew. Feet moved, heads swayed; there was no audience, no performers—everyone breathed music as they breathed air. Sam was clinched with the piano in some joyous struggle both knew. A yellow youth in a black beret charmed his saxophone like a snake, with its own weaving voice. The bass thumped along for dear life under the enchanted hand of a man with the bearded, black delicate face of an Assyrian king. A fat boy with a pock-marked face jumped with rubber knees into a little clearing; girls began to swing this way and that from their partners' hands, like springs coiling and uncoiling. (WS, p. 120)

In such passages the physical landscape of South Africa, rural and urban, is rendered with great skill.

Characters, too, are created with the sharp economy Miss Gordimer practises in her short stories. There are the pompous British consul and his gauche oppressed mate: "a dumpy, lumpy little woman with tiny features buried in a big, round face. Bunches of curly brown hair, to which some sort of reddish dye gave a bright nimbus, made her face seem even bigger. . . . Her florid cheeks had rounds of another tone of red overlaying them. It was an astonishingly innocent face, in all its coarse crudity" (*WS*, p. 11). Or the desperately conventional caretaker of Toby's apartment: "she wore her fur coat, a long-haired animal with tawny stripes that made a chevron down her bosom, and her huge regularly-painted face confronted me like a target in a shooting game" (*WS*, p. 205). Discovering that Toby is entertaining Blacks, this common woman loses control of herself and becomes shrill and vindictive: " 'Yoo can't bring kaffirs in my building,' she screamed. 'Sitting there like this is a bloody backyard location, I mean to say, the other tenants is got a right to 'ev yoo thrown out' " (*WS*, pp. 205–206).

The strength, then, of *A World of Strangers* is documentary, its creation of the *external* world—buildings, places, minor characters— within which the main characters, Toby and Sithole, operate. Much less assured is its account of the relations *between* character and environment.

3

Such weaknesses cannot be discussed in formal terms alone, simply as failings in the novelist's craft or as issues of technique. Wider questions are always involved in criticism of South African literature, for, as Miss Gordimer herself has noted, the artist there is never unconditioned by, or independent of his environment:

> All that is and has been written by South Africans is profoundly influenced, at the deepest and least controllable level of consciousness, by the politics of race. There is no country in the Western world where the creative imagination, whatever it seizes upon, finds the focus of even the most private events set in the overall social determination of racial laws.[6]

It is here, in its presentation of "the politics of race" and the manner in which it formulates the connections between "private event" and the circumference of apartheid, that *A World of Strangers* appears vulnerable. To be specific: the problem is the imbalance between the lightness of the novel's liberal commitment to private life and the harsh solidity of those forces shown arrayed against personal fulfilment. Indeed the novel's success in its recreation of the strains of living in a Police State actually militates against the ideology it seems to endorse. The repression and cruelty are so effectively drawn that they seem to dwarf the proffered alternatives.

Toby, the narrator, is central to the novel's imbalance. The son of "leftist" English parents, he has been sent out to Johannesburg to head the family publishing house. His upbringing amidst causes and enthusiasms has made him profoundly sceptical of any political involvement. In reaction against his earnest parents he believes that the freedom which they had sought was only "an empty international plain where a wind turns over torn newspapers printed in languages you don't understand" (WS, p. 32). "Luxury," he holds, "was one of the most important things in life" (WS, p. 20); and he only wants to be allowed to live the private life of his choice. He refuses to pretend to indignation; he reserves the right not to take a stand; he won't be "a *voyeur* of the world's ills and social perversions" (WS, p. 33). His code is aggressively private and self-centred:

> I want to live! I want to see people who interest me and amuse me, black, white or any colour. I want to take care of my own relationships with men and women who come into my life, and let the abstractions of race and politics go hang. I want to live! And to hell with you all! (WS, pp. 33–34)

A World of Strangers follows the form of *Gulliver's Travels* or *Robinson Crusoe* by placing a traveller, an outsider, in a strange new environment.

At first Toby manages to keep his balance in three worlds: he enjoys the parties of the rich Whites; the company of Anna Louw in no man's land; and the exuberance of his Black friends in the shebeens. Most valued of these is Steven Sithole who had opted out of the recent (1952) Defiance Campaign—in which 8,500 Blacks went voluntarily to jail—and, like Toby, claims to be apolitical, not "bothered with black men's troubles" (WS, p. 96). Each is seeking a haven within the repressive State. Toby finds Sithole attractive because he too is "in rebellion against rebellion" (WS, p. 116). For some time Toby continues his dual role, living by instinct, enjoying alike the comforts of his rich White friends and a sense of liberation and relaxation in the townships. He can listen both to the Whites' talk about the struggle between the Nationalists and the United Party and to Black discussions of A.N.C. tactics. However all is changed by the death of Steven in a car accident during his escape from a police raid. Deeply shocked, Toby recognizes that he had loved Steven as a "brother" (WS, p. 240) and finds a measure of consolation in the friendship of Sam and Ella Mofokenzazi. Yet he fears that their faces will represent the commitment he has always fled; he fears to lose to them "the aimless freedom that had hung about [his] neck so long" (WS, p. 246). In the final chapter of *A World of Strangers* Toby, leaving town on a short business trip, reads that Anna Louw has been arrested on a treason charge for her work as a legal adviser to a women's organization. This news and the support of the Mofokenzazis bring home to Toby that he is part of the world of protest and commitment he had always evaded, "the world of dispossession" (WS, p. 253). Engagement, the novel asks us to believe, had come to him through personal relations, rather than through ideological struggle or political involvement.

Toby's emotional life, we can see, will now revolve around Sam, Ella and his Black friends, yet the conclusion leaves us wondering whether these affections will issue in any wider, political activity. We cannot help doubting whether mere friendships are an adequate response to the death of a "brother" which had resulted from the State's interference in private lives. The novel's endorsement of what one critic has called the paradox "of a non-ideological ideology, almost an uncommitted commitment" scarcely seems commensurate with the potency of those forces marshalled against privacy and self-realization.[7] As the Lorca epigraph had hinted, the terms of the novel's conclusion are too restricted; yet the whole novel had confined itself to the social, domestic and private. Significant in this connection is the large number of parties in A World of Strangers; most of the novel's eighteen chapters are devoted to accounts of social intercourse. Miss Gordimer's decision to structure the novel around a series of private episodes excludes any attention to the world of work and of political activism. Most of the novel's characters do, in fact, work— Toby as a publisher, Steven as an insurance agent, Anna in trade union and legal-aid activities—but this aspect of their lives reaches us only mediately, through report and anecdote. The novel's preoccupation with personal relations and its presentation of them in such sealed hermetic terms encourages us to forget what else was occurring in South Africa at this time: the "Congress of the People" meeting in June 1955 or the beginning of the protracted Treason Trial at the end of 1956. Later novels, in particular A Guest of Honour and The Conservationist, will seek to define personal relations in much larger, more inclusive terms, as being affected by the kind of public events excluded from A World of Strangers.

Furthermore, even within its own restricted range A World of Strangers is oddly incomplete. A novel's concern with individual sensibilities ought to ensure that the hero's emotional life is fully presented, yet in the case of Toby there are certain unilluminated areas. The quotation of a passage from the beginning of the novel may illustrate the difficulty we have in understanding Toby's deepest needs and drives. Soon after his arrival in Johannesburg he goes to his office and meets for the first time his secretary, "Miss McCann, who was one of those common little girls to whom anaemia gives a quenched look which may be mistaken for refinement, and who, appropriately, smelled of sickroom cologne." The girl, then, is strikingly ordinary and the hero's comment in the next sentence—"I should have to find some means of getting rid of her" (*WS*, p. 38)—appears too sweeping, too excessive for such an unremarkable person. Later the publisher and secretary do part company, when the girl objects to his entertainment of Non-Whites in the office, and on this occasion the high feelings of both people are comprehensible. In the quoted passage, however, the problem is that Miss Gordimer has not enabled us to understand the source of Toby's loathing. Is it perhaps a matter of class (the girl is "common")? Or of misogyny? Or even perhaps that Toby just dislikes White women? We do not know; we are left adrift, uncertain how to make sense of the incident.

This episode, in itself so trivial, is representative of the novel's failure to clarify Toby's sexual identity. He will have two affairs with White women, with Cecil and Anna, but both are unspontaneous, unexciting, arbitrary, even dutiful. Their inability to move him is indicated by his bored description of intercourse with Cecil as a participation in "the ancient ritual of oneness" (*WS*, p. 241). In other novels—in, for example, the affair between Gideon and Anna in *Occasion for Loving* or in the powerful lust depicted in *The Conservationist*—Miss Gordimer is perfectly capable of describing heterosexual attraction, but it is clear that this is not the driving force in Toby's affairs. On the contrary the most powerful scenes in the novel are those depicting his friendship for Steven Sithole. Part One, for example, reaches its climax in their flight from a police raid. They escape by climbing over fence and roof:

> With one impulse we scrambled over a curling galvanized iron fence and found ourselves on the roof of a low shed among pumpkins put out to ripen. Steven put a pumpkin under his head, as you might use a plump quilted cushion for a sofa nap. We lay there panting and laughing in swaggering, schoolboy triumph.
> All at once, it was morning. (*WS*, pp. 97–98)

This adventure, reminiscent of the communion evoked by Twain in descriptions of Huck and Jim, seals the friendship and after his death Toby will acknowledge Steven as his brother, recording that he "loved him as a man" (*WS*, p. 245). Yet it is not a homosexual relationship and we cannot feel that its memory is sufficient to account for Toby's decision to remain in Johannesburg's Black world at the end of the novel.

Thus neither his relationship with the two White women nor his friendship with Steven is presented as being the compelling force in Toby's life. A third alternative available to the novelist would have been the creation of an affair with a Black *woman*. Indeed such an involvement is half expected. Black strangers in the townships find Toby's presence there inexplicable precisely because his motives are not sexual. Steven himself remarks pointedly on his failure to interest

Toby "in a nice African girl" (*WS*, p. 204) and though this is said humorously Toby understood

> that he meant what he said, it was a cover for some reservation he had about me, some vague resentment at the fact that I had not been attracted by any African woman. (*WS*, p. 204)

Love for a Black woman would certainly have helped to solidify Toby's decision in the final chapter to live in the Black world. As it stands, however, without the ratification of either sexual or strong political compulsion, this move seems oddly unfounded, as unrooted and unspecific as "the arrival of the reign of the ear of corn." It is difficult not to suspect that, for all his commitment to them, Toby is incapable of sustaining human relationships.

4

In an interesting attempt at explaining the novel's weakness Kevin Magarey has drawn attention to the possible influence of the novelist's own Jewish background.[8] The hero's name, Toby Hood, might reflect The Book of Tobias, a Jewish romance of private life. Toby might have rejected any political or sexual commitment not in the name of individual freedom but because Miss Gordimer has given him "a Jew's extensive, almost voracious range of sympathy and the continuous sensibility from which this stems."[9] In this reading *A World of Strangers*, with its relaxed acceptance of life as given, becomes a distinctly Jewish book, the author's "appetite for the human," her "universal sensibility" in some way absorbing and transcending the reader's anticipation that she will specify the sources and possible outcome of her hero's stance at the end.[10] Magarey grants that the fact that Toby is a Gentile is an awkward contradiction. Furthermore it is also a fact of South African history that a Jewish background has not prevented many people from joining the opposition to apartheid and developing very firm political allegiances. (Doris Lessing's *Golden Notebook* indicates the close connections Jews forged with the freedom movements in southern Africa in the forties and fifties.)

Magarey's is an interesting argument though he probably would not go so far as to claim Miss Gordimer as a "Jewish writer" if this were to suggest that her work could be placed alongside, say Saul Bellow's or the poems of A. M. Klein. Most of her major characters are, in fact, Gentiles, and her fullest portrait of a Jew, Boaz Davis the musicologist of *Occasion for Loving*, scarcely emphasizes Jewish traits. Miss Gordimer's Jewish connections seem to have been deeply assimilated. In essays and interviews she hardly mentions her origins and it would appear from these statements as if she considered her nationality a more crucial factor than her communal connections.

Tellingly she does not link herself with Dan Jacobson as *Jewish* writers, but as *South Africans*. *A World of Strangers* is, then, a markedly "South African" novel and especially a strongly "liberal" work, as that word was understood there at the time of its publication. The novel's weakness stems, I shall suggest, from the peculiar position adopted by liberal intellectuals in South Africa in the fifties.

The novel's sympathy with "liberalism" is made plain in the Prologue. Here Toby, relaxing at Mombasa en route to South Africa by boat, goes for a swim in the tepid Indian Ocean:

> After the dreary wet summer and the cold wet autumn at home—after a whole lifetime of dreary English winters and wet English springs—I was enchanted with the slack, warm beauty of the place. I seemed to feel an actual physical melting, as if some component of my blood that had remained insoluble for twenty-six years of English climate had suddenly, wonderfully, dissolved into free-flowing. . . . The last jagged crystal in my English blood melted away. (WS, p. 14)

The moment of thawing and release is important and will be confirmed, in similar terms, when Toby visits the much less beautiful, unenchanting townships. Also important is the way such a change is recorded, with its emphasis on the hero's feelings, his "blood" (twice) and heart. This is not a development registered in moral or intellectual terms but rather as an expansion of the sensibility. It is deeply self-centered, self-aware, independent of the presence of another human being. Later, Toby's reaction to the townships will be similarly narrated. These impoverished ghettos do not arouse in him moral or intellectual outrage. Rather they minister to an emotional nourishment:

> The life of the townships . . . seemed to feed a side of my nature that had been starved; it did for me what Italy or Greece had done for other Englishmen, in other times. It did not change me; it released me and made me more myself. (WS, p. 154)

External reality, here the landscape of repression and legislated blight, is primarily of value in that it can be absorbed and exploited for the purposes of individual realization. This is a latterday version of the gentlemanly "Grand Tour," yet the comparison between Johannesburg and the classical ruins of Athens or Rome seems cruelly inapt, evidence only of Toby's blindness to the surrounding misery. Mention of Italy may also remind us of the slight Edwardian fictions of E. M. Forster, of *Where Angels Fear To Tread* (1905) and *A Room With A View* (1908), where the English "underdeveloped heart" is quickened through contact with Mediterranean vitality.

Miss Gordimer, then, has drawn Toby so that the possibility of "change" is frustrated by her stress on his more private intuitive life. Even the mediation of other people cannot penetrate the shell of his self-absorption. Nevertheless Forster's accounts of the effects of Italy on Anglo-Saxon inhibitions, novels imbued with the spirit of G. E. Moore and "The Apostles," may provide an unsuitable paradigm for *A World of Strangers*, for the crucial point is, I think, that we expect Toby to change morally and ideologically just because South Africa should affront and insult his humanity. He should, we feel, be forced by his experiences there to revise his rather callow notions about "the abstractions of race and politics." The novel has indeed shown him that his "brother's" death is not an "abstraction"; nor is the breakdown of Anna Louw's marriage to an Indian, under public scrutiny and pressure, metaphysical or theoretical. These two events are shown to have been caused, in large measure, by the State's invasion of home and bar. *A World of Strangers* indicates all too plainly the insufficiency of Toby's code, and yet the novelist's own apparent sympathy with him prevents her from elaborating the necessity of moral and intellectual renewal. Toby is immune to the pressures of events, so much so that it is his own creed of self-development that appears to be the "abstraction."

Moreover, the inadequacy of Toby's position, central to the novel's implausibility, is analogous with the recorded history of the Liberal Party in South Africa. The Party's engagement with Black interests was never more than partial, conditional. In the 1920s, for instance, when Joint Councils of Blacks and Whites were established, Liberals urged Blacks "to abandon militancy, believing that by education, moderation, and patience Africans could win white sympathy."[11] Later, in 1952, the nonviolent Defiance Campaign—which Sithole has ignored in *A World of Strangers*—was opposed by the Liberals, who in this respect aligned themselves with the Nationalist Government. The Liberal Party's affirmation of "the dignity of every human being, his right to develop, and his right to participate in political activities" was always to stop short of support for a universal franchise and the Party's hesitancy on this crucial issue aroused the suspicion of the A.N.C.[12] In 1955 the Party refused to attend the celebrated "Congress of the People" and in the sixties and seventies, after the period spanned by the novel, it was to become increasingly isolated and anachronistic. Miss Gordimer's recent "Letter from South Africa" documents the abyss between White liberals today and the young Black militants of Soweto: "There is not much sign that whites who want to commit themselves to solidarity with blacks will be received by the young anonymous blacks who daily prove the hand that holds the stone is the whip hand."[13] There is now no place for "liberalism" in South Africa; it is a bankrupt ideology, without viability or respect. *A World of Strangers* foretold its present insolvency.

Miss Gordimer has claimed that she is the only South African writer to have investigated this development, "the decline of a liberalism, black-and-white, that has proved itself hopelessly inadequate to an historical situation."[14] The claim is supported by the novels that followed *A World of Strangers;* by *Occasion for Loving* (1960), *The Late Bourgeois World* (1966) and even, though it is not set in South Africa, by *A Guest of Honour* (1971). Here indeed the novelist treated liberalism dispassionately, ironically, critically. Jessie Stilwell, Elisabeth Van Den Sandt and James Bray in these novels are all aware of the limitations in their creeds and, crucially, are amenable to change. None of them is as cocooned, as isolated from political reality as the earlier Toby Hood. The interest, then, of *A World of Strangers* is that it enables us to trace the development of a critique of liberalism in Miss Gordimer's work and to situate the later novels within the context of earlier, less formed views. Though it has been cruelly overtaken by later events the early novel is valuable for its documentation of the innocence, vulnerability and impracticality of the liberalism of the fifties. Its weakness as a novel is, then, inseparable from its worth as an historical record.

Notes

1. "Preface," *The Selected Poems of Federico Garcia Lorca,* ed. F. G. Lorca and D. M. Allen (New York, 1961), p. x.

2. *A World of Strangers* (London, 1958), p. 75. All subsequent quotations refer to this edition, abbreviated *WS.*

3. See Paul Fussell, *The Great War and Modern Memory* (London, 1977).

4. Ursula Laredo, "African Mosaic: The Novels of Nadine Gordimer," *Journal of Commonwealth Literature,* 8, No. 1 (June 1973), p. 49. A much cruder attack on *WS* was mounted by Robert F. Haugh, *Nadine Gordimer* (New York, 1974), ch. 4. Haugh disapproves of the contrast between White sterility and Black vitality, calling it "this transparent aesthetic agitprop." He accuses Gordimer of unsubtlety: "anger at racial bigotry does indeed jar a fine instrument out of tune."

5. She has collected the best of these in a recent one-volume edition: *Selected Stories* (London, 1975).

6. Nadine Gordimer, "English-Language Literature and Politics in South Africa," in *Aspects of South African Literature,* ed. C. Heywood (London, 1976), p. 100.

7. Kevin Magarey, "The South African Novel and Race," *Southern Review* [Adelaide], 1 (1963), pp. 27–45.

8. *Loc. cit.*

9. Ibid, p. 42.

10. Ibid, p. 44.

11. Mary Benson, *The Struggle for a Birthright* (Harmondsworth, 1966), p. 47.

12. Ibid, p. 160.

13. "Letter from South Africa," *New York Review of Books,* 23, No. 20 (December 9, 1976), pp. 3–10.

14. "The Novel and the Nation in South Africa" (1961), in *African Writers on*

African Writing ed. G. D. Killam (London, 1973), pp. 33–52. The passage cited is from a later "Appendix" dated 1972.

Gordimer's *A World of Strangers* as Memory
Stephen Gray°

"A place without a memory,"[1] comments Nadine Gordimer's narrator, Toby Hood, in *A World of Strangers.* Johannesburg is the city, and it is a thrown-away, unself-conscious aside, not meant to be taken very gravely. First published by Gollancz in 1958, *A World of Strangers* kept its own internal memory very much intact. Written in the firm social style of the British novel overseas, it probed to the very corners of the urban complex, connecting point of view and ironic observation in a web of fictional design greater in scope than the worlds available to its characters. The main metaphor was a South African city as a conglomerate of separate "countries," with secret "passports" (passes), "border posts" and the no-man's land between—the appropriate terrain of a voyeuristic visitor like Toby. The roots of his history are there intact, too; Toby had his grandfather buried in the Boer War at "Jagersfontein" outside town; Jagersfontein becomes a black free-hold settlement, is to be cleared—Toby meets the very woman who is attempting to postpone evictions. Keep making the connections, and the vision of the fictional world is complete.

But it is now some thirty years since *A World of Strangers* first appeared. The British colour bar society the novel protrays was to settle into the amnesia of the Afrikaner apartheid system. Many of the events just about to precipitate this great oblivion are quite accurately foreseen: Sharpeville, the demolition of Sophiatown, the outlawing of black resistance in the form of the ANC and PAC, the Treason Trial, and the flight of artists and intellectuals, black and white, into exile. For those who remained behind more cosmopolitan schooling was to be replaced by Bantu Education, the widened no-man's land to be patrolled with guns. Banning brings down the curtain of the thriving literature of resistance, and the '50s which *A World of Strangers* so celebrates floats off into limbo, is lost. Rereading the novel today is indeed like reclaiming a past unknown, one which it is now very much the vogue to reconstruct.

The landscape was different, then. Of his early days in Johannesburg Gordimer has Toby remark: "We left the city . . . and crossed the new Queen Elizabeth bridge. I twisted my head to look back and I must say that from there, it all looked rather fine; the

° From *Ariel* 19 (1988):11–16. Reprinted by permission. © Stephen Gray.

rectangular buildings, bone and sand and stone colour, pale as objects picked up on a beach, made a frieze of clean, hard shapes against a sky that was all space"(48). The queen's two-laned coronation bridge, then the main access route from the north, is now six lanes wide, and today for an aerial view Johannesburgers have encircling flyovers. Like that of any modern city, the skyline has been transformed by redevelopment. At a recent screening of *Come Back, Africa,* the American Lionel Rogosin's secretly-made hand-held camera documentary of Johannesburg and its people of 1958—shown here on public circuit for the first time this year—Johannesburgers guffawed in utter disbelief: could that flat dorp once have possibly inspired such awe?

The subtropical and Edwardian Carlton Hotel, complete with pinkly-lit Palm Court orchestra, from which Toby started out now rises sixty floors high. Glassy skyscrapers, cut like the diamonds they represent, blink coldly gold in the sun, and even the old lantern-shaped cooling towers are imploded.

Newtown is no longer new, and the colourful Market is now the Africana Museum—and the famous theatre complex where the children of the '50s go in other colours to see musicals like *Sophiatown* about their past. In these musicals not even the music of the original ghetto is accurately recollected; it's all disco and soft liberation anthems now. Gordimer's milieu in *A World of Strangers* is (one dreads to remark) full of chronic song in the streets:[2] pennywhistles, kwela and jive. Indoors is the jazz of saxophones and Todd Matshikiza—his look-alike in the novel, Sam Mofokenzazi, writes an African jazz opera, the prototype of *King Kong.* Even Miriam Makeba appears for a few guest numbers (as Betty Ntolo with the Township Ten [92–93]). Now the songs are unaccompanied at funerals; either that, or rehashed in gutless high-tech showbiz. *Drum* magazine, that during the '50s unleashed the fervour of a much romanticized Johannesburg school—to which Gordimer's own verve is not unrelated—is owned these days by the government.

On the other hand, Coca-Cola—which so amazingly fills Gordimer's pages as a novelty—is still here, though disinvested due to sanctions and bootlegged in from Swaziland (!). Her fintailed Studebakers and Cinemascope of such vogue persist in the leisured boulevards and desegregated venues in uninterrupted modernizations, but out of the central business district in the white bunkers to the north. Meanwhile, not only has a rival dormitory city, one of the largest in Africa—Soweto—been spawned to the southwest, but it has irresistibly flowed back into downtown.

Hillbrow in *A World of Strangers* was still notorious for its townships in the sky (that is, servants' quarters on the roofs of apartments). Toby's landlady chewed him out for having blacks inside

the building: " 'Yoo can't bring kaffirs in my building,' she screamed"
(216) . . . those were the days! Now the older parts are occupied
from the ground floor up by those servants' middle-class children.
After thirty years of residential segregation, South Africa has achieved
an undemolishable "grey area," housing near to a million contentedly
integrated citizens, living happily in sin.

Today nostalgia for the '50s has become a growth industry in
the arts in South Africa. The experience of Sophiatown, which was
destroyed, is relived in three or four books a year;[3] Alexandra Township (described in the novel from page 130), after a generation of
being threatened with removal, has been partly renewed; accordingly
it has accumulated none of the other place's apocalyptic glamour.
The illegal drinking dens or shebeens that commanded Toby's delighted awe, where prohibition-type hoods rubbed elbows with intellectuals and drunks—the spirit of Can Themba and Lewis Nkosi
haunts A World of Strangers—are now legalized; there is even a
union of shebeen-owners, a few of the members being millionaires.

One feels nostalgic for Gordimer's version of the '50s, I suppose,
because in the post-Forster, "Passage to Africa" type tradition of
British fiction in which she wrote there could be some certainties.
It is not just a matter of the "Belgian Congo," "Northern and Southern
Rhodesia" and even Harry Llewellyn's famous horse, Foxhunter, still
being talking-points; "Mau Mau" and the name Nkrumah were already
evident. Gordimer could believe in a kind of Afro-European evolu-
tionary progress; of Sithole she had Toby write: "He was a new kind
of man, not a white man, but not quite a black man, either—a kind
of flash—flash-in-the-pan—produced by the surface of the two societies in friction" (134).

For the liberal novel there was evolution, continuity, to be driven
by the type of acuity and disengaged observation from the sidelines
such as Gordimer offered. There was the confidence to ruminate on
the human condition, relax into a faultlessly satirical commentary.

We don't need to be reminded now how even that has changed.
The twists and contortions of Gordimer's later vision show her loss
of cool, her embattled, confrontational position, and how the issues
in South Africa have polarized since then.

And, returning to A World of Strangers after such cultural de-
privation, the contemporary reader finds it is nothing like what it
was intended to be. It has turned into a documentary, an archive of
the writer's lost possibilities. The Stratford bar in Commissioner Street
(39), in a building owned by the same Oppenheimer group to which
an author like the late Alan Paton[4] made such a personal appeal for
charity in racial matters, is gone (in favour of a cut-rate supermarket)
. . . but so is the Imperialism it implied. In fact, about all of the
'50s that is left as a landmark is the literature. A World of Strangers

can now be seen as the "conglomerate night-cry" (her expression [131]) of memory; accurate, truthful, to be recaptured in full.

But this process of reclamation cannot proceed as innocently as the reception of the return of the '50s in general has proceeded.[5] Toby the Britisher, like Gordimer's later Bray in *A Guest of Honour*, derives his non-committal attitudes to life in reaction to his leftist, cause-championing intellectual family. For the novelist his non-partisanship is useful, gets him places. But Toby is also a conscienceless drifter; he can make no decisions other than in the end to quit, and he is guilty of moral dereliction (which, one fears, in those days passed all too easily as authentic existential angst).

Some of the judgments he makes we see with hindsight are unforgiveable. The myth of the Nietzschean south, which Gordimer quite schematically transposes from Forster's Italy to her southern Africa, must finally be seen as unfortunate, even libellous. Italians are entitled to feel as offended as are South Africa's blacks that some old northern European dialectic of otherness renders them "opposites," "outsiders"—in short, excluded. True, Gordimer frequently has him talk of "the feeling that the age-old crystals of the North were melting away in my blood" (129), and to some extent that is what *A World of Strangers* is really about, but they don't melt, give up, find a new chemistry. Nor does the novel; in the end it merely appropriates Johannesburg, never emotionally joins it and its wonderfully dispersed, derelict people.

There are also some heresies practised in the novel, unintentionally for sure. For example, the only character Toby encounters whose full autobiography is given is Anna Louw, an early portrait of an Afrikaner dissident. Through Toby, Gordimer rightly admires her— but is it her Afrikanerhood or her dissent which is so fascinating? If the former—well, Afrikaners have presented themselves as the only *true* South Africans for thirty years now, so that any overattention paid them in the literature, when it is at the cost of other true South Africans, receives little sympathy these days. If the latter—then Gordimer was thinking wishfully; revolt from within the ranks was not to come in the literature for another generation.

Many recent critics of Gordimer, herself included, would probably also react to her "township scenes" as too generalized, too panoramic. One has only to read works like Mongane Serote's *To Every Birth its Blood* (1981) to realize how hopelessly naïve they are: "And they lived, all the time, in all the layers of society at once: pimps, gangsters, errand boys, washwomen, school-teachers, boxers, musicians and undertakers, labourers and patent medicine men—these were neighbours, and shared a tap, a yard, even a lavatory" (130).

Apparent classlessness for class-crippled Toby is a democratic wonder, maybe, but Gordimer seems to endorse this romantic gush, rather than analyse it. Through the pane of glass that is privilege, plain common sense—impartiality—becomes distorted, the picture outside too idealized. Today Gordimer is the last author to be accused of over-simplification, but a reductive tendency was certainly there in her early work. The turnabout that most liberal thinkers of old have had to perform on this issue has obvious causes—apartheid thrives on gross, schematic simplifications and deceits—human rights, for example, become social engineering—and the system will certainly not fall through furthering that process.

Yet the new radical critics, guilt-stricken, can often not appear to be generous-spirited towards the old liberal style. At present its grievous ideological and tactical faults are anathema, its concealed paternalism and condescension out. Yet, confronted across the divide of forgetfulness with *A World of Strangers* once again, I believe it has taken on a newly promising value for us. It is one of the few works to tell us how things in Johannesburg really *were*.

Notes

1. All quotations from *A World of Strangers*, Penguin edition. "The street was one of those newly old streets that I saw all over Johannesburg—a place without a memory" (64).

2. "Outside my flat, piccanins shuffled and jerked their backsides to tin whistles and a banging on old tins" (189) is a characteristic remark.

3. Notably in Don Mattera's *Gone with the Twilight* (London: Zed, 1987), published in South Africa by Ravan with the more apt title, *Memory is the Weapon*. See also *Sophiatown Speaks*, Pippa Stein and Ruth Jacobson eds. (Johannesburg: Junction Avenue, 1986), which contains a retrospective interview with Gordimer on the '50s (25–30). Athol Fugard's novel, *Tsotsi*, first published only in 1980, is the outstanding example.

4. Paton's *Cry, the Beloved Country* (1948) is addressed to Sir Ernest Oppenheimer—surely the most misaimed appeal in modern letters.

5. Stephen Clingman's *The Novels of Nadine Gordimer: History from the Inside* (1986) is the necessary corrective.

The Degeneration of the Great South African Lie: *Occasion for Loving*   Abdul R. JanMohamed°

Gordimer's next novel, *Occasion for Loving*,[1] focuses on the problems of historical responsibility and amnesia. In fact, this am-

° From *Manichean Aesthetics: The Politics of Literature in Colonial Africa* (Amherst: University of Massachusetts Press, 1983), 101–7. © 1983 by the University of Massachusetts Press. Reprinted by permission.

bitious novel sets out to examine the nature of the *occasion* for loving as it is defined by contradictions between two fundamental matrices of human endeavor: the diachronic and the synchronic. Gordimer's novel scrutinizes the relevance, importance, and culpability of the Western development of these two matrices for the specific problems and conditions of South Africa; she analyzes the causes and effects of apartheid in terms of an awareness and acceptance of historical heritage and in terms of a more detached, atemporal, structuralist-scientific approach to society. Through a juxtaposition of these two major components of Western culture she is able to show that the particular configuration of apartheid and other colonial societies is produced by a studied negation of the democratic tendencies inherent in the development of Western countries and valorized by their histories.

Nadine Gordimer is able to ensure the success of this highly abstract undertaking by presenting her characters as specific, concrete human beings as well as analogues of larger cultural forces. Her characteristic ability to depict people and places, the psychological and social aspects of reality, with great clarity and precision prevents both the concrete and the analogic levels of meaning from over-whelming each other. The consequent balance and tension result in a brilliant novel that can be read simultaneously as a tragic love story and as an analysis of the effects of the contradiction between the diachronic and the synchronic on the South African "occasion," that is, on the possibilities of love and compassion in a manichean society.

Once again Gordimer's characterization is stylized, though not as dramatically as in the previous novel. Tom Stilwell, a historian, and his wife, Jessie, are analogues of the historic, communally oriented, diachronic tendencies, whereas Boaz Davis, a musicologist studying primitive African music, and his wife, Ann, are analogues of scientific, individually oriented, synchronic tendencies; the Stilwells have been born and bred in South Africa and are committed to staying there, whereas the Davises (who are living with the Stilwells while in South Africa), though born in southern Africa, have been living in Europe and plan to return as soon as Boaz's research is completed. The stylization is further enhanced by differences in the male/female functions within the analogic representations. Tom and Boaz respectively embody the objective, theoretical concerns of the diachronic and synchronic tendencies, whereas Jessie and Ann manifest them through their subjective, internalized, and personal actions and preoccupations. The major cast of analogic characters is completed by the introduction of Gideon Shibalo, a black painter, who represents the black South African conflict between historic and ahistoric tendencies, and who activates the plot of the novel by falling in love with Ann.

The theoretical side of the diachronic tendencies is represented by Tom's current project—a history of the European invasion of Africa that will neither valorize European superiority nor romanticize pre-colonial African cultures. On the practical and political level, Tom's commitment to a complex diachronic world is reflected by his fight against the government's ultimately successful attempts to bar Africans from the university where he happens to be teaching. The denial of advanced education, which is a cumulative product and an embodiment of Western history, would in effect isolate the black African from the material and intellectual products of Western culture as well as from its history. Thus Tom's commitment to history is theoretical, practical, and political.

Jessie's relation to the past is far more personal and affective. It manifests itself incidentally in her views of Christmas and the African miners' dance, both of which have been deprived of their traditional significance. Although she does not wish for a resurrection of the African past, she is horrified by the strangulation, the sudden end, of that culture; its past is destroyed, its present abominable, and its future ambiguous and problematic. However, Jessie's main historical concern is personal; throughout the novel she is engaged in an extended meditation focused on how her given "occasion"—that is, her personal and social relationships with her parents and with Morgan, her son from a previous marriage—affects the nature and strength of her love. Just as Tom, in his commitment to historical accuracy and continuity, fights the attempt to withhold Western education from blacks, so does Jessie, in her efforts to love in spite of her parents' selfishness, refuse to accept the diachronic disorientation produced by the absence of love and compassion. Through her analysis and subsequent transcendence of past handicaps she is able to love her current husband, Tom, and their children, and throughout the novel she makes a strenuous and finally successful effort to love Morgan. She overcomes the lack of adequate verbal communication between her son and herself by personally retracing his escapades in bars and bordellos. Her attempt to put herself in Morgan's place by experiencing his alterity and her commitment to live according to a code of "decency" by treating others as subjects become the sole means of solving the problems of her personal heritage.

Thus Jessie's heritage reflects certain aspects of the moral and political morass created by apartheid, and she shows a way out of those dilemmas by successfully liberating herself from that heritage. The selfishness and avarice that define her personal "occasion" imply, on the analogic level, the exclusionist and materialist tendencies of white South Africa; the absence of love indicates the lack of compassion in South African society; and the personal discontinuities she experiences correspond to the disjunction between European values and colonialist practice. By rejecting democracy, that is, by treating blacks as the *objects* of their self-centered desires, the white South Africans have radically disconnected themselves from the political development so central to the Western history and theory of progress and meliorism. Jessie's transcendence of diachronic and synchronic interpersonal distance implies that Europeans in South Africa can similarly overcome racial antipathy by individually subjecting themselves to a thorough and open-minded experience of black alterity.

The synchronic representation of Western culture is manifested in Boaz's "scientific" musicological studies which allow and in fact oblige him to examine selected parts of South African reality with "impartial" and "disinterested" eyes. He is only interested in the atemporal structure of African music and instruments, and not in their historic development. Although he is personally emancipated from racism, he insists that he intends to shun "politics" and to avoid the whole question of apartheid and moral responsibility because it has no bearing on his work. Yet Jessie prophetically warns him that it will not be easy to do so in South Africa where apartheid has contaminated all modes of human relations.

The disregard for historical context and development, deliberately espoused by Boaz as a professional necessity, is an intrinsic and natural essence of Ann's personality. She confines herself to a radically synchronic view of life: "The present was the only dimension of time she knew; she woke every day to her freedom of it" (*OFL*, 93). Her egotism and self-absorption exclude not only the past and the future but also intellectual abstraction; she is incapable of being moved by general notions of injustice and only responds to concrete suffering that she can witness. And Gideon falls in love precisely with her aura of concrete freedom, which she generates with her spontaneity, enthusiasm, and innocence, and which includes her childlike ignorance of race as an explosive issue in personal and social relations in South Africa.

In contrast to her, Gideon is a frustrated man, bitterly aware of his bondage. He is a talented painter who has been forced to relinquish a scholarship to Italy by the government's refusal to issue him a passport because of his political activity. His subsequent decision to refuse an exit permit, which would allow his departure but prevent his return to South Africa, has turned him into an aimless, brooding character who can no longer paint. Thus apartheid, by isolating him from the larger, diachronic movement of Western and world art, deprives him of a personal, synchronic outlet for his creative energies. This severe limitation propels him, like other black individuals, into renouncing personal desires and committing himself further to a communal fight against apartheid. He knows that only through this collective effort can he achieve an identity and a sense of historical direction.

Yet the social situation creates contradictions of which Gideon is unaware and which he cannot overcome easily. In spite of his support of a collective diachronic movement he, unlike Jessie and Tom, is intellectually unaware of the importance of history. During a discussion of African history at the Stilwells, Gideon insists that the African must forget his past, for when he accepts what Western civilization has to offer at present, he also accepts the future that it implies, and because the African past is irrelevant to that future he must not cling to it. Yet as Jessie clearly realizes, Gideon's past, his life in the brutal, squalid locations to which apartheid has condemned him, is an experience that permeates his life and actions. Gideon's personal connection with the African past, Jessie feels, gives him a continuity which is magical in its power to attract others. According to her, Gideon possesses an innocent, unconscious awareness of history which, unlike the Stilwells' deliberate, conscious analysis and understanding of the past, is not weighed down by inherited burdens and responsibilities. It is this historic innocence of Gideon, as well as his bondage and frustration, that makes him very susceptible to the synchronic vitality of Ann. She models for him, inspires him to recommence his painting, and rekindles his desire for personal freedom. The affair between Gideon and Ann is strong enough to flourish in a benign environment, but too weak to withstand the frustrations created by racial segregation. Unable to cope rationally with the pressures of a manichean society, Ann suddenly returns to Europe with her husband, once again shattering Gideon's hopes for freedom.

At the analogic level of meaning, Gordimer's treatment of the Davises and the affair between Gideon and Ann implies a powerful criticism of the cultural forces, whether scientific and technological or personal and avaricious, that are historically irresponsible. Gordimer demonstrates that even if one deliberately or spontaneously ignores one's involvement in the general, inclusive process of culture and history, one will not be left untouched by them: Boaz's attempts to eschew the politics of race are utterly futile. Through Ann's fantasy about Gideon's death, Gordimer condemns the colonialist's typical need to resolve his own conflict between his desire to dominate the native and his consequent guilt by wishing, and sometimes practicing, the annihilation of the colonized subject. Finally, through the sudden departure of the Davises, Gordimer also indicts those who, at the first sign of "trouble," abandon the problems they have created in the colonies in order to return to their home country, which they believe to be the only repository of "civilization." What Gordimer clearly identifies and criticizes is the ahistorical, exclusionist mentality of the colonialist who either wishes to dominate the native or chooses to ignore his existence.[2]

With the departure of Ann and Boaz, Tom, Jessie, and Gideon

are left to suffer the consequences of their encounter with the Davises. For Gideon the repercussions are drastic: he drinks himself into a stupor much as he had done when the passport and, therefore, the scholarship had been withheld from him. Ann's abandonment of Gideon implies that apartheid and those Europeans who tacitly support its existence have once more denied him the chance to live freely and to realize his individual artistic potential. If we treat Gideon as a tragic hero, then the flaw in his character has to be his attempt to strive for self-fulfillment and his hubris has to be his belief that his personal desires can be, or have a right to be, satisfied in a society deformed by apartheid. Thus by writing a quasi-tragic novel Gordimer poignantly shows that the kinds of personal freedom that most of us take for granted are extremely risky luxuries for those condemned to live in the fascist society created by apartheid. But Gordimer's novel is not tragic; that is, it is not concerned exclusively with the fate of a heroic individual; rather it focuses on the *occasion*, the social circumstances that produce freedom and bondage. Therefore, through Jessie's and Callie's constant reminders to Gideon, Gordimer insists that the latter's and his compatriots' only freedom lies in committing themselves to the political and historical necessity of overthrowing apartheid. For Jessie and Tom, two historically aware people, there is a modicum of redemption; Jessie and Morgan are reconciled at the end of the novel by having witnessed and experienced together the anguish, humiliation, and absurdity of the story of Ann and Gideon. Reconciliation between mother and son is made possible not through discursive dialogue but through a common experience of Gideon's history. However, there are negative repercussions for them too. Their belief in "the integrity of personal relations against the distortions of laws and society," a belief that is a part of their Western historical inheritance, is badly shaken.

Yet the gloomy ending of the novel, which implies an unavoidable racial conflict, is belied to some extent by the existence and nature of the novel itself. *Occasion for Loving* is a product of a project similar to the one to which Tom and Jessie have committed themselves: a clear-headed analysis of South African history designed to culminate in an unsentimental definition of its present condition. The end of the novel, then, warns us to remember its contents. It implies that the manichean racial tension and opposition in South Africa can still be resolved if those who have produced and supported apartheid are willing to recognize their responsibility through a thorough analysis and understanding of the South African *occasion*. The absence of compassion in the South African political system can only be remedied through a clear awareness of the history that produced it—through a comprehension of how democratic Europe was able to create a perfectly fascist regime in South Africa in the name of civilization.

The conclusion of the novel also clarifies the ever-present contradiction between the desire to stay and the desire to leave. The
need to depart, now clearly associated with the Davises, implies
historical irresponsibility whereas "staying," associated with the Stilwells' commitment, indicates an acceptance of the culpability for the
problems created by colonialism and a dedication to resolve them no
matter how much personal suffering and danger this may entail. With
this clarification and commitment Nadine Gordimer ceases being a
"colonial" writer to the extent that the colonialist mentality is marked
by its belief that "home" and "civilization" are located back in
Europe, that life in the colonies is a temporary exile in an outpost
surrounded by savagery and barbarism.

These three books form a coherent group to the extent that they
are all novels of recognition. All of them culminate with the shocking
realization that apartheid is indeed appalling and that the liberal
creed is useless in this setting. Yet this knowledge is followed by a
relative stasis. There is no action in any of the novels to change
society; rather they end with a desire to leave that is eventually
conquered and with expressions of intentions, of promises to continue
the struggle. However, the narrative repetition is balanced by a
progressively deeper understanding of the historical causes of apartheid. In fact, the problem of historical determination itself increasingly
becomes one of the central issues. And one would suspect that a
historical understanding of one's present "occasion" would eventually
result in imperatives for future action. Indeed the second group of
novels is distinguished from the first by its greater commitment, no
matter how vague at times, to the forces opposed to apartheid.

Notes

1. Nadine Gordimer, *Occasion for Loving* (New York: Viking Press, 1960). All
further references to this novel will be abbreviated as *OFL* and incorporated in the
text.

2. Rose Moss argues that the unsuccessful affair between Gideon and Ann implies
a corresponding failure in Gordimer's imagination—"her imagination sometimes seems
blocked at the point where the road leads out of the territory she shares with the
authorities she detests." See her article "Hand in Glove/Nadine Gordimer: South
African Writer: a Case Study in Censorship," *Pacific Quarterly Moana* 6, nos. 3/4
(1981): 106–22. However, it seems to me that this approach ascribes an intention to
Gordimer and then criticizes her for not fully realizing it. Gordimer firmly subordinates
her imagination to the realities of apartheid and racism; she is less concerned with
portraying ideal possibilities (the hypothetical transcendence of racial barriers) and
more with depicting the debilitating effects of those barriers. As I argue later in this
chapter, Gordimer deliberately confines herself to the "territory" of apartheid in order
to chart it as thoroughly as possible.

A *Guest of Honour:*
A Feminine View of Masculinity   Elaine Fido[*]

The political material which fills out Nadine Gordimer's *A Guest of Honour*,[1] and which is used to establish the milieu of the central theme, is not the most important aspect of the novel. Critics, however, frequently examine the novel from the point of view of politics. Robert Haugh[2] and Robert Green,[3] for example, have compared it with Conrad's *Nostromo* but come to different conclusions. Haugh criticizes the amount of political material in Gordimer's novel, whereas Green praises the critical realism of the whole work and its recognition of the extent to which politics affects the entire scope of human experience. As Green observes: "*A Guest of Honour* is preoccupied with the nature of political and individual change,"[4] and he bases his thesis on the judgment that Gordimer sees truly into Black African politics:

> Gordimer's achievement here, in understanding the historical forces at work in independent, black Africa and giving them such real embodiments in fiction, is made still more remarkable in that this insight doesn't result from long residence in emancipated Africa.[5]

Green's praise, however, obscures the fact that as a political novel *A Guest of Honour* deals rather too much in commonplaces: neo-colonialist versus neo-Marxist; liberalism distressed by political realities; industrial action versus organized authority being treated as subversion; political thugs enjoying violent rampages in the name of the Party. It is like a collection of news reports of recent years, and not only from Africa. Haugh also notes the naivete of the political material: "the novel reveals a stubborn and outmoded liberalism, with the dream of socialism—if we are to take Bray's ideas seriously— still overriding the hard facts of human nature."[6] There are, indeed, serious weaknesses in Gordimer's handling of political material, in terms of convincing the reader of the validity of this fictional African state. One of these is the newspaper report on Mweta's Preventive Detention Bill, whose language suggests *The Times* rather than an African newspaper:

> There is no doubt that this country sees its destiny always as part of the greater destiny of the African continent . . . no doubt that President Mweta, the day he took up the burdens of office, has taken along with responsibilities at home the ideal of an African that would present an entity of international cooperation to a world which has so far signally failed to resolve national contradictions. (p. 147)

[*] From *World Literature Written in English* 17 (1978):30–37. Reprinted by permission.

Mweta's country, itself, is an obvious mixture of aspects of recognizable African states: Eastern and Southern African geographical details predominate, but there are political echoes of West Africa. Dando, for example, recalls Nkrumah's Geoffrey Byng[7] to some extent. The result of this is that while Gordimer cannot be accused of poorly portraying a particular location, the reader is forced to suspend skepticism at the way in which facts of Mweta's society are supposed to hang together.

The country Gordimer has created is just barely plausible and not nearly so politically interesting as modern Africa. Her characters tend towards the well-sketched type: the new African civil servant Aleke, the Police Chief Lebaliso, the settler-farmer Boxer, the European Club Secretary, the amoral businessman Gordon Edwards.[8] There is even an Indian tailor, Mr. Jeesab. In the capital, an unlikely group of whites manages a blissfully easy-going relationship with their African colleagues. A liberal, Hjalmar Wentz, runs a bar, having moved up from South Africa against the usual tide of white migration.

These characters support the major four: Bray, Mweta, Shinza, and Rebecca Edwards. But Mweta and Shinza are seen only from the outside, in accordance with Gordimer's unfortunate, recent concession to the effects of the apartheid:

> I now believe that Georg Lukacs is right when he says that a writer, in imaginative creation and the intuition that comes with it, cannot go beyond the *potential* of his own experience. That potential is very wide; but living in a society that has been as deeply and calculatedly compartmentalized as South Africa's has been under the color bar, the writer's potential has unscalable limitations.[9]

By this she means that some aspects of black experience are closed to a white writer and vice versa. Critical acclaim for Gordimer's faithful portrayal of the politics of a black African country must be reevaluated if the author asserts that her understanding of black politicians is limited. Rebecca Edwards has only the last part of the novel in which to establish herself with the reader independent of Bray's assumptions, but like the rest of the book, Part Six is dominated by James Bray.

Bray is an Englishman, but has spent his working life in Africa. A colonial officer at one time, he was recalled to England for siding with the African independence movement in his province. He is in his mid-fifties when the novel opens, but he resents the idea of old age. He thus contains within himself enough conflicting facts to provide an interesting study of a search for identity. Gordimer shows him returning to Africa from the safe but suffocating comfort of his Wiltshire retirement, looking for a job to do to restore his sense of himself as a fit and useful man. She further protects herself from having to grapple too closely with inner lives of her black characters by channeling all the novel's experience through Bray's until the last section. At the same time, because Bray is so familiar with the African scene, Gordimer can include a great many details of place and society which qualify the novel as African by her own definition:

> African writing is writing done in any language by Africans them-
> selves and by others of whatever skin color who share with Africans
> the experience of having been shaped, mentally and spiritually, by
> Africa rather than by anywhere else in the world.[10]

Nevertheless, her work is closer to European models than to the novels of Achebe, Soyinka, or Ngugi, and in *A Guest of Honour*, with its emphasis on the character and the final tragedy of Bray, Gordimer is following a Western tradition of fiction. Furthermore, by examining the relationship of masculinity to power and therefore to politics, Gordimer shares concerns with a growing number of feminist writers.

Gordimer emphasizes certain key details of Bray's experiences which highlight his pursuit of the masculine illusion that sexual potency makes a man more effective as a public figure. Most important and most obvious is his obsession with Shinza's recent paternity. Some readers have felt that the love affair between Rebecca and Bray is a weakness of the novel, a sop to female readers, and a surprising return to conventional novelistic material. But it is essential to the theme of masculinity and power. When Bray, previously monogamous, copulates with Rebecca without even looking at her, he thinks urgently of Shinza and the sense of power and of life. He has taken away from his first reunion with him an image of vibrant masculinity: "the vigour of Shinza's breast, rising and falling, the strong neck shining a little with warmth—a body still a man's body and not an old man's" (p. 120). Bray thus reveals a personal distinction between aging and maturity, and his fear that the former does not inevitably allow the latter. Bray is determined to fight against the role he was being encouraged to play in Wiltshire: the gentle grandfather, reading Proust with his wife, doing a little gardening, and writing his history of Mweta's country. Instead of such a life of secure pleasure and scholarly usefulness, he prefers to return to Africa, to serve as best he can.

Such is the man who arrives for the Independence ceremonies, still using the careful self-control built up over a working life in which paternalistic kindness and self-effacement became the most valuable aids he could develop in himself to further the cause of African nationalism. By the end of the novel, Bray is accidentally killed whilst on his way to negotiate resouces for Shinza's rising. He has become a political agent of his own choosing and so exposed to the dangers of a destabilized country. Although his death is not directly related to his own activity, he is at that time aware of the danger to his course of action, if Mweta discovers it.

The most important single event in the chain leading Bray from one mode of action to the other is his first meeting with Shinza. In Bray's eyes, Shinza becomes a symbol of masculinity, someone to emulate and ultimately to follow and serve. As a result of experiencing Shinza's careless arrogance, of being made to feel naive by him, and most of all, of seeing Shinza as a sexually potent man, Bray starts to release himself from the control which monogamous marriage and liberal altruism have long placed on his powerful personality.

For Bray is experiencing a reprieve from old age. He is free of permanent responsibilities: children, a wife, a long-lasting career. When Mweta asks him to return to Africa, he feels "a strong consciousness of his own being . . . as if a stimulant had been injected into his veins" (p. 5). He does not take up an airline booking already made to return to Olivia, his wife, after the Independence celebrations, because Mweta gives him a job. This is the first rebellion against the life-long ties of loyalty and affection to his wife. Much later in the novel, Bray thinks of the mutual pleasure which he and Olivia shared sexually. Yet in bed with Rebecca, he behaves like any feminist's idea of the classic male chauvinist, concerned with the performance and power: "he brought a small yell of triumph from her; and again" (p. 143). After some time in this affair with Rebecca, he assumes, with the realization of his arrogance, that Olivia's sexual life is over anyway, and that he is the survivor in that respect, reviving himself with a younger woman.

It is not far from this sexual emulation of Shinza to political adherence. While Bray bristles at the idea that Mweta wants him to spy on Shinza, he allows Shinza to use him as messenger to Switzerland, although he dies before he can achieve his purpose. At the Party Congress, Shinza claims his loyalty, "that's my man" (p. 365). The phrase has a special meaning in the light of the novel, since it is masculine identity which Bray is seeking.

The post-colonial white man in Africa has to rethink his role, in Bray's opinion. He himself worked for the abnegation of his own power and the new dispensation should therefore worry him less than most expatriates. But he worries that Mweta is still looking to him as mentor, and he thinks that it is difficult for a white man in Africa to see himself as anything but that. He is strongly aware of his size, his height, his solidity, his pinkness, "almost like some form of aggression he wasn't responsible for" (p. 35). The old equation of white with power emerges again even now when Bray is approached by a school master to help a relative into agricultural college. The paternalism of the District Officer returns; Bray is polite and speaks the man's language, but nevertheless, they are not equals.

Paradoxically, then, Bray wanted to control and ultimately give up the extent of his power during the colonial period, and now, as a free agent, he begins to want some, first sexually, and then as a means to effecting a situation of which he approves in the new African state. But the basis of his actions remains a desire to bolster his sense of himself as an active man. He is disarmingly aware of himself as partly ridiculous; he and Olivia used to joke about men with "a last kick of the prostate" (p. 321). He worries that he is becoming a "boy scout," (p. 214), or that he is virginal, taking on a "sort of priggish absurdity" (p. 214) with his high-mindedness about Mweta's methods. But increasingly, through the novel, we watch a physical attraction to Shinza become an emotional involvement with the man. Political affiliation follows, gradually, in a much more reasoned manner. Mweta's inability to cast a physical spell over Bray is a significant factor in the change of heart that Bray experiences.

Presented as a delicately built man, with fastidious habits and a clear, if not extraordinary, mind, Mweta takes every piece of aspic from his cold duck. He has "womanish curly eyelashes" (p. 194), and is "small" (p. 5) and "quick" (pp. 5, 69). Bray can see delicacy and can associate it with strength, as when he thinks of African convicts breaking stones with beautiful hands or when he sees Shinza's delicate ears. But Mweta is not physically imposing, while Bray, like Shinza, is a big man and very conscious of it. At best, Bray notices him as handsome, in the Congress. But the adjectives "handsome" (p. 266, 270) and "small," (p. 266) are used by him for Gordon Edwards, Rebecca's husband, for whom Bray feels only a slight jealous contempt. Finally, there is an implicit relationship between Mweta's solid marriage and political compromises, just as there is between Shinza's romantic sexuality and dreams of a revolution.

The novel thus examines the kind of illusion concerning liberation and sex which is being increasingly exposed by feminist writers. Germaine Greer linked the idea of sexual impotence and feminine submission in The Female Eunuch,[11] where she called for sexual emancipation and social freedom at one and the same time. Shulamith Firestone in The Dialectic of Sex[12] devoted a whole chapter to her assertion that racism is basically a sexual phenomenon, since sexual power structures dominate society. Kate Millett, in Sexual Politics,[13] cites and attacks a 1947 popularizer of Freud, referring to penile erection: "Here it is that mastery and domination, the central capacity of the man's sexual nature, must meet acceptance or fail."[14] Clearly, then, Gordimer is in line with feminist thought in examining the relation of sexual potency and political drive in the masculine psyche. Like other feminists, she criticizes, in the person of Bray, paternalism and patriarchal domination. Bray is initially portrayed as the product of paternalistic colonialism and even despite his own rebellion against its racial prescriptions, he practises a retreat into his "elderly" voice when, to steady himself, he wishes to reject his intimate relationship with Rebecca. During the course of the novel, he grows away from this paternalism, thought not entirely, to a more equal footing with Rebecca and to a recognition of Shinza's intellectual as well as physical strength. There never was any chance to patronize Shinza, who has a more sophisticated mind and is better educated than Mweta.

Gordimer, then, has managed to achieve in fiction an analysis of sex and power similar to that which other feminists have accomplished in essays, with the clear difference that she has a novelist's concern for the character which she has created, and a sympathy with the forces that restrict men to specific attributes and roles. The novel shows, among other points, that the kind of *machismo* which Shinza exerts is compelling for a man brought up with traditional ideas of the male role.

Because of her central concern with Bray, Gordimer does not detail the fate of Rebecca or Olivia or any of the other women in the novel, and, indeed, casts them in rather familiar models as women who in various ways play supportive roles to their husbands. Rebecca must be seen as a victim for Bray to love her. Further, Rebecca betrays an old prejudice of women which supports the *machismo* drive when she says she finds Hjalmar Wentz weak and therefore irritating. Bray remembers Olivia as a pretty young girl, and refers to her as writing a letter to him in Gala whose tone suggests a spoiled child. Olivia never emerges out of the cocoon of her domestic roles. But like Jane Austen, Gordimer is acutely aware of the nature of responsiveness between men and women.

Degrees of masculinity are portrayed; Dando and his old steward argue like a pair "of old-maid sisters" (p. 17), Dando is "indiscreet" and even in a masculine context, he seems like "an old seal, long outcast from lordship of the harem by the young bull" (p. 185). Boxer, when staying with Bray, seems "old maidish" (p. 288) and Bray contemplates the possibility that Boxer is impotent by now. Hjalmar Wentz seems "an old woman giving a confidence" (p. 335) as he talks to Bray. All these men are white and elderly. Bray is alone amongst them in seeking a new vitality. Without change, he would become anachronistic, like the two spinster sisters, Adelaide and Felicity, because his old role does not fit into the new state. One particularly interesting example of the irreversibility of Bray's change is his rejection of Kalimo, the old steward, who comes out of retirement to serve Bray, as in the old days. Now, however, he is old and inefficient, but more important, Bray will not allow himself to sink into the bachelor state of being cared for by an elderly servant, a surrogate wife in domestic chores.

The passage which highlights Bray's recognition of the contrasting emotions he feels for Mweta and Shinza deserves to be quoted at length:

> Bray had never had with Shinza the sense of affection he had with Mweta, the affection that of course meant a certain physical affinity too. . . . That was partly what the girl meant when she said once that he "loved" Mweta. . . . But with Shinza, who knew him so much better than Mweta did, between Shinza and himself there was something of physical hostility. He remembered once more the moment, the day he had first seen Shinza again, with the boy-child he had begotten on a young girl, feeble in his hand. A moment of pure sexual jealousy. (p. 353)

This passage sums up the growing tensions between Bray and his two African friends. It is shortly after this that Bray turns towards Shinza positively. This passage also makes more sense of the realization in Bray that he is now both unreasoning and "whole." He has revived the full strength of his manhood, and yet succumbed, to do it, to a dangerous fascination with possibly irresponsible power.

The novel concludes, nicely, with Bray's immortalization in "the Bray report." Mweta, now that Bray is safely dead, can afford to be generous. If the art of politics is the art of maintaining power, then Mweta is a strong denial of Bray's feeling that the stronger masculine personality is the best political bet.

A Guest of Honour is an important novel, since it breaks new ground in theme, but also, and more importantly, because Gordimer is developing a capacity which contradicts her reliance on Lukacs' remark. She is able to cross over into the "other" experience of men, and yet retain her female perspective on experience and transmit it. Gordimer manages to fuse both masculine and feminine, giving a rich sense of the way in which people, men and women, relate to each other. Gordimer's skill in this novel, then, is to make politics seem to grow naturally out of the sexual nature of men, rather than to make experience subordinate to politics.

Notes

1. Nadine Gordimer, *A Guest of Honour* (London: 1971). Subsequent references to the novel will be found in body of the essay.

2. Robert F. Haugh, *Nadine Gordimer* (New York: 1974). pp. 145–160.

3. Robert J. Green, "Nadine Gordimer's *A Guest of Honour*," *World Literature Written in English*, Vl. 16, No. 1, (April 1977), pp. 55–65.

4. Green, p. 59.

5. Green, p. 56.

6. *Nadine Gordimer*, p. 159.

7. The British Labour Politician who served in Kwame Nkrumah's Cabinet until Nkrumah was deposed.

8. This character is of a type which is in life reflected in "Tiny" Rowlands, the Anglo-Indian businessman whose manifold black and white contacts across Africa enabled him to build the small London and Rhodesian Mining Company into a multi-million pound African business with four hundred subsidiaries.

9. Nadine Gordimer, "The Novel and the Nation in South Africa" in *African Writers on African Writing*, ed. G. D. Killam (London: 1973), p. 52.

10. Nadine Gordimer, *The Black Interpreters* (Johannesburg: 1973), p. 5.

11. Germaine Greer, *The Female Eunuch* (London: 1971).

12. Shulamith Firestone, *The Dialectic of Sex* (New York: 1970; London: 1971).

13. Kate Millett, *Sexual Politics* (London: 1971), p. 209.

14. Millet, p. 209. The quotation is taken from Ferdinand and Lundberh and Marynia F. Farnham, *Modern Woman, The Lost Sex* (New York: 1947), p. 241.

Landscapes Inhabited in Imagination: *A Guest of Honour*   John Cooke°

Gordimer described the setting of *A Guest of Honour* in 1970 as "a nonexistent, composite central African country. Imagine a place somewhere between Kenya, Tanzania, Zambia, Rhodesia, and Angola—you know, just make a hole in the middle of Africa and push it in—that's where it takes place."[1] It's a large hole, particularly by contrast with the limited urban settings of earlier novels. And the filling is different. For the first time in Gordimer's novels, the central figures are political men and the major events public spectacles, from the independence celebrations which open the novel to the party congress near the close. As in many of the states Gordimer mentions, these spectacles are the battleground for factions advocating different shapes for this new African state. The faction in power, led by Adamson Mweta, accepts, if reluctantly, a continued reliance on colonial economic and social structures; the opposition, led by Mweta's former mentor Edward Shinza, urges an African socialist path. Gordimer proves surprisingly deft in introducing not only the large cast of characters on both sides but of the many disoriented by the rapid transition to self-rule, like the servant that James Bray greets on his return as a guest of honor for the independence celebrations:

> Bray greeted the servant in Gala with the respectful form of address
> for elders and the man dumped the impersonality of a servant as

° From *The Novels of Nadine Gordimer: Private Lives/Public Landscapes* (Baton Rouge: Louisiana State University Press, 1985), 134–48. Reprinted by permission of Louisiana State University Press. © 1985 by LSU Press.

if it had been the tray in his hands and grinned warmly, showing some pigmentation abnormality in a pink lip spotted like a Dalmation. The ex-Governor looked on, smiling. The servant bowed confusedly at him, walking backwards, in the tribal way before rank, and then recovering himself and leaving the room with an anonymous lope. (p. 28)

Gordimer includes scores of characters like this servant in a vast canvas covering Mweta's capital, Shinza's rural Bashi Flats, and the old colonial outpost of Gala to which Bray returns.

Bray, who had been a district commissioner in Gala but removed ten years previously for supporting African demands for self-rule, is himself transformed during the course of the novel by learning how to participate in Shinza's attempts to transform the new country. He begins by assuming that his role in the new state will be simple: with the colonial era ended, he will facilitate the foundation of a new African society by serving as Mweta's educational advisor. His response during the celebrations to the servant in the traditional African way and his perception of the ex-governor as a smiling on-looker are but two small indications of his certainty that one era has passed, another begun. Bray eventually learns, however, what is most succinctly put in a passage from Frantz Fanon that he reads midway through the novel: "Everything seemed so simple before: the bad people were on one side, and the good on the other. The clear, the unreal, the idyllic light of the beginning is followed by a semi-darkness that bewilders the senses" (p. 292). Bray, a friend of both Mweta and Shinza, must learn to first accept this semi-darkness, then act within it, as he finally does by trying to assist Shinza. Indeed, the novel opens with him in the semi-darkness between waking and sleeping: "A bird cried on the roof, and he woke up. It was the middle of the afternoon, in the heat, in Africa; he knew where he was" (p. 3). This claim is unconvincing, for Bray immediately drifts into an extended recollection of the English country estate he has just left. It will take most of the novel for him to renounce the moderate, liberal values that are appropriate in that setting but finally, he learns, inappropriate in the new African country.

For most of the novel, Bray persists in a mediatory posture between two sets of contradictory allegiances: on the one hand, Mweta and his wife Olivia, whom he finally realizes were "linked at some level of his mind"; on the other, Shinza and Rebecca Edwards, a woman through whom the fifty-year-old Bray finds a revivified sensuality (p. 377). The depth of conflict he feels is indicated by Mweta's given name, Adamson. Which son of Adam is he, Bray tries to see, a betrayed Abel to Shinza's Cain or vice versa? From these two pairs grow other larger oppositions: between Mweta's city and Shinza's country worlds, neocolonialism and socialism, rationalism and intuition, a life of the present and a life governed by a sense of history. Bray must learn to operate in the world of semi-darkness these oppositions create. He finally does so when he comes to understand shortly before his death "that one could never hope to be free of doubt, of contradictions within, that this was the state in which one lived" (p. 465).

Bray learns how to act in the face of these contradictions through a process which is the reverse of Gordimer's early protagonists. He begins by attempting to read the "outward signs" in the landscape, but he gradually finds that only by allowing the landscape to inhabit him can he sense a role for himself. He comes to trust less in his vision of the landscape, more in envisioning within its presence. He articulates this change near the novel's close when he realizes that his future with Rebecca had been presaged by his first view of the lake near Gala:

> If he had been able to see it, the girl was there ahead in that presence. He had the feeling that the area of uncertainty that surrounded him visually when he took off his glasses was the real circumstance in which he had lived his life; and his glasses were more than a means of correcting a physical shortcoming, they were his chosen way of rearranging the unknowable into a few outlines he had gone by. (p. 431)

The external world, the lake here, holds signs, but they must be sensed as a "presence," not through acuity of sight which gives the false promise of a pattern which can be read in a discrete landscape. Bray finally learns to accept that his world is an "area of uncertainty" which can be negotiated only by means of what he terms "a kind of second intelligence." He finds that a developing history can be sensed in such presences as the lake; the continuity Jessie Stilwell found in the African kraals cannot be seen or described, only felt.

From the novel's outset, environment plays a much more significant role than in the earlier works. It is not simply something that can be observed; rather, it enforces a kind of life. The environment has the same insidious power that the personal bonds to mothers had for Helen Shaw and Jessie Stilwell. Its power is first revealed through the effect of Olivia Bray's furnishings of the Wiltshire house that she and Bray were to inhabit during their retirement. She had taken out her family's furniture and possessions "and, putting them in place, inevitably had accepted the life the arrangement of such objects provided for": "In the room they had decided on for his study, the desk from her great-grandfather that had naturally become his—a quiet field of black-red morocco scratched with almost erased gold—was a place to write the properly documented history of the territory (Mweta's country) that had never been done before" (p. 7).

This description gives the sense that not just the furniture but the inhabitants are "put in place." Not simply a kind of life, but the very way one looks at the world seems determined by this external order. Bray is "naturally" put in the role of the detached observer when put at "a place to write the properly documented history." Even when Bray imagines the house, after months away from it in Gala, its power of place reasserts itself:

> The house in Wiltshire with all its comfortable beauty and order, its incenses of fresh flowers and good cooking, its libations of carefully discussed and chosen wine came to Bray in all the calm detail of an interesting death cult; to wake up there again would be to find oneself acquiescently buried alive. At the same time, he felt a stony sense of betrayal. Olivia moved about there, peppermints and cigarettes on the night-table, her long, smooth-stockinged legs under skirts that always drooped slightly at the back. A detail taken from a painting, isolated and brought up close to the eye. (p. 130)

Bray's very thoughts of the house's order cause it to come to him in "calm detail" and finally to resolve itself into the detail from a painting. The sense of the environment's dominance is created by presenting the atmosphere of the house, then describing Olivia's place in it, ending with her legs as a detail taken from the larger whole of Bray's "painting."

By the time of this recollection, Bray has obviously begun to reject, because it is unchanging, this world which can be pictured, in which Olivia's skirts "always" drooped. This house is not somewhere Bray can "wake up"; in this passage "wake," bracketed by "death cult" and "buried alive," clearly suggests a funeral. His movement away from this visioning of life is made possible by Gala's environment in which he becomes, less and less, a detached observer. His movement toward merging with what he observes is revealed in thoughts of Rebecca occasioned by his use of the phrase "for a lifetime" in a letter to Mweta:

> For a lifetime—lying suddenly in his mind, the word associated with advertisements for expensive Swiss watches: lifetime. The habits of a lifetime. He felt himself outside that secure concept built up coating by coating, he was exposed nakedly as a man who has been shut away too long from the sun. The girl presented herself face-to-face, fact-to-fact with him, a poster-apocalypse filling the sky of his mind. Thought could crawl all over and about her, over the steadfast smile and the open yellow eyes and in and out the ears and nostrils. (p. 269)

Bray's engagement in this scene is revealed most obviously by the two references to its being in his mind, the trite phrase "lying" there, Rebecca more actively "filling" it. The choppy phrasing and the abrupt transitions reinforce the sense of internal images, feeling rather than intellect, in operation. The pictorial comparison remains, but the picture is without form and certainly not seen from the detached perspective of the Wiltshire house; rather, Rebecca is taken into Bray, face-to-face. This world of engagement has its dangers too. In fact, this vision foreshadows Bray's own apocalypse, his being murdered while attempting to leave the country to raise funds for Shinza. Rebecca's "yellow eyes" suggest Balzac's *La Fille au Yeux d'Or* that Bray will use as the password for securing funds in Switzerland. As in his thoughts about the lake above, this scene—"if he had been able to see it"—portends not only his private engagement with Rebecca but engagement in a Sartrian sense as well, for the trip to Switzerland is in aid of Shinza's political cause. The scene thus reveals a future intuitively apprehended, a claiming of a life-in-death with Rebecca and Shinza, a rejection of a death-in-life with Olivia and Mweta.

Reaching this point requires a radical change in Bray. At the novel's outset he attempts to comprehend the current condition of the African state, from which he has been absent ten years, through picturing it in much the same way as Toby Hood had Johannesburg in *A World of Strangers.* During the independence celebrations Bray provides descriptions of the town's buildings, such as the Great Lakes Hotel and the Silver Rhino bar, which, as their names imply, embody the colonial era which Bray assumes will soon cease to exist. On his first visit to Mweta's new house, Bray finds yet another colonial remnant:

> It was neo-classical, with a long double row of white pillars holding up a portico before a great block of local terracotta brick and mica-tinselled stone, row upon row of identical windows like a barracks. The new coat-of-arms was in place on the façade. The other side, looking down upon the park as if Capability Brown had been expected but somehow failed to provide the appropriate sweep of landscaped lawn, artificial lake, pavilion, and deer, was not so bad. The park itself, simply the leafier trees of the bush thinned out over seven or eight acres of rough grass, was—as he remembered it—full of hoopoes and chameleons who had been there to begin with, anyway. (p. 56)

Bray is unsettled by Mweta's having occupied the governor's mansion, especially perhaps because of the uncanny resemblance of this mansion to the house Bray himself has left behind. The Wiltshire house also has an imposing façade and an extended grassy look-out down through a long valley behind it. Bray takes solace in the African aspect of the park, which seems to be merely thinned-out bush. Yet, while he refuses to acknowledge them, the details reveal the beginning of

Fanon's semi-darkness. The mansion and grounds have more of an English than an African aspect. Not just the neo-classical portico but even the so-called local aspects have a European flavor: the local brick is terracotta; the hoopoes and chameleons are European as well as African animals. Bray thinks that this house can be easily ignored. At the end of a walk in the park with Mweta, Bray concludes, "It was so easy, very tempting—he looked at the empty house looming up in their way—one could walk round the past they had inhabited, as one does round a monument" (p. 69). As in so many of the novel's descriptions, this house carries signs of a future as yet unapprehended by Bray and indications that the past cannot be walked around. The house, as the depiction of the windows indicates, will become a barracks during an insurrection near the novel's close. And the house is one means by which Mweta will show his desire to continue the colonial regime he inherited; he will later reject the non-English aspects of the park by closing a window looking on to it and commenting, "We're not in the bush in Gala anymore" (p. 162). Mweta does seem to expect that an architect like Capability Brown, so named for his finding "capability" in the most unprepossessing sites, might yet transform the African bush into an English country garden.

As Bray leaves the capital for Gala, where he has agreed to serve as Mweta's educational consultant, the landscape he observes also reveals his desire to see the colonial era as coming to a neat close. The pattern he perceives in the landscape is the same pictured by Helen Shaw and Toby Hood—the city, then the encircling gold mines, and finally the mine properties:

> Then there were the landscaped approaches to the mine properties themselves, all flowery traffic roundabouts, sign-boards, and beds of cannas and roses, and then the stretches of neat color-washed rectangles of housing for the African miners, a geometric pattern scribbled over by the mop-heads of paw-paw trees, smoking chimneys, washing lines, creepers and maize patches, and broken up by the noise and movement of people. In twenty minutes it was all gone; he passed the Bush Hill Arms, its Tudor façade pocked with wasp nests and a "For Sale" notice up (someone else "getting out"), and then there was nothing at all—everything; the one smooth road, the trees, the bamboo, and the sudden open country of the *dambos* where long grasses hid water, and he saw at last, again, the single long-tailed shrike that one always seemed to see in such places, hovering with its ink-black tail-plume like the brushstroke of a Chinese ideograph. (p. 76)

Bray is quick to notice that the Bush Hill Arms (like his own and Mweta's residences) has an English façade, which marks it as a superficial remnant of empire left by another colonial "getting out." This end of the colonial era is signaled to him as well by the intrusion of the African landscape and people into the neat "geometric pattern" of housing created by the mine owners, which is "scribbled over" by indigenous trees and "broken up" by the Africans' noise and movement. Bray's need to see the country's history in such neat terms is also revealed as he moves out into the veld. Its formlessness causes him to distance himself by resolving it into a composition, the bird giving it the form of a Chinese ideograph. He still feels the need to control "the sudden open country" by keeping it at a distance, a picture to be viewed. It will require time for him to come up close to this world as he does, for instance, when that phrase "for a lifetime" lay "suddenly in his mind," leading to his vision of merging with Rebecca. Here he reacts as Helen Shaw did to the sudden stretch of open veld outside the mines; his conceiving it as a composition is the counterpart of her retreat to the order of the clearly focused picture of the colonials playing tennis.

On entering the town of Gala, Bray finds a history in the landscape which shows even more emphatically his belief that the colonial era need no longer be reckoned with. He thinks of the outpost Tippo Tib established nearby as part of his slave network, then of the British colonial settlement:

> Walls had fallen down in the village but trees remained; too big to be hacked out of the way of the slave-caravan trail; too strong to be destroyed by fire when British troops were in the process of subduing the population; revered by several generations of colonial ladies, who succeeded in having a local by-law promulgated to forbid anyone chopping them down. Their huge grey outcrops of root provided stands for bicycles and booths for traders and crafts-men; the shoemaker worked there, and the bicycle and sewing-machine repairer. (p. 90)

This landscape shows not just that the colonial era has passed but that it never really took effect. The slave caravans, British troops, and colonial ladies made no lasting impact on the native environment, for those trees remained. The two references to bicycles also show Bray's attempt to deny the continuing colonial presence, for his allegiance to Mweta, long after his maintenance of colonial policies should be clear to Bray, is due to his image of Mweta as "the boy on the bicycle" journeying from village to village in the campaign for self-rule. Bray has indeed walked around that governor's mansion to avoid seeing that the boy on the bicycle has become part of the colonial system he previously fought. Bray, in short, persists in viewing the colonial era as past. As he thinks shortly afterwards, his own role before independence had been dictated by "a particular historical situation, a situation that no longer existed. Not objectively, and not for him; he had been away and come back clear of it" (p. 92). This

easy and tempting view is clearly bound up with his lack of involvement with the society to which he returns. So long as he persists in
separating what is "objectively" out there from himself, he will remain
"clear of" the troubling semi-darkness around him.

Soon after Bray's arrival, Gordimer introduces the beginnings of
the engaged perspective which will lead to his choice of Rebecca
and Shinza. This new perspective, prompted by Bray's first thoughts
of the lake, serves as a comment on the simple historical view he
has maintained thus far:

> As he went in and out of the Fisheagle Inn he was sometimes
> arrested, from the veranda, by the sight of the lake. The sign of
> the lake: a blinding strip of shimmer, far away beyond the trees,
> or on less clear days, a different quality in the haze. For a moment
> his mind emptied; the restless glitter of the lake, the line of a
> glance below a lowered lid—for it was not really the lake at all
> that one saw, but a trick of the distance, the lake's own bright
> glare cast up upon the heated atmosphere, just as the vast opening
> out of pacing water to the horizon, once you got to its bush-hairy
> shores, was not really the open lake itself at all, but (as the map
> showed) only the southernmost tip of the great waters that spread
> up the continent for six hundred miles and through four or five
> countries. It was then, just for a moment, that this symbol of infinity
> of distance, carrying the infinity of time with which it was one,
> released his mind from the time of day and he was at once himself
> ten years ago and himself now, one and the same. It was a pause
> not taken account of. (p. 93)

Instead of two separate roles in two different historical situations,
Bray is at once himself then and now. He is led to this feeling of a
continuing history, "an infinity of time," through experiencing the
lake, "an infinity of distance," which casts its glare around him in
the atmosphere. This change derives from the disillusion of his observer role; he is captured ("arrested") by the lake, which is not
kept "out there," as the two references to his mind indicate, but
experienced within. This vision, moreover, prefigures the form of his
future awareness. The "blinding" lake foreshadows that his awareness
will come not through observing but when, his glasses removed, he
will merge with the landscape he inhabits. The passage, more specifically, points to the consequences of this more involved perspective,
for the reference to "the line of a glance below a lowered eyelid"
is echoed by his appearance after his murder (p. 474). The passage
thus reveals Bray experiencing his past, present, and future as one
through a new participatory mode of perception. That this mode
requires development is indicated by the momentary intrusion of an
objective construct in the reference to the map. Bray's development

will come as such pauses, unlike here, are "taken account of" without such distancing.

A more conscious acknowledgment of this change in perspective comes to Bray as he arrives in Shinza's Bashi Flats after a long trip:

> On the morning of the sixth day the Volkswagen was poled across the river and the silent motion, after the perpetual rattling of the car, was a kind of presage: Shinza was on the other side. In the light, sandy-floored forest he came upon movement that he thought, at a distance, was buck feeding; it was women gathering sour wild fruit, and they turned to laugh and chatter as he passed.
>
> The trees ended; the scrub ended; the little car was launched upon a sudden opening-out of flowing grass and glint of water that pushed back the horizon. He had always felt here, that suddenly he saw as a bird did, always rising, always lifting wider the ring of the eyes' horizon. He took off his glasses for a moment and the shimmering and wavering range rushed away from him, even farther. (p. 115)

The passage incorporates many of the same elements as the moment of arrest at the Fisheagle Inn, from the "glint" and "shimmering" qualities to the premonitions of death in the removal of his glasses and the Charon-like poling across the river. The passage points up the consequences of two modes of perception he might choose to employ. His attempt to observe this scene fails—he mistakes the women for bucks—whereas the movement culminating in the removal of his glasses provides a broadened viewpoint within himself. Two contrasts with his earlier observations reinforce this sense of change: instead of using a bird to create a portrait as he had on leaving the city, he identifies with it, and the "sudden opening" of the landscape here provokes him to "suddenly" see. In short, this landscape is not viewed; it evokes a sympathetic response in him.

The consequence of this moment's being "taken account of" is immediately apparent in his perception of a different history in the landscape than he had on first entering Gala:

> Feeling his way through the past, he drove, without much hesitance at turnings, to Shinza's village. A new generation of naked children moved in troops about the houses, which were a mixture of the traditional materials of mud and grass, and the bricks and corrugated iron of European settlement. Some of the children were playing with an ancient Victorian mangle; Belgian missionaries from the Congo and German missionaries from Tanganyika had waded through the grass all through the last decade of the nineteenth century, dumping old Europe among the long-horned cattle. (p. 116)

In equating wading "through the grass" with "through the last decade of the nineteenth century," Bray conjoins landscape and history much more concretely than in his view from the Fisheagle Inn. This land-scape, unlike those Bray had previously perceived, shows a continuing colonial presence, with Europe and Africa mixed in the houses, the "Victorian mangle" with the cattle. And, unlike the first view of Gala, in which the trees overshadowed European attempts at intrusion, Bray does not present a simple argument about the country's history. He is "feeling his way through the past" without the false security of a single bicycle in sight.

Bray's development is occurring through a series of contrasts between his initial tendency to observe his world and his taking into account "sudden" moments in which he internalizes the landscape. Gradually the tendency to observe dissipates and the power and concreteness of the envisioned scenes increase, carrying with them more explicit presentiments of his future. Looking at Gala from his desk outside his bungalow one day, he begins once again by estab-lishing a detached perspective; he sees "foreshortened" figures in the village below, and he finds "himself held in a kind of aural tension—something cocked within him, as in an animal in the dream that is grazing" (p. 201). Bray uses Henri Rousseau's "The Sleeping Gypsy" to give his feeling shape, but the picture is internalized, a correlative for his condition. And instead of distancing him from the scene, the picture leads him into a dream vision:

> Nothing happened in the open in this small, remote, peaceful crossroad. All change was a cry drowned by the sea of trees. A high-pitched note, almost out of range. (In a noon pause, one morning, he experienced in fantasy this same quiet of sun and heavy trees existing while things went wrong—he saw a car burning, bleeding bodies far down under the shifting shade-pattern of the trees. It lasted a vivid moment; his skin contracted—it seemed prompted physically, like the experience of *déjà vu*. . . . (pp. 201–202)

As at the novel's outset, Bray is awakened by a bird's cry, which leads here to a vivid presentiment of the scene of his death, where his body will lie bleeding near a burning car. Again, the landscape evokes a corresponding state in Bray. Its timelessness—it is morning at noon—induces him to experience in the present his future death which has the feeling of *déjà vu*. He not only perceives but experiences the continuity Gordimer's earlier characters sought.

This scene reflects as well Bray's growing acknowledgment that the process of change as he had first conceived it is too simple, for nothing happens "in the open" at this crossroad. Bray reveals a more conscious sense of a complex historical pattern when he states shortly afterward that "a profound cycle of change was set up here three or four hundred years ago with the first of us foreign invaders. We're

inclined to think it comes full stop, full circle, with Independence
. . . but that's not so . . . it's still in process—that's all" (p. 210).
With this statement, Bray renounces his easy certainties about historical stages. Moreover, the statement shows Bray's inklings that his
own personal history, which he had foreseen when "things went
wrong" in his vision above, is connected with a history "in process"
since he is responding here to a query of Rebecca's about his use of
the phrase "when things go wrong."

Bray can never articulate what this "cycle of change" is, but he
does know that it involves change, not Mweta's attempts to frustrate
it by shoring up colonial structures. His coming break with Mweta,
which does not find expression until the party congress near the
novel's close, is indicated in another scene in which observing yields
to an inner landscape. Bray and Rebecca stand "looking out across
the neat *boma* garden . . . down the slope to the town half-hidden
by the cumulus evergreen," where the activities of the town are "all
in the frame of vision":

> The usual bicycles and pedestrians moved in the road, bicycles
> bumping down over the bit where the five hundred yards of tar
> that had been laid in front of the *boma* ended and there was a
> rutted descent to the dirt. He had the feeling—parenthetic, pre-
> cise—that they were both suddenly thinking of the lake at the same
> time. The lake with its upcurved horizon down which black pirogues
> slid towards you. The lake still as a heat-pale sky. (p. 295)

Here the neat, observed view, with its allusions to "the boy on the
bicycle," is replaced by the lake, which begins to inhabit Bray's
imagination as the pirogues slide toward him.

While Bray supports Shinza at the party congress and agrees to
aid him by going to Europe, the attraction of Mweta does not fade
until literally minutes before Bray's death. Appropriately, his final
dispatching of Mweta comes as he thinks of the obliteration of Mweta's
colonial residence from his consciousness. He envisions himself "actually walking up the steps to the red brick façade," but supposes
that this image will fade "into an empty wall" (p. 466). Only with
Mweta's habitation removed from his own inner landscape can Bray
tell Rebecca that he will do whatever he can for Shinza.

Bray can act for Shinza because he has accepted the uncertainties
of the world with which he has engaged. Shortly before his death,
Bray thinks, "There was no finality, while one lived, and when one
died it would always be, in a sense, an interruption"; and his final
thought while being bludgeoned to death is "I've been interrupted,
then—" (pp. 465, 469). This acceptance is credible because Bray's
development has occurred through many sudden interruptions of what
had been his accepted way of viewing life: his being "arrested" by

the lake, the "sudden opening out" when removing his glasses at Shinza's, the "vivid moment" when he envisioned his death, the "parenthetic" appearance of the pirogues. These moments have given him a sense of a continuous personal existence and of his life's accord with a cycle of history, which allows him to act in the semi-darkness he inhabits. As Gordimer said of his death, "He's killed by mistake, it's gratuitous, fortuitous, it doesn't make sense to the world. But it would have made sense to him, because he'd made his moral choice there, he'd accepted the risks it carried. He'd accepted the fact that what he had to offer the country was no longer sufficient, and ineffectual. He had taken the risk, moral and physical, of *action*."[2]

A *Guest of Honour* could well end with Bray's life being interrupted, but Gordimer chooses to emphasize the worth of his moral choice through a long coda to the novel. She begins by giving him an honorable mourning ceremony by the local Africans. She underscores the consequences of failure to develop a sense of felt history and act in accord with it through two of Bray's friends: one chooses a private retreat and ends doddering about Bray's garden in Gala; the other remains in the thrall of Mweta and increasing amounts of alcohol. But Gordimer affirms Bray's choice best in a portrait of the man he might have become had he continued simply to observe, not act in, his world. While waiting in Mozambique for a plane to Europe, Rebecca sees a man sitting at a nearby table. He had "a very dark Mediterranean face, all the beautiful planes deeply scored in now, as if age were redrawing it in a sharper, darker pencil. Brilliantly black eyes were deep-set in a contemplative, amused crinkle that suggested disappointed scholarship—a scientist, someone who saw life as a pattern of gyrations in a drop under a microscope" (p. 489). The man is clearly what Bray was likely to become had he remained in Wiltshire with Olivia: a contemplative scholar writing his "carefully documented history," observing the patterns of life, and hardening into a picture, a product of the kind of perception he has had of the world. For the child with him, the man has drawn "a picture of great happiness, past happiness, choppy waves frilling along, a gay ship with flags and triumphant smoke, birds sprinkled about the air like kisses on a letter" (p. 489). Rebecca's sense that the child is "all he has left" is confirmed by this picture, a happy child's picture. Its "past happiness" and the man's focus on the child reveals a life drawn back into the past without the sense of a future. The picture shows, in short, the contemplative death-in-life which Bray, writing at the desk of Olivia's grandfather, forsook for a life of action, his own.

The very fact that Bray's death is so consistently misunderstood serves only to highlight, as Gordimer stated, that *his* choice was what mattered. *Time* labels him Mweta's "trusted White Man Friday"; an acquaintance calls him one of "those nice white liberals getting mixed up in things they don't understand" (pp. 488, 502). Bray, accepting the uncertainties of the semi-darkness in which he lived, had antic-ipated such responses when he observed of his choice of Shinza, "It was either a tragic mistake or his salvation . . . I'll never know, although other people will tell me for the rest of my life" (p. 465). Indeed, when Bray thought that the party congress "would be swept up in the historian's half-sentence some day," he foresaw the kind of attention he is given by a British writer who gives him fleeting attention as one of those who renounced "empirical liberalism" and was prepared to accept "apocalyptic solutions, wade through blood if need be, to bring real change" (pp. 359, 503). This historian's half-sentence is half-right. Bray renounces liberalism and accepts the apocalypse. But he has learned to proffer no solutions, and the blood is his own.

Notes

1. E. G. Burrows, "An Interview with Nadine Gordimer," *Michigan Quarterly Review*, IX (Fall, 1970), 233–34. Gordimer traveled extensively in Southern Africa in the decade prior to the novel's publication. See "Report and Comment: Tanzania," *Atlantic*, CCXXXI (May, 1973), 8–18; "Zambia," *Holiday*, XXXIX (June, 1966), 38–47.

2. Stephen Gray, "Landmark in Fiction," *Contrast* XXX (April, 1973), 81.

The Motif of the Ancestor in
The Conservationist   Michael Thorpe*

In contemporary black African literature, which is much con-cerned with establishing links with the precolonial past, an exacting theme is that of the forgotten, or neglected ancestor. One of the earliest and most celebrated examples of the ancestor motif is Wole Soyinka's *A Dance of the Forests* (1960). There the link with the ancestor has an ironic doubleness: "illustrious" ancestors are desired by the living to glorify past greatness, but instead the supernatural powers send to Nigeria's Independence Feast too-human ghosts the living would rather forget. Only by acknowledging the whole of one's past, only by recognizing one's flawed humanity, it is Soyinka's implicit message, can man begin to build in the present. The necessity to embrace the whole ancestor is similarly a leading theme in the work of Achebe, Awoonor, Armah and Bessie Head, among the foremost

* From *Research in African Literatures* 14 (Summer 1983):184–92. Reprinted by permission.

black African writers. This has been duly noticed. It is a curious fact, however, that in South Africa this task and insight have so far been the achievement of a white novelist, Nadine Gordimer, in *The Conservationist* (1974). It is still more curious that, though central to the complex ironies of this widely admired novel, the ancestor motif seems to have received only passing notice.[1]

The most striking aspect of the narrative that has been overlooked is its punctuation with quotations from the Reverend Henry Callaway's *The Religious System of the Amazulu*, first published in 1870 by the Springdale Mission Press, reissued in facsimile by C. Struik, Cape Town, in 1970.[2] A rare and important acknowledgement of this book's existence is that of Elias Canetti, in 1981 the winner of the Nobel Prize for Literature:

> Among the Zulus in South Africa the relationship between the living and their ancestors was particularly intimate. The reports which the British missionary Callaway collected . . . provide the most authentic account of their ancestor cult. He lets his authorities speak for themselves, taking down their words in their own language. His book, *The Religious System of the Amazulu*, is rare and for that reason too little known. It is among the essential documents of mankind.[3]

Clearly, Gordimer wished to make it better known, but her extracts from it are probably ignored by many readers as an indigestible excrescence or else vaguely understood without further enquiry. It must be said that, whatever Gordimer expected, the reader finds that her use of Callaway yields its full meaning only if one goes to the source.

The ancestor motif in the novel centers upon the unknown man who near the beginning is found murdered on Mehring's farm. Rightly, the corpse's symbolic significance—reminiscent, initially, of the *Waste Land* corpse[4]—has been recognized as a warning Mehring at first ignores, but which by the end of the book has shattered his mind. What needs to be recognized, with equal force, is what it signifies for the blacks who, to begin with, are as eager as Mehring to expel it from consciousness.

When the corpse is found, Jacobus, the black overseer, is linked with Mehring in abrogating responsibility for it. Mehring thinks, "It is not anyone one knows. It is a sight that has no claim on him."[5] Jacobus, questioned closely by Mehring, points away to the shanty town: "Nobody can know this man. Nothing for this man. This is people from there—there—" (p. 18). Jacobus reiterates this rejection of the corpse and its "people" in a later conversation about the incident with the Indian shopkeeper: "Is not our trouble," he curtly concludes (p. 35). It is after this that we meet the first of ten quotations, punctuating the narrative, from Callaway's *The Religious System of the Amazulu*[6]: "I pray for corn, that many people may come to this village of yours and make a noise, and glorify you" (p. 39). These words are quoted by one of Callaway's Zulu informants as being addressed by the head man of a village to the Amatongo (spirits of the dead) after the sacrificial slaughter of a bullock.[7] Though Gordimer supplies no such contextual gloss, the effect is to introduce suddenly a sharply contrasting glimpse of another world, of ordered customary ritual, of a relation between the human and a supernatural spirit world utterly apart from that of the novel. It precedes the blacks' Sunday rite, a "beer-drink," a chapter in which Mehring is back on "[his] bit of veld," dozing on the pasture—only to wake, with a premonitory shock, sprawled "with earth at his mouth" in the dead man's posture (p. 41). In the next chapter, on the same day, Mehring entertains Boer neighbors and there is discussion of "a kaffir doll . . . they used for magic" (p. 55), which Mehring tells de Beer would doubtless interest an American museum. The ironies of this are patent.

The next extract from Callaway continues the first, the head man's petition to the Amatongo[8]: "I ask also for children, that this village may have a large population, and that your name may never come to an end" (p. 61). With double irony, it follows the first of Mehring's thoughts of the son, the inheritor for whom he conserves—who is to prove a homosexual and alienated liberal—and also prefaces an episode in which Jacobus, the black overseer, discusses how to find work for a jobless migrant, a fragment of the broken tribe.

A brief chapter (pp. 66–68) allows an insight into the blacks' suppressed awareness of "that," the dead man, "something one never spoke of." Mehring has noticed "they don't come down here"—to the pasture—"any more" (p. 75). We have yet to learn why.

On page 83 we meet the third extract from Callaway[9]: "once at night he was told to awake and go down to the river and he would find an antelope caught in a Euphorbia tree; and to go and take it." This conjures a suggestion of a mysterious scriptural injunction, of a supernaturally directed purpose. It precedes two brief chapters, the first of which records the bewildered impressions of some older children from the farm who walk to school on the location—images of rubbish dumps, squalor, and random violence—while the second treats the beating up of Solomon by two strangers who "came out of the dark." Now arises "the legend . . . that he was attacked in the night by a spirit": this is linked with "something . . . still there" in the third pasture (p. 92). The third epigraph has been drawn from Callaway's story of James, one afflicted by delusions, apparitions, voices, and dreams. These were believed to have been sent by unappeased, dissatisfied Amatongo: at this point no such contextual meaning is evident, though the theme of the unappeased spirit will later be developed in the narrative itself. Perhaps, enigmatically, Gordimer hopes to send the reader to Callaway.

The anecdote of the search for the antelope is continued in the next extract (p. 93) and completed thus: "That was the end of it, and he was not again told by anything to go and fetch the antelope. They went home, there being nothing there" (p. 113). These last words echo the close of the previous chapter—of the fire, Mehring's reflections upon the deeper claims of his possessions (the farm) to those of his fretful ex-mistress (his conscience?), and upon the now cleansed, purified state of "the poor black scum," the corpse: "It will be as if nothing ever happened down there" (p. 111). "Nothing" has been the keynote of the chapter. Mehring follows his wishful desire to bury truth, that is, an intimation of a truth beyond the self and material security—"forgotten and (for him) non-existent gods" (p. 95). Fittingly, this ironic contrast extends also to our insight into "the Indias" in the next chapter (pp. 114–125). They, too, with Mehring's aid hope to buy literal possession of the land.

We have now reached the novel's center. Gordimer's narrative has kept returning, in both "white" and "black" episodes, to the symbolic center—the murdered man's unceremoniously buried corpse and what that signifies. The epigraphs, with their suggestions of ritual and ceremony, have not yet centered there explicitly. We now learn, in the chapter where Mehring's son returns from Namibia to accuse him and, thus, become one with the absent mistress, Antonia, that "the wife of Phineas she's want to be witch-doctor" (p. 144). There is to be a ritual trial of her powers and a goat will be sacrificed. Mehring accompanies his son to the third pasture, thinks of what lies beneath and links it inwardly with: "their ancestors. No one knows who they were either. No way of making known" (p. 148). Thought of the blacks' buried ancestry converges with sounds of their debased drumming: "Ordinary Castrol drums. . . . They don't know how to make the real thing any longer" (p. 156). The chapter ends with Mehring's full ironic illusion of possession: "He's at one with it as an ancestor at one with his own earth" (p. 161).

Immediately after, comes this from Callaway[10] (p. 163): "The Amatongo, they who are beneath. Some natives say, so called, because they have been *buried beneath the earth*. But we cannot avoid believing that we have an intimation of an old faith in a Hades or Tartarus, which has become lost and is no longer understood." This comes from a passage that notes that if a man dies after the diviner's instructions for averting death have been followed people would say, "He is summoned by those who lie beneath" (i.e. the Amatongo). An "old faith" lost—however we may judge it—is set against the meaningless worlds of both white and black: it is significant that, in the next chapter, Phineas's wife, in whom traces of the old faith persist, is one "people laughed at privately" (p. 164). She dreams of the "snakes that are men and if killed will come to life again; speaking of the spirits, amatongo" (p. 166);[11] "she feels the amatongo in her shoulders" (p. 169).[12] At the same time Solomon, who was attacked and left for dead near "that other one . . . who . . . had never been buried by his own people" (p. 169), has nightmares about lying there dead himself. To relieve him of his trouble a sacrifice is made, in the manner Phineas's wife has dreamt of, to Solomon's parents, but it is a debased ritual. They have no cattle to "cleanse the kraal," so a goat must do—and everyone is more interested in feasting on it than in the perfunctory invocation to "Bengu, father of Solomon, Nomsa, mother of Solomon" (p. 171).[13]

In the next two chapters Mehring continues in his abstracted, divided world of surface social life and buried inner life, but the claims of this buried inner life grow more insistent, like a death wish, a desire for sweet oblivion.

The next epigraph (p. 193)[14] is taken from the words of a convert, voicing to Callaway his skepticism about the legend that "the Amatongo were created by the first man," for "there is no one who tells us that Unkulunkulu first came into being, and what was his wife's name, and that he had a son. But we hear the missionaries say that Jesus is the Son of God."[15] In the following chapter Mehring, disturbed by the suicide of a business associate whose daughter he had been tempted to seduce, digs further for solace into his imagined "companionship . . . with nature"—shared, subconsciously, with *"him"* (p. 200). If the epigraph may be interpreted, it seems to point toward Mehring's ironic relationship with the Amatongo chosen for him, as it were, with a double irony, the beliefless "white man" whose own ancestors introduced the Zulus to God (p. 193). The next chapter, in which Mehring shares with Jacobus a New Year's Eve bottle of whisky, further underscores the black and white complicity in unknowing: "Nobody," Jacobus stubbornly repeats, "can know for this man. Nothing for this man" (p. 208). Disowning kinship with the ancestor, he continues the divisive process begun by the missionaries a century ago.

The next extract (p. 213) from Callaway gives one of his informants' descriptions of the origins of white and black—part, Callaway notes, of the "prevalent . . . tradition that man and all other things came out of the earth":[16] this seems an essential gloss upon "came out" in the passage Gordimer quotes. It is typical of those pervasive African legends that ironically date white opportunism to the beginning of things. Aptly, it precedes the chapter in which the young Indian, mimicking liberal white youth, paints a peace sign on the water-tank, watched by the uncomprehending black, Isak. With a more sinister aptness Mehring is soon after sucked into a mudhole on his farm and feels as if "a soft cold black hand" clutched his ankle; he struggles in a panic to escape, but when he does he "feels as if part of him is still buried" (p. 228). He has almost been sucked back into the undifferentiated beginning of things. Next comes the flood.

The next extract[17] suggests, without explicit statement, that the poisoned Umkqaekana was a martyred raindoctor. This is indeed the case, as we learn from Callaway's section on "Heaven-doctors, etc.";[18] there, the destruction of the murderers' gardens "by a flood" suggests heavenly retribution. In *The Conservationist* the floods flush out the murdered man's remains. Mehring returns afterwards to inspect the damage. He sends Jacobus to the fateful third pasture and waits, thinking "For everything in nature there is the right antidote, the action that answers" (p. 245). Jacobus returns "panting," Mehring knows what he "is going to say" (p. 246).

The last and longest extract[19] reverts to Callaway's first book, *Unkulunkulu,* and is one of his informants' clearest statements of the meaning of ancestor worship—though, again Gordimer's quotation needs tracing to its source for its full effect. The informant concludes there, "It is I myself who am an uthlanga," and this is because he is "the father of children."[20] "Uthlanga," Callaway notes, may refer to both the primal source of being *and* any other source of being (e.g., father, mother). The statement signifies ancestral continuity and a secure sense of inheritance: both, Mehring has been driven to realize, denied him despite his wealth and apparent possessions. The dead man's return to the surface ironically attests this: "The only thing that is final," Mehring acknowledges in his horror and revulsion, "is that he's always there" (p. 251). So powerfully is his appalled identity with the man evoked in the penultimate chapter that some have read the last two pages as an account of Mehring's burial.[21] It is, of course, the murdered man's remains Jacobus and his people at last do their human duty by. As we have seen, they have never forgotten. We are reminded on the last page of the haunting of Phineas's wife by the spirits of the restless dead. In burying him at last with due ceremony they acknowledge him as in a deep sense "one of them"; it no longer matters that "Nobody can know this man" (p. 16). Gordimer says (p. 267): "The one whom the farm received had no name. He had no family but their women wept a little for him. There was no child of his present but their children were there to live after him. They had put him away to rest, at last; he had come back. He took possession of this earth, theirs; one of them."

The dead man's belated "second burial,"[22] an act of atonement by his fellow blacks, contrasts with the callous indifference of the whites who, as Mehring cries when his buried conscience surfaces, "shovelled him in as you might fling a handful of earth on the corpse of a rat" (p. 263).[23] The close thus restores to living significance the black "ceremony of innocence" (Yeats's phrase seems apt here) that has been glimpsed throughout in the quotations from *The Religious System of the Amazulu* as a reminder of a more ordered world that, whatever its flaws, was their own, a "system" to live by. The blacks, converted and then abandoned by the whites, a broken people made fearful by their insecurity of even the simplest reverential act, are finally granted an opportunity to reenact an age-old rite and duty— in earth they, for that purpose, repossess.

Clearly, however, the dead man is neither a revered elder of the tribe (which, anyway, is broken) nor a family member: there is no customary obligation to him, and indeed the prime motive of the goat sacrifice has been to avert the evil influence of a potentially hostile spirit, of one who has left no heirs and not benefited his people. The murdered man was associated with the evil ones of the shanty town and might have been a victim of gang warfare. Nevertheless, Jacobus and his people bury him and so accept him as "one of them." In doing so, they not only accord him a dignity his life lacked, but also rise above their conditioned fear and superstition.[24] Thus Gordimer appears to move beyond the strict limits of her source, the traditional ancestral rites of the Amazulu, which contributes— beyond the ironic effects I have noted—an allegorical dimension to the novel. Only by accepting the darker side of their humanity, can the Africans themselves hope to create a new moral order in the earth they must repossess from the bankrupt white order whose possession rests upon an amoral assertion of power. No more than in the open-eyed work of Soyinka or Awoonor, is there here a simplistic assumption of black virtue, but if there is hope it must lie with the blacks—if they can renew old sanctities and feel and act as *one people,* not practicing among themselves a callous, terrified apartheid.

Notes

1. Robert L. Bemer, in *World Literature Today,* Summer 1975, p. 597, notes that the passages quoted "from the legends of the Amazulu . . . in their clarity and simple dignity serve as appropriate commentaries on the tangled web of Mehring's predicament." Michael Wade, in the most detailed commentary on the novel [*Nadine Gordimer* (London: Evans Brothers, 1978), pp. 183–227], notes the necessity the Africans feel to appease the murdered man's spirit and draws a passing parallel between the surfacing of the corpse and the emergence of the ancestors from the earth in *A Dance of the Forests.* He ignores the allusions to Callaway.

2. Also reissued by the Folk-Lore Society, 15 (London: 1884), with the original pagination.

3. *Crowds and Power* (Harmondsworth: Penguin Books, 1973), p. 308 (first published 1960).

4. "That corpse you planted last year in your garden, / Has it begun to sprout?" (T. S. Eliot, *The Waste Land*, I:71–72).

5. *The Conservationist* (New York: Penguin, 1978), p. 13; all subsequent references will be in the text.

6. "The Amazulu are so called . . . from Uzulu, an ancient chief. He, however, may have obtained that name from the ascription to him of heavenly power. U-izulu, Thou art the heaven, became soon converted into the proper name, Uzulu" [Callaway, *The Religious System of the Amazulu* (Cape Town: C. Struik, 1970), p. 124].

7. Ibid., p. 182.

8. Ibid.

9. Ibid., p. 194.

10. Ibid., pp. 12–13.

11. "They say that a man dies, and when he is dead, he turns into a snake; and they gave that snake the name of Itongo, and they worship it by sacrificing cattle, for they say the cattle too belong to it; it is it that gives them cattle," ibid., p. 140.

12. "That is the place where black men feel the Amatongo," ibid., p. 159.

13. For an earlier ironic treatment of the debasement of the ritual significance of cattle in customary African life see Doris Lessing, "A Home for the Highland Cattle," in *Five* (London: Michael Joseph, 1953).

14. See the novel for the full text, p. 193.

15. Callaway, pp. 134–136. Unkulunkulu: "means the old-old-one, the most ancient man" (Callaway, p. 1).

16. Ibid., p. 76. See the novel for the text of the extract, p. 213, and Callaway, pp. 77–79.

17. See the novel for the text, p. 231.

18. Callaway, p. 392.

19. See the novel for the text, p. 247.

20. Callaway, pp. 15–16.

21. Cf. Jonathan Raban, reviewing *The Conservationist* in *Encounter*, 44, no. 2 (February 1975), pp. 80–82; the dead man escapes all mention.

22. The "second burial" is an essential final rite of passage that may take place a few weeks or months after death, "to make the grave firm" and "separate off the dangerous powers of the dead finally from the living," Geoffrey Parrinder, *Religion in Africa* (Harmondsworth: Penguin Books, 1969), p. 83.

23. Cf. Callaway: "When we were with the Dutch they . . . said that we black people should be burnt; and that we have no spirit, but are like a dog, which has no spirit," p. 10.

24. "only evil people or those with highly infectious diseases . . . are refused burial," Parrinder, p. 82. Mehring thinks of his "gangster's (most probably) savage life," *The Conservationist*, p. 110–11.

Prospero's Complex: Race and Sex in Nadine Gordimer's *Burger's Daughter*

Judie Newman*

Nadine Gordimer has remarked that all South African novels, whatever their political intentions, involve the question of racism: "There is no country in the Western world where the creative imagination, whatever it seizes upon, finds the focus of even the most private event set in the social determination of racial laws."[1] There are those who have argued that the white South African novelist is automatically corrupted by a privileged position, that Gordimer's audience can only be other privileged whites, and that the products of her creative imagination are therefore intrinsically a part of a racist society.[2] In *The Conservationist* Gordimer focused upon the disjunction between the internal, subjective reality of her white protagonist and the external reality of political consensus, employing as her principal strategy the translation of political problems into other languages, particularly into sexual terms. In the novel sexual fantasy functions as a surrogate for colonial lusts. The sexual body of woman, the body of a murdered black, combine to form one massive image of colonial guilt. As her use of the language of Zulu culture, and Zulu dreams, indicates here, Gordimer is clearly aware of the dangers of solipsistic art, an art which may articulate only the dominating power of the white imagination.[3]

Rosa Burger begins her tale with the recognition that: "one is never talking to oneself, always one is addressed to someone . . . even dreams are performed before an audience."[4] In *Burger's Daughter* Gordimer focuses upon the fantasies of the white subconscious, in order to undermine their power. Once again, a body lies below the level of conscious articulation, here the body of a white woman. In the opening scene of the novel Rosa is presented as she appears to other observers, as seen by casual passers-by, as reported on by her headmistress, and as transformed by the rhetoric of the Left, which converts her into "Little Rosa Burger" "an example to us all" (p. 12). The later Rosa reflects on her invisibility as a person: "When they saw me outside the prison what did they see? I shall never know . . . I saw-see-that profile in a hand-held mirror directed towards another mirror" (pp. 13–14). As the daughter of a Communist hero, it is assumed by others that Rosa's views reflect her father's. Rosa is thus trapped in a hall of mirrors, an object in the eyes of others whose internal reality remains unknown. A figure in an ide-

* From *Journal of Commonwealth Literature* 20 (September 1985):81–99. Reprinted by permission.

ological landscape, she is placed by observers only in relation to their own political position: an image of the struggle in the "bland heroics of badly written memoirs by the faithful" (p. 14), a suspicious object to State surveillance. This public rhetoric of South Africa contrasts with a bleeding body, invisible to all shades of South African opinion. For Rosa these external views are eclipsed by her awareness of the pains of puberty: "real awareness is all focussed in the lower part of my pelvis . . . outside the prison the internal landscape of my mysterious body turns me inside out" (p. 15). In the novel Rosa's sexuality forms the point of entry to an exploration of the topography of the racist psyche. The disjunction between external and internal realities is rendered in the form of the novel, in the alternation of first and third person narratives, narratives which interact in order to explore the roots of racism.

Burger's Daughter poses the question of racism as primary or secondary phenomenon. Is racism the product of a political system (capitalism) as Lionel Burger would argue? Or is racism a screen for more primary sexual insecurities? The central images of the novel are drawn from an informed awareness of the principal arguments involved here. Racism has been generally understood by various commentators as a product of sexual repression. In his early, classic study of prejudice Gordon Allport[5] notes that to the white the Negro appears dark, mysterious and distant, yet at the same time warm, human and potentially accessible. These elements of mystery and forbiddenness are present in sex appeal in a Puritanical society. Sex is forbidden, blacks are forbidden; the ideas begin to fuse. White racism expresses itself in response to ambivalence towards the body, conceived of as both attractive and repugnant. In White Racism: A Psychohistory Joel Kovel[6] developed the argument, describing aversive racism as the product of anal repressions. In his view the Negro is not the actual basis of racism but a surrogate or substitute. In white culture bodily products are seen as dirt. The subject therefore splits the universe into good (clean, white, spiritual) and bad (dirty, black, material). Things associated with the sensual body are dirty; those things which may be seen as nonsensuous are clean. Racism therefore depends upon the displacement of "dirty" activities onto an alter ego. Fantasies of dirt underlie racism, which is a product of sexual repressions.

Octave Mannoni[7] offers a rather similar analysis, though with greater emphasis on sexual fantasy. Nadine Gordimer entitled her Neil Gunn Fellowship Lecture 'Apprentices of Freedom' quoting Mannoni.[8] In Prospero and Caliban Mannoni argues that colonial racism simply brings to the surface traits buried in the European psyche, repressed in Europe but manifest in the colonial experience. Colonial countries are the nearest approach possible to the archetype of the desert island. Colonial life is a substitute life available to those who are obscurely drawn to a world of fantasy projection, a childish world without real people. For Mannoni, European man is always in inner conflict between the need for attachments which offer emotional security, and the need for complete individualization. Revolt against parents is an important factor here. When a child suffers because he feels that the ties between him and his parents are threatened, the child also feels guilt, because he would also like to break those ties. He therefore dreams of a world without bonds, a world which is entirely his, and into which he can project the untrammeled images of his unconscious. This desire to break every attachment is impossible, of course, in fact. But it is realized by the colonial when he goes into a "primitive" society, a society which seems less "real" than his own. In the modern world this urge may be realized by the substitution of depersonalized links for original attachments. Mannoni cites the film star and pin-up girl as examples. These people are still persons, but only just enough for the subject to form unreal relations with them. The more remote people are, the easier they appear to attract our projections. Prospero's relation with Caliban and Ariel, Crusoe's with Friday, are cases in point. In Gordimer's *July's People*[9] a similar relationship obtains between white woman and black servant. Maureen Smales comes to realize in the course of the action that the traits she admired in July were not his real character but only assumed characteristics, assumed in order to conform to Maureen's mental image of him. In the literature of colonialism the native woman is more commonly a focus for this type of projection. The white colonial marries the native girl because her personality is so little externalized that it acts as a mirror to his projections. He may then live happily among these projections without granting that the Other has autonomous existence. In Mannoni's words: "It is himself a man is looking for when he goes far away; near at hand he is liable to come up against others. Far-away princesses are psychologically important in this respect" (Mannoni, p. 111). As will become evident, Rosa Burger almost becomes identified with the image of the far-away princess, inhabiting a world of erotic fantasy, though in her case Europe becomes the magic island, and her guilty revolt against her father is only temporary.

In this connection Mannoni's analysis of the roots of racism in a patriarchal system is particularly important. For Mannoni the antagonism between Caliban and Prospero in *The Tempest* hinges upon Miranda's presence as the only woman on the island. Having first treated the black (Caliban) as his son, Prospero later accuses him of having attempted to rape Miranda, and then enslaves him. In short, Prospero justifies his hatred of Caliban on grounds of sexual guilt. Analyzing the "Prospero complex" Mannoni draws a picture of the paternalist colonial whose racism is a pseudo-rational construct to rationalize guilty sexual feelings. In his view the sexual basis of racism is revealed in the old cliché of the racist: But would you let your daughter marry one? Uneasy incestuous feelings in the father are disturbed by this argument. For Mannoni it is easy to see why it is always a daughter, sister, or neighbor's wife, never his own, whom a man imagines in this situation. When a white man imagines a white woman as violated by a black man he is seeking to rid himself of guilt by projecting his thoughts onto another (Caliban), putting the blame for his "dirty" sexuality upon someone else. In *The Tempest* Prospero's departure from the colonial island is accompanied by his renunciation of his art, in this case magical arts which enable him to dominate a world created in his own image. Caliban remains behind, however, as disowned son and slave. There are clearly extremely interesting connections here with the character of Baasie (adopted as a son by Lionel Burger but later abandoned) with Rosa's relationship with her father, in whose shadow she lives, and with the nature of Gordimer's art.

Mannoni's is, of course, a highly ambivalent analysis of the colonial enterprise. His central thesis, that the dependence and inferiority complexes are present in rudimentary form in everyone, too easily elides into the untenable hypothesis that people are colonized because they want to be colonized, at least subconsciously. Communists, in particular, have denounced the search for psychological solutions, as too easily providing an alibi for those who refuse to confront political problems. In *Black Skin, White Masks* Fanon[10] contested Mannoni in detail. While Fanon allows that the "civilized" white may retain an irrational longing for areas of unrepressed sexuality which he then projects onto the Negro, he argues that this image of the sexual-sensual-genital Negro can be corrected: "The eye is not merely a mirror, but a correcting mirror. The eye should make it possible for us to correct cultural errors" (Fanon, p. 202). For Fanon, sexuality need not remain at the level of frustration, inauthenticity, or projection. True authentic love is "wishing for others what one postulates for oneself" (Fanon, p. 41). Confrontation of one's psychic drives is only a necessary part of a process of cultural evolution: "The tragedy of the man is that he was once a child. It is through the effort to recapture the self and to scrutinize the self, it is through the lasting tension of their freedom that man will be able to create the ideal conditions for a human world. . . . Was my freedom not given to me in order to build the world of the *You*?" (Fanon, pp. 231–232).

Burger's Daughter charts just such a process of self-scrutiny. Rosa remembers and observes her past self, in an extensive attempt to recapture and reconstitute it, and to engage with the world of the "You." Rosa's first person narrative is directed to three people, each addressed as "You": Conrad, a surrogate brother with whom she enjoys childish erotic freedom, Katya, a sexually permissive replacement mother, and finally Lionel Burger, the father to whom she eventually returns. "You" is obviously also the reader, who is initiated into these three identities. The reader participates in the fantasy while also measuring the distance between these surrogate people and himself. At key points Gordimer adopts Fanon's phraseology. For Conrad, the significant dynamic is "the tension between creation and destruction in yourself" (p. 47). Rosa describes Lionel, however, in antithetical terms: "the tension that makes it possible to live lay, for him, between self and others" (p. 86). In the novel Gordimer's narrative technique draws the reader into a tension of freedom, progressing from Conrad's inner psychological existence to a fresh orientation towards the world of the autonomous other. The alternation between first and third person narrative creates a tension between external image and internal voice, between "She" and "I." As "You" the reader continually mediates the two, correcting the errors of the eye, emerging from the spell of the internal voice. The reader is therefore offered a choice. He may place the voice addressing him as initiating him into a secret intimacy. Or he may refuse to identify with a surrogate "You" and thus register the possibility of a world in which communication is not limited to depersonalized stereotypes.

In the first movement of the novel, Rosa Burger disowns her original attachments in order to enter a world in which surrogate brothers and mothers replace them in a fantasy landscape. She does so largely as a result of ambivalence towards the body, as one example will indicate. When Rosa meets Marisa Kgosana (gorgeously regal while buying face cream) their embrace is described as a step through the looking glass. "To enter for a moment the invisible magnetic field of the body of a beautiful creature and receive on oneself its imprint—breath misting and quickly fading on a glass pane—this was to immerse in another mode of perception" (p. 134). To the salesgirl Marisa appears in the image of the sensuous black woman, distant and unreal. She asks, "Where's she from? One of those French islands!" (p. 139). Marisa, however, has returned, not from the exotic Seychelles or Mauritius, but from Robben Island, the island to which white racist attitudes have banished her husband. From Marisa, Rosa's mind moves at once to Baasie, who is remembered quite differently as a creature of darkness and dirt. Rosa remembers Baasie wetting the bed which they shared as children: "In the morning the sheets were cold and smelly. I told tales to my mother—Look what Baasie's done in his bed!—but in the night I didn't know whether this warmth . . . came from him or me" (pp. 138–140). Quite obviously the two images suggest the twin racist strategies delineated by Kovel and

Mannoni—the attempt to use blackness as a way to sensual liberation (Marisa), the attempt to blame "dirty" actions on the black (Baasie). Rosa exists in tension between these two forms of racism, but it is a tension Gordimer's complex art transforms into a political challenge. Key terms and images—island paradise, incestuous desires, projection onto mirrors, far-away princesses—recur in the novel from Mannoni's thesis, as do images of dirt, guilt, bodily products and repugnance, taken from Kovel. The language of racism is exploited, however, in order to confront the reader with a series of questions. Which vision of Rosa do we accept?—that of a white woman who is part of a racist society and who can address a "You" who exists only in her own projections? Or that of a woman confronting and correcting a stereotyped image and painfully learning to address herself to a world of other autonomous beings? It is my contention that the complex narrative art of *Burger's Daughter* refuses to maintain the text at the level of private fantasy or dream, and also avoids the danger of the depersonalised image. Gordimer employs the terms of the white racist subconscious in an attempt to free her art from Prospero's complex, and to direct it towards a world where "You" is not a fantasy projection, but real.

Gordimer's daring strategy, here, is to select as the focus of the novel a white woman attempting to achieve autonomy by emerging from her father's dominance. As the daughter of a white Afrikaner Communist, Rosa is an extremely complex figure. She may be defined in terms of sex, race, and position in the class struggle, and thus encapsulates the warring explanations of South African racism. In order to assert her autonomy Rosa can rebel only against another rebel. Her father is fighting political repression, so to fight his psychological influence is to join with the forces of political repression. This paradoxical situation is made evident from the beginning. In the eyes of the faithful, Rosa is desexualised and infantilised, maintained in the image of the faithful daughter. In the opening scene Rosa is described as having already "taken on her mother's role in the household" (p. 12) "giving loving support" (p. 12) to her father. That father cheerfully permits Rosa to have boyfriends while laughing at them for "not knowing she was not for them" (p. 17). In the Burger household the children have few exclusive rights with their parents (p. 84) for whom intimate personal relationships are subordinate to the struggle. As a young woman Rosa gains her parents' approval by posing as the fiancée of Noel de Witt, a device to enable him to receive visits in prison. Decked out, scented, "a flower standing for what lies in her lap" (p. 68) Rosa presents herself as a sexual object in prison, conveying a political subtext beneath innocuous lovey-dovey phrases. She returns to her mother's welcoming expression, the expression reserved for her "as a little girl" (p. 67) returning from school, and to her father's "caress" (p. 67). Rosa's parents are blind to the fact that she *is* actually in love with Noel. They are happy to cast her in a surrogate sexual role, a role which denies the reality of her emotions, confining her sexuality within prison walls. In the overall action of the novel, Rosa moves from prison to prison. Infantilised as "Little Rosa Burger" at the start, she becomes in the final pages, once more a child. Flora describes her at the end: "She looked like a little girl . . . About fourteen" (p. 360). In the eyes of the faithful Rosa has not changed at all. She is still her father's daughter, and is living out the historical destiny prepared for her by him. Imagistically, the prison is connected to the dichotomy of "inside" and "outside" in the novel. The reader, with access to Rosa's internal voice, knows that Rosa defected from her father in a belated revolt against the ideology of the parental generation. Does Rosa return from France to continue the political struggle, making a free choice on the basis of internal understanding? Or has Rosa simply fled from the erotic life of Europe in order to return to a desexualised security, a prison of women where she is once more her father's daughter? Rosa is finally imprisoned on suspicion of abetting the schoolchildren's revolt—a revolt informed by consciousness of black brotherhood, and directed against paternalism, whether white or black. Rosa's return follows her encounter with Baasie who denies her "brotherhood." In external political terms the white is rejected by blacks and retreats into paternalism. In internal psychological terms, however, the position is more complex.

That Rosa's rejection of her father is connected to sexual assertion is made clear in the scene with Clare Terblanche, daughter of Dick and Ivy who have been as surrogate parents to Rosa. Rosa is tempted by the parental warmth of their welcome and recognizes their attraction: "In the enveloping acceptance of Ivy's motherly arms—she feels as if I were her own child—there is expectance, even authority. To her warm breast one could come home again and do as you said I would, go to prison" (p. 114). Clare Terblanche lives with her parents and her life is devoted to their cause. As a result she is desexualised, in contrast to Rosa who is beginning to emerge. Clare appears at Rosa's door as a shadow which "had no identity" (p. 118) glimpsed through a glass panel. In Rosa's eyes, Clare is still her childish playmate, sturdy as a teddy-bear, suffering from eczema and knock knees which went uncorrected by parents for whom the body is unimportant. Where Rosa's is a body with "assurance of embraces" (p. 121) Clare, faithful to her father's ideals, has "a body that had no signals" (p. 122) and is "a woman without sexual pride" (p. 123). Clare has two purposes here—to recruit Rosa as a political intermediary, and to rent a flat for her lover. The first is clearly the dominant motive. Rosa refuses on the grounds that she will not conform to her parents' image of her: "Other people break away. They live completely different lives. Parents and children don't understand each other . . . Not us. We live as they lived" (p. 127). One event specifically links Clare to the earlier Rosa. When Rosa shows Clare the vacant apartment, Clare discovers a used sanitary towel in a cupboard. As they leave she removes this unmentionable object to the waste-bin, "and buried her burden . . . as if she had successfully disposed of a body" (p. 129). Disposing of her body is, of course, what Clare has done. Supposedly involved with the people's struggle, her background isolates her from the realities of the body.[11] Irony cuts both ways here, however. In the background a radio announcer is "reciting with the promiscuous intimacy of his medium a list of birthday, anniversary and lover's greetings for military trainees on border duty" (p. 119). Rosa's refusal to help Clare aligns her with this promiscuous intimacy. In South Africa there appears to be no possible mediation between the desexualized image and an erotic intimacy which is the voice of the repressive state.

This erotic intimacy is developed in the person of Brandt Vermeulen. Breaking her attachments to the original family, Rosa sets out to obtain a passport, aligning herself with an alternative family. In order to defect, she makes a series of visits to Afrikaners "whose history, blood and language made (Lionel) their brother" (p. 173). Of them all, she selects as her ally Brandt Vermeulen, member of the Broederbond, the Afrikaner political "brotherhood" which runs South Africa from within Parliament. Brandt's house expresses the psychological reality of colonialism. The façade is that of a Boer farmhouse of seventy or eighty years ago. Within, however, all the internal walls have been demolished to create one large space of comfortable intimacy, with glass walls giving access to a secret garden. Behind the façade of historical legitimacy there exists a vast personal space, inhabited by the erotic male. Brandt runs an art publishing house, and is about to publish a book of erotic poems and woodcuts. By participating in a racist political system Brandt has found sexual liberation. Rosa's attempt to escape from her father has brought her to a "brother" whose façade of reverence for the traditions of his fathers conceals a sophistic eroticism. Rosa is placed here against a highly representative background of *objets d'art*. Brandt's walls are hung with Pierneef landscapes, modernist abstractions, a print of the royal Zulu line, and images of tortured bodies. The room is dominated, however, by a sculpture, a perspex torso of a woman's body, set upon a colonial chest. Described as suggesting both the ice of frigidity and the hardness of tumescence (p. 182) the sculpture presents an image of erotic woman as a reified object of display, possessed by the male and existing only in his internal space. It is on this erotic object that Brandt's more "sophisticated" art depends, as Prospero's art draws upon a complex of sexual motives. In the garden a small black boy plays, amidst chairs spattered with messy bird-droppings, indicating his place in Brandt's internal landscape. To escape desexualisation by a father Rosa has entered a landscape organized by a surrogate brother to reflect his own fantasy.

Conrad is another such "brother." (The watchman for whom he places bets describes him to Rosa at one point as "Your brother" (p. 149). Rosa's relation with Conrad is foreshadowed in the visit she pays to the Nels' farm when first separated from her jailed parents. At the farm "More and more, she based herself in the two rooms marked Strictly Private—Streng Privaat" (p. 55). On the door hangs a wooden clock-face on which visitors mark the time of their call. To Rosa it is "immediately recognizable to any child as something from childhood's own system of signification. Beyond any talisman is a private world unrelated to and therefore untouched by what is lost or gained. . . ." (p. 55). The dummy clock marks the entrance to the timeless world of the child's psyche, a place to which Rosa returns when separated from her parents. The visit to the Nels also marks the disappearance from Rosa's life of Baasie. Rosa recalls that she and Baasie had both been given watches, but that Baasie ruined his in the bath. To Rosa, Baasie has become timeless, existing only in her memory. When Rosa is permanently separated from her parents, she sets up house with Conrad in a world which is also outside time and place. Their cottage, soon to be demolished in favor of a new freeway, is let without official tenure at "an address that no longer existed" (p. 21). Set in a jungle of palms, beneath a bauhinia tree, the house is "safe and cosy as a child's playhouse and sexually arousing as a lovers' hideout. It was nowhere" (p. 21). In the dark of their secret cottage, Conrad and Rosa act out their dreams of a private erotic world in which parents are no longer controlling. For Conrad, a man with no political affiliations, only psychological events matter: Sharpeville passes unnoticed, obscured by the realization that his mother had a lover. Freed from his Oedipal conflicts by the awareness that his mother was no longer the sole possession of his father, Conrad became obsessed with her. "I was mad about her; now I could be with someone other than my father there already" (p. 44). Rosa admits a kinship with Conrad: "We had in common such terrible secrets in the tin house: you can fuck your mother and wish your father dead" (p. 63). Conrad's reaction to Lionel's death is "Now you are free" (p. 40). Freedom from the father liberates Rosa sexually, but is attended by guilt. She wished for this freedom. She obtained it on her father's death. She concludes, "I know I must have wished him to die" (p. 63). In the psyche there is no distinction between what she has actually done and what she has imagined. This criminality of the white imagination is seen as liberating by Conrad. For him

Rosa can only begin to live once she blasphemes her father's ideology. He quotes Jung in his support: "One day when he was a kid Jung imagined God sitting up in the clouds and shitting on the world below. His father was a pastor . . . You commit the great blasphemy against all doctrine and you begin to live" (p. 47).

As Conrad's choice of example suggests, he and Rosa are still inhabiting a world structured around the opposed terms of racist language. When Rosa ends her relationship with Conrad she does so in terms which suggest important connections with Lionel and Baasie:

> I left the children's tree-house we were living in, in an intimacy of self-engrossment without the reserve of adult accountability, accepting each other's encroachments as the law of the litter, treating each other's dirt as our own, as little Baasie and I had long ago performed the child's black mass, tasting on a finger the gall of our own shit and the saline of our own pee . . . And you know we had stopped making love together months before I left, aware that it had become incest. (p. 70)

Rosa recoils from Conrad's erotic activities—activities which depend upon the replacement of the father—because these activities are perceived as dirty and incestuous. The closer Conrad becomes to Rosa, the more he blasphemes against her family's beliefs, the more he approaches Baasie, the black "brother" with whom her first "dirty" acts were performed. For Rosa sexual freedom is forever connected to images of the black, and to imperfectly suppressed incestuous desires. Significantly Conrad later sails off upon a yacht to islands in the Indian Ocean. Rosa departs for Paris—an unreal place, "Paris—a place far away in England" (p. 56) as she describes it to the Nels' maids—and thence to the South of France, to the arms of a surrogate mother, Lionel's first wife, who placed erotic freedom before the needs of the Party.

Rosa's arrival in the South of France is described in terms which establish it as the enchanted land of fantasy. "The silk tent of morning sea" (p. 214) tilts below her plane, glimpsed through the distorting glass of the window. Below, tables outside a bar become "tiny islands" (p. 217) in "a day without landmarks" (p. 217). On the verge "roadside tapestry flowers grow" (p. 217) and in the background "a child's pop-up picture book castle" (p. 217) stands against a landscape of sea and flowers, where "People were dreamily letting the car pass across their eyes an image like that in the convex mirror set up at the blind intersection" (p. 217). Rosa's perceptions are dazed here, as if entering a dream world, a world drowning in sensuality. Katya's dining room appears as "swimming colours, fronds blobbing out of focus and a sea horizon undulating in uneven panes of glass" (p. 220). Katya's reminiscences of the Party—vodka, parties, sexual affairs—accompany Rosa's meal while she is "dissolving" (p. 222) in the pleasures of wine, and French sights, sounds, and tastes. A room has been prepared for Rosa at the top of the house, full of feminine bric-à-brac, flowers, mirrors, and peaches: "a room made ready for someone imagined. A girl, a creature whose sense of existence would be in her nose buried in flowers, peach juice running down her chin, face tended at mirrors, mind dreamily averted, body seeking pleasure. Rosa Burger entered, going forward into possession by that image" (pp. 229–230). Rosa is thus presented with an image of herself as sensual woman, created by Katya, an image which she delightedly assumes, enjoying the sensual pleasures of an unreal country, where her projections are reflected back to her, where she ceases to be her father's daughter and becomes instead the mistress of Bernard Chabalier. The particular features of the landscape—islands, tapestry, flowers, mirrors, silk tent—are focussed in the tapestry series, *"La Dame à la Licorne"* which is presented to the reader after Rosa's return to Africa.

Rosa's lover plans to show her these tapestries. He also takes her to see an exhibition of paintings by Bonnard. As he says, "In Africa, one goes to see the people. In Europe, it's paintings" (p. 286). The white in Africa sees people as objects to be contemplated, objects which mirror their own projections. In Europe art offers a timeless substitute reality. To Rosa the paintings of Bonnard are just as real as the French people she lives among. These people are "coexistent with the life fixed by the painter's vision" (p. 286). Bernard points out that Bonnard's style and subjects never changed. The woman painted in 1894, the mimosa painted in 1945 during the war are treated in the same way. In the fifty years between the paintings there was the growth of fascism, two wars, the Occupation, but for Bonnard it is as if nothing has happened. The two paintings could have been executed on the same day. In Bernard's analysis, the woman's flesh and the leaves around her are equal manifestations: "Because she hasn't any existence any more than the leaves have, outside this lovely forest where they are . . . Your forest girl and the vase of mimosa—C'est un paradis inventé" (p. 287). With Bernard, Rosa lives in a similar invented paradise, a world of sensual pleasures, divorced from the world of historical events, cut off from both future and past, a world in which she is only a timeless image. Rosa meets Bernard for the first time in the bar owned by Josette Arnys, a Creole singer. The bar is mirrored and suggests the solipsism of France for Rosa. "In the bar where she had sat seeing others living in the mirror, there was no threshold between her reflection and herself" (p. 272). In the background runs a recording of Arnys' unchanging voice, singing about "the island where she and Napoleon's Joséphine were born" (p. 269). Arnys is quite unaware of the naive political content of the song. For her, art is timeless in its eroticism. She argues at one point that "the whole feminist thing" (p. 270) will mean the death of art, as women will no longer be able to sing of love. In her view, "the birds sing only when they call for a mate" (p. 270). Katya is associated with the same vision, when she takes Rosa to hear the nightingales singing. Rosa's final rejection of this world is linked to a different voice—that of Baasie—and to the image presented in the tapestry series.

The tapestries of the Musée de Cluny have been very variously interpreted both by artists and scholars. Discovered by George Sand, who featured them in her novel *Jeanne*,[12] they were also the inspiration for a ballet created by Jean Cocteau in Munich in 1953.[13] Rilke was also attracted to them, and celebrates them in one of his Sonnets to Orpheus, which begins "O dieses ist das Tier, das es nicht gibt." (This is the creature that has never been.)[14] Rilke also described the tapestries in detail in The *Notebooks of Malte Laurids Brigge*. The hero, Malte, has found that growing up is a process of reducing and distorting experience to make it fit conventional categories, thus acquiring a false identity or mask. To his horror that mask becomes more real than his inner self; the self he sees in the mirror is more real than the person it reflects. When he observes the tapestries, however, Malte feels a restored sense of totality. From the tapestries he gains a sense of total or simultaneous time, with no sense of an absent future. "Expectation plays no part in it. Everything is here. Everything forever."[15] Forced as she grows up into a similar assumption of a fixed role, Rosa is also attracted at first to the tapestries, as part and parcel of her assumption of the role of Bernard's mistress. "Bernard Chabalier's mistress isn't Lionel Burger's daughter; she's certainly not accountable to the Future; she can go off and do good works in Cameroun or contemplate the unicorn in the tapestry forest. 'This is the creature that has never been'—he told me a line of poetry about that unicorn, translated from German. A mythical creature. Un paradis inventé" (p. 304).

Scholars have suggested various interpretations for the tapestries, seeing them as representing a Turkish prince and his lady, as celebrating a marriage between two noble houses, as an act of homage to the Blessed Virgin Mary, and most importantly, as a celebration of the five senses, to name only a few of the available explications.[16] A particular focus of difficulty is the sixth tapestry, in which the lady, on a blue island, against a rose background strewn with tapestry flowers, stands in front of a silk tent over which hangs the banner motto "A mon seul désir." The Lady appears to be taking a necklace from a box and the tapestry has thus been understood as celebrating a gift of love. Nadine Gordimer draws upon both Rilke's vision of the tapestries and the most recent scholarly explanation. In the text, she describes the first tapestry, in which the lady holds a mirror in which the unicorn is reflected, and then simply lists the four following tapestries as "the representation of the other four senses" (p. 340), hearing, smell, taste and touch. The text then moves to the sixth tapestry which is described in more detail. In 1978, Alain Erlande-Brandenburg[17] agreed that the tapestries represent the five senses, but suggested that the meaning of the sixth tapestry lay not in the acceptance of a gift, but rather in its renunciation: the lady is not receiving the necklace but replacing it in the box. The sixth tapestry may therefore be understood as signifying the need not to submit to the power of the senses, but to exercise free will in their control. The necklace is therefore a symbol of the renunciation of the passions, which may interfere with our ability to act morally. "A mon seul désir" translates as "by my own free will" and is linked to the *Liberum arbitrium* of Socrates and Plato. Where formerly the tapestries were seen as celebrating the senses, as embodied in a beautiful woman, the understanding of the sixth panel has now corrected the eye of the observer.

On the simplest level, therefore, the tapestries indicate that Rosa's decision to abandon the luxuriant sensual joys of life with her lover is an act of free will, and a renunciation of the fantasy eroticism of projection, mirror images and magic islands. Life with Bernard would remove her from her historical destiny to a "place" outside time; Gordimer's description of the tapestries is entirely in the present tense, a timeless participial present which creates an impression of enchanted stillness. "The Lion and the Unicorn listening to music. . . . The Lady weaving . . . The Lady taking sweets from a dish . . ." (p. 340). In France Rosa has been possessed by an image of herself as sensual, floating like the lady on "an azure island of a thousand flowers" (p. 340), hearing nightingales sing, delighting in the taste of French foods and the sights of France, enjoying the touch of a lover. For all their beauty, however, the tapestries were executed in "the age of the thumbscrew and dungeon" (p. 341). Bernard would take Rosa away from a similar world of pain and imprisonment in order to sequester her in a private world of sensual joy and art, a world in which he could show her the tapestry he loves—"to love you by letting you come to discover what I love" (p. 341). What Bernard loves is an image of Rosa to which she does not entirely correspond. In the extremely complex presentation of the tapestries, Gordimer describes a woman gazing at them, a woman who has all the time in the world to do so.

> There she sits gazing, gazing. And if it is time for the museum to close, she can come back tomorrow and another day, any day, days.
> Sits gazing, this creature that has never been. (p. 341)

In the "Sight" tapestry the lady is also gazing, into a hand-held mirror, but she sees only the reflection of the unicorn, the mythical creature which has never existed outside the human mind. In the tapestry the oval face of the lady with her hair twisted on top is echoed in the oval frame of the mirror and the unicorn's twisted horn. Rosa Burger may become, like the lady, a gazer into a hand-held mirror which reflects back to her only an unreal and mythical creature, a woman who has only existed in the projections of others. In returning to South Africa, however, Rosa chooses not to be such an image, an object to be displayed and desired, a figure in an erotic or political iconography. In South Africa, Rosa, like Rilke's Malte, acquired a false identity imposed upon her by others. Pursuing a personal erotic course, however, simply creates an alternative mask. Rosa's progress towards autonomy involves coming to terms with the mythic masks which men have fastened over the female face—whether desexualised or erotically reified—and correcting the errors of her own internal eye.

Where the tapestry series articulates the necessity of correcting the errors of the eye, Baasie's voice establishes the autonomous existence of "You." Rosa wakes in the night to "the telephone ringing buried in the flesh" (p. 318) and in the darkness at first assumes it is her lover, Bernard. When she realises it is Baasie she tries to put him off. When Baasie keeps telling Rosa to put on the light, Rosa refuses on the grounds that it is late; she will see him "tomorrow— today, I suppose it is, it's still so dark" (p. 319). Rosa would very much like to keep this conversation in a timeless darkness. To her, Baasie is not a person with an autonomous existence, but a creature of her own mind. "The way you look in my mind is the way my brother does—never gets any older" (p. 323). She addresses him as Baasie. The childish nickname, insulting in the world of *baasskap*, infantilises and desexualises an adult male, converting him into a "boy." For Rosa his real name—Zwelinzima Vulindlela—is unknown and unpronounceable. Infantilised and desexualised by Rosa's impersonal greeting at the party, Baasie angrily insists that he is not her "black brother" (p. 321) and doesn't have "to live in your head" (p. 323). He will not enter into a relationship with her in which he functions as a psychological surrogate. His insults force Rosa to put on the light, transforming his voice: "the voice was no longer inside her but relayed small, as from a faint harsh public address system" (p. 320). Baasie's insults externalize his voice, no longer a part of Rosa, but a person in his own right, challenging her. By taunting her, "he had disposed of her whining to go back to bed and bury them both" (p. 322).

Burying the body is a part of Rosa's strategy, as much as it is Clare Terblanche's. She, too, would like to live in a world which corresponds to childish projections, a world in which the childish magical landscape is more real than a "Suffering Land" (Zwelinzima). In the conversation, Baasie can only be "You," a voice without pronouncable identity. Up to this point in the novel Rosa may be said to have addressed a "You" of fantasy. Now, however, "You" answers back. At the end of the conversation, vomiting in front of the bathroom mirror, Rosa sees herself as "Ugly, soiled" (p. 324), "filthy" (p. 329) and "debauched" (p. 329). She comments, "how I disfigured myself" (p. 329). Disfiguration is an essential step in Rosa's progress to autonomy, an autonomy which depends upon confrontation with her real body, repugnant as well as beautiful, a body which cannot be split into good, clean, white or bad, dirty, black.

The realisation is also a product of the subject of Rosa's conversation with Baasie—their respective fathers. In the conversation Rosa tries to assume responsibility for Baasie's father. She says that she was responsible for getting a pass to him, a pass with which he was caught, and as a result died. Baasie, however, refuses to allow whites to assume responsibility for blacks: "it's nothing to do with you . . . who cares whose 'fault' " (p. 322). Baasie rejects Lionel as spokesman for the black cause, as he rejects white paternalism. Rosa's desire to assume responsibility for her "brother's" father's death is finally checked here, as she emerges from the world of the psyche into the light of conscious action. What Baasie says to her ends her fantasy guilt over a white father, but does not absolve her from political responsibilities. She leaves behind an incestuous psychological world, in the recognition that blacks are autonomous beings, who are not bound to her by imagined ties of dependence.

Rosa returns to South Africa to take up her father's work again, in two senses: firstly in terms of a renewed political commitment, and secondly in the tending of black bodies. As a physiotherapist, Rosa (like her doctor father) restores feeling to the nerves of injured black people. Rosa's return is to a world of repugnant bodies— horribly mutilated in the Soweto riots—but she is now able to face these bodies and act in their world. When Rosa is charged with "aiding and abetting of the students' and schoolchildren's revolt" (p. 356) the reader knows of no external evidence for the truth of the accusation. Internally, however, Rosa had participated in a schoolgirl's revolt against paternalism, a revolt which has brought her to political consciousness. The novel ends with a revolt against parents which is not the product of white fantasy, but a political and historical reality. The schoolchildren's revolt in Soweto is directed at the white paternalist state, but also at the political compromises of black fathers. Fats Mxenge is such a father, a man who appears at the end of the novel like "someone brought abroad out of a tempest" (p. 343).

The extent to which she has left Prospero's complex behind is indicated in the art of Gordimer's novel. Two points are important here. In the final pages of the novel the third person view is emphasised and Rosa appears flatter and more distant than before. Gordimer also introduces into these final pages a statement from the Soweto Students Representative Council, ungrammatical, misprinted and rhetorically crude. Rosa comments: "They can't spell and they can't formulate their elation and anguish. But they know why they're dying" (p. 349). In the prison Rosa obtains drawing materials and produces paintings which are also crude in their expression. Failures in aesthetic terms, they are however politically valuable. One drawing is a Christmas card. Ostensibly an innocuous group of carol singers, the card represents the clumsily drawn figures of Marisa, Rosa and Clare, signalling to its recipients that the women are in touch with each other. In the prison Marisa sings—not of love—but in order to announce her presence to the other prisoners. Rosa has also found her political voice and as a result her inner voice has become silent. The other picture is a "naive imaginary landscape that could raise no suspicions that she might be incorporating plans of the lay-out of the prison" (p. 355). In this crude drawing tiny boats appear "through some failure of perspective" (p. 355) to be sailing straight for a tower. Rosa's drawing is an analogy to the art of Gordimer's novel, which takes the landscape of the racist psyche and inverts it to political ends. At the end of the novel Rosa is distanced as a result of a creative change in the reader's perspective. The "You" of fantasy has disappeared, replaced by the political voice of autonomous blacks (the S.S.R.C. statement). The internal voice has been silenced in favor of communications directed towards the world of the Other. *Burger's Daughter* opens with the epigraph "I am the place in which something has occurred." Gordimer's aesthetics are directed against the constructs of a racist imagination, constructs which depend upon psychological displacement, in order to relocate the individual in a real political perspective.

Notes

1. Nadine Gordimer, "Literature and Politics in South Africa," *Southern Review*, 7, 3, 1974, 205–206.

2. See, for example, Ronnie Mutch, "Growing Up with Gordimer," *The Literary Review*, January, 1982, pp. 44–45.

3. As I have previously argued. See Judie Newman, "Gordimer's *The Conservationist:* 'That Book of Unknown Signs,' " *Critique: Studies in Modern Fiction*, 22, 3, 1981, pp. 33–44.

4. Nadine Gordimer, *Burger's Daughter*, London: Jonathan Cape, 1979, p. 16. All subsequent references follow quotations in parentheses.

5. Gordon W. Allport, *The Nature of Prejudice*, Cambridge, Mass.: Addison-Wesley, 1954, pp. 376–382.

6. Joel Kovel, *White Racism: A Psychohistory*, London: Allen Lane, The Penguin Press, 1970.

7. Octave Mannoni, *Prospero and Caliban: The Psychology of Colonization*, translated Pamela Powesland, New York: Frederick A. Praeger, 1956. First published as *Psychologie de la colonisation*, Paris: Editions du Seuil, 1950.

8. Nadine Gordimer gave the Neil Gunn Fellowship Lecture in Edinburgh on 29 May, 1981, published as "Apprentices of Freedom," *New Society*, 24–31 December 1981, ii–v. Mannoni uses the phrase "an apprentice to freedom" on p. 65 of *Prospero and Caliban*.

9. Nadine Gordimer, *July's People*, London: Jonathan Cape, 1981.

10. Frantz Fanon *Black Skin, White Masks*, translated Charles L. Markmann, London: MacGibbon and Kee, 1968. First published as *Peau Noire, Masques Blancs*, Paris: Editions du Seuil, 1952.

11. A point instantly seized by one reviewer. Seen Z. N., "The Politics of Commitment," *African Communist*, 80, 1980, pp. 100–101.

12. George Sand, *Jeanne*, edited Simone Vierne, Grenoble: Presses Universitaires de Grenoble, 1978, pp. 132–133. Sand also described the tapestries in detail in "Un Coin du Berry et de la Marche," *L'Illustration*, 3 juillet, 1847, pp. 275–276.

13. René Gilson, *Jean Cocteau*, Paris: Editions Segher, 1964 p. 39. Cocteau rejected courtly and allegorical explanations in order to place the tapestries in the tradition of Beauty and the Beast.

14. Rainer Maria Rilke, *Sonnets to Orpheus*, translated J. B. Leishman, London: Hogarth Press, 1946, pp. 94–95.

15. Rainer Maria Rilke, *The Notebooks of Malte Laurids Brigge*, translated John Linton, London: Hogarth Press, 1930, p. 122. I am indebted to E. F. N. Jephcott, *Proust and Rilke: The Literature of Expanded Consciousness*, London: Chatto and Windus, 1972.

16. For details of the various interpretations see Pierre Verlet et M. Francis Salet, *La Dame à la Licorne*, Paris: Braun, 1960, and Charles Dédéyan, *Rilk et la France*, Paris Sedes, 1964.

17. Alain Erlande-Brandenburg, *La Dame á la Licorne*, Paris: Editions de la Réunion des Musées Nationaux, 1978. I am grateful to John Frankis, of the University of Newcastle upon Tyne, for assistance in obtaining this documentation.

Masters and Servants:
Nadine Gordimer's *July's People*
and the Themes of Her Fiction   Rowland Smith°

In the introduction to her *Selected Stories*, published in 1975, Nadine Gordimer writes: "I was obliged to read through my five existing collections of stories and saw how there are some stories I

° First published in *Salmagundi* 62 (Winter 1984):93–107, issue devoted to Nadine Gordimer. Reprinted by permission.

have gone on writing, again and again, all my life, not so much because the themes are obsessional but because I found other ways to take hold of them."[1] Taken at face value, this statement would appear to be at odds with commonplace critical praise of the freshness with which each new novel by Gordimer reveals a new stage in the political and social history of her native South Africa. Later in the same introduction, however, she asserts: "The change in social attitudes unconsciously reflected in the stories represents both that of the people in my society—that is to say, history—and my apprehension of it; in the writing, I am acting upon my society, and in the manner of my apprehension, all the time history is acting upon me" (pp. 12–13). It is the "other ways" with which Nadine Gordimer "takes hold" of those repeated themes that reflect both history itself and her own apprehension of it. Even when the tale is told again and again, the difference in perspective or emphasis reveals the changes which the author embodies in her work. To chronicle changes in the attitudes and values of her particular society is especially difficult because its overriding problem is intractable.

Each of Nadine Gordimer's South African novels published after 1960 has revealed a dead end, although the nature of that impasse has varied. The inevitably tainted context of liberal gestures towards political commitment or natural relations between black and white was investigated in *Occasion For Loving* (1963) and *The Late Bourgeois World* (1966). The mood of white liberal failure in those works was replaced with the even more arid mood of monolithic, intransigent, white "occupation" in *The Conservationist* (1974) and *Burger's Daughter* (1979). With the publication of *July's People* in 1981, the immediate deadlock appears to be removed. Its setting during an imagined revolutionary war of the future offers a context in which white power is tottering, if not already fallen.

In its verisimilitude, the picture of an increasingly chaotic guerilla struggle for the industrialized, gold-mining belt of the Transvaal gives *July's People* a startling, almost sensational opening which distinguishes it both from more flaccid accounts of the coming struggle in novels like C. J. Driver's *Send War in Our Time, O Lord* and from the more leisurely openings of Gordimer's own recent work. This fragmented and yet vivid account of escalating black attack on the hitherto impregnable core of white power and affluence so graphically captures the aura of a final breakdown of the old order that it also suggests a break with Gordimer's old preoccupations. In its very daring—to create the almost unimaginable crumbling of white mastery—*July's People* could be seen as primarily prophetic and admonitory, its warning incorporated at every stage in the depiction of the alien roles thrust on its white protagonists forced to flee their threatened white city to the protection of their servant's tiny, anonymous village in the bush. To relegate to the past all the trappings of white invulnerability, to imagine them irretrievably destroyed, could be seen as the central intention of the novel. On the surface, that is the impact in this depiction of Maureen Smales' waking moments on her first morning in the refugee hut: "At first what fell into place was what was vanished, the past. In the dimness and traced brightness of a tribal hut the equilibrium she regained was that of the room in the shift boss's house on mine property she had had to herself once her elder sister went to boarding school."[2]

But the pastness of Maureen Smales' past—what has vanished— is both asserted and denied. What falls into place in her totally alien new surroundings is a reassertion of her old identity as the white shift boss's daughter. The book itself has begun two pages earlier with the surprising evocation of the typical beginning to a white master's day:

You like to have some cup of tea?—
    July bent at the doorway and began that day for them as his kind has always done for their kind.
    The knock on the door. Seven o'clock. In governor's residences, commercial hotel rooms, shift bosses' company bungalows,
master bedrooms *en suite*—the tea-tray in black hands smelling of Lifebuoy soap.
. . . .
    No knock; but July, their servant, their host, bringing two pink glass cups of tea and a small tin of condensed milk, jaggedly opened, specially for them, with a spoon in it. (p. 1)

Inescapably grotesque in their dependent new circumstances, the Smales' privileged status is what preserves the decorum of their relation with July and his village. The specially opened luxury of condensed milk and the prized glass cups (an earlier gift to July's wife appropriated by him for the whites) are the point of contact between the city past and the village present. They preserve the possibility of communication with July. Other roles are unknown. That ambiguity of role is built into every situation in the novel. "July, their servant, their host" is as inextricably enmeshed in the conflicting claims of past and present relationships as is the bourgeois family he serves, protects, governs and obeys. Who possesses whom becomes as confused an issue in the novel as is the syntax of its title. July's people are both subjects and objects of possession, their roles and identities compromised by a patterned response produced by generations of white masters and black servants. The Smales cannot pass beyond their former relationship with July. To see him from any perspective other than that of liberal, self-confident white overlords is impossible, and that hopelessly compromised position is the impasse the novel investigates. In spite of its context of a revolution that has utterly changed all, such a dead end is a familiar one in Nadine Gordimer's fiction.

Many of her repeated stories reveal the hiatus between white and black in specific situations. And these frequently involve the commonplace points of friction and contact in the apartheid state: violent robbery, servants and masters, enlightened attempts at non-racial friendship and collaboration. The sickening battle between Maureen and July in the latest novel culminates in an insulting exchange in which each reviles the other with conventional racist slurs: dishonest black servant; alien white employer. At the same time as she is spitting out her hostility towards July, Maureen realizes that her own view of herself in the past—as tolerant, humane, non-racist—has been false. Confronted with this denial of the values assumed in the past to define herself and her marriage, Maureen flees, headlong, irrationally in the final pages of the novel towards the undefined and possibly illusory escape of a lone, unidentified helicopter that lands near the village. Her act is inconclusive and yet final. What she is running towards is unpredictable. What she leaves behind in the village is the emptiness of her new, unprivileged life, the evaporation of her marriage as she used to know it, and the previously inconceivable knowledge of her past status as an overlord. She has no future as the descendant of the shift boss identified in the opening pages.

Flight from impasse is a common feature at the end of Nadine Gordimer's fiction. One of her earliest stories is entitled "Is There Nowhere Else Where We Can Meet?" and describes the terror, guilt and ultimately evasive reaction of a young white bourgeoise confronted by a ragged black purse-snatcher. His threat to her is vividly described as a mixture of the sexual, the violent and the otherness of his pathetic, outcast condition. Thankful to have escaped him she arrives at the first house on the empty road where she can raise the alarm:

> She thought of the woman coming to the door, of the explanations, of the woman's face, and the police. Why did I fight, she thought suddenly. What did I fight for? Why didn't I give him the money and let him go? His red eyes, and the smell and those cracks in his feet, fissures, erosion. She shuddered. The cold of the morning flowed into her.
>
> She turned away from the gate and went down the road slowly, like an invalid, beginning to pick the blackjacks from her stockings.[3]

White authority is still unshaken in this early story. It first appeared in the South African magazine *Common Sense* in 1947. Even as an object of violence, the narrator conceives herself in control of the choices involved in the situation. The black robber is obviously the real victim in her perception of the crisis, and she retreats like an invalid from the knowledge.

A sense that change is possible—even a change of heart—is what distinguishes so early a piece from later fiction. In the penultimate chapter of *The Conservationist* (1974) the protagonist shows a much more profoundly disorienting urge to flee hydra-headed threats to the materialistic world he seeks to conserve. The immediate cause of panic is the appearance of a mysterious white authority figure observing Mehring, the conservationist, in an outdoor sexual groping with a cheap woman hitch-hiker:

> He's going to leave her to them. He's going, in a matter of seconds— mustn't give himself away by so much as glancing towards the car— he's going to make a dash for it, a leap, sell the place to the first offer, jump in, the key's there in the ignition, and drive off reversing wildly first through the trees, the open door on the passenger's side swinging and crashing, breaking branches and tearing leaves. He's going to run, run and leave them to rape her or rob her. She'll be all right. They survive everything. Colored or poor-white, whichever she is, their brothers or fathers take their virginity good and early.[4]

Terror that he will be caught and exposed with the anonymous woman pick-up is only part of Mehring's explosion of panic. Fear of robbery— that quintessential South African anxiety—also merges with the other phobias of his privileged dead end: the burden of his weekend farm and the boorishness of all "them" around him. In spite of his status, power and possessions, there is nothing left in Mehring's existence but to run.

Maureen Smales' flight from her family, her past and July reveals an even more radical collapse of identity. Her husband and children themselves are merely familiar aliens in the animal panic with which she runs towards the landed, idling, invisible helicopter:

> She is running through the elephant grass, dodging the slaps of branches, stooping through thickets of thorn. She is running to the river and she hears them, the man's voice and the voices of children speaking English somewhere to the left. But she makes straight for the ford, and pulling off her shoes balances and jumps from boulder to boulder . . . She runs: trusting herself with all the suppressed trust of a lifetime, alert, like a solitary animal at the season when animals neither seek a mate nor take care of young, existing only for their lone survival, the enemy of all that would make claims of responsibility. She can still hear the beat, beyond those trees and those, and she runs towards it. She runs. (pp. 159 and 160)

These panic-stricken routs are both all encompassing and inconsequential. What they reveal is a total inability to live with the present. Because they embody rejection alone, they lead to an unrevealed future. In fact the consequences of each flight are inaccessible. Even speculation is impossible, so total is the concentration in the writing on the intolerable present. This absence of summatory statement leaves Gordimer's later novels delicately balanced on the fulcrum of conflict which they have investigated. The impotent frenzy of Mehring's and Maureen's fleeing clinches the sense of traumatic impasse which the books reveal.

Frozen immobility—caused by fear, by guilt, by incarceration in prison—creates a similarly traumatic deadlock. *The Late Bourgeois World* concludes with the protagonist, awake in bed, contemplating the terrifying possibility of treasonable action at the request of a friend in the black underground. Here the immediate consequences of action are open to assessment, but her situation is still stifling: "I've been lying awake a long time, now. There is no clock in the room since the red travelling clock that Bobo gave me went out of order, but the slow, even beats of my heart repeat to me, like a clock; afraid, alive, afraid, alive, afraid, alive. . . ."[5] There is no sense that her cooperation with the underground will offer anything conclusive except risk.

In an early short story, "Ah, Woe Is Me," also first published in *Common Sense* in 1947, the inconclusive gesture with which the story closes is contained within the myopic world of white suburban privilege. The obtuse narrator is finally moved to embarrassment by the misery of her ex-servant's daughter. The daughter has called regularly since her mother's departure from service because of illness. On each occasion the present servant gives her bread and tea and the mistress gives her cast off clothing. On this occasion the daughter breaks down at the moment of departure:

> But what's the matter, my girl, I said. What's wrong? You mustn't cry. What's wrong? Tell me?
>
> She tried to speak but her breath was caught by the long quavering sigh of tears. My mother—she's very sick . . . she said at last.
>
> And she began to cry again, her face crumpling up, sobbing and gasping. Desperately, she rubbed at her nose with her wet arm.
>
> What could I do for her? What could I do?
>
> Here . . . I said. Here—take this, and gave her my handkerchief.[6]

The narrator's impotent gesture serves the same function as similar gestures in later works and crystallizes the intractability of the relationship investigated in the story. The focus of attention (up to the fifties) is on white obtuseness. In her passive and victimised position the wretched daughter has no range of response open to her. All the cards are in the hands of the complacent, blinkered white protagonist. And there *is* a sense that white holders of power do have cards to play, still have choices open to them, in much of Gordimer's early fiction. The claustrophobic dead end of the later works results from the absence of these possibilities. At the same time there is a change in the kind of white protagonist who is shown to be trapped. Well-meaning, liberal-minded whites are frequently involved in the later fiction. Black rejection of white bona fides is a new element in work written after 1960. Blacks are no longer portrayed as choiceless, and this intensifies the trauma of derailed relations between black and white.

Occasion For Loving (1963) ends with an early presentation of this theme. The sympathetic white female protagonist who has observed and sheltered a searing love affair between a white English guest in her house and a black artist from the Johannesburg townships comes across him at a typically liberated party of the 1950s in white Johannesburg. His white lover has left him and he is drunk. At Jessie Stilwell's approach he mumbles: "White bitch—get away." The novel concludes with a rueful reflection on the end to their friendship: "When Jessie saw Gideon again, he clearly had no memory of what he had said to her. They continued to meet in a friendly fashion, sometimes in the Lucky Star, occasionally at the houses of friends, but the sense of his place in the Stilwells' life and theirs in his, that she felt that night, never came again. So long as Gideon did not remember, Jessie could not forget."[7]

Such an articulate depiction of blocked affection is a far cry from the irrational panic with which later protagonists run away from blockage. But the active role played by the black person in this mutual failure indicates the shift in scope between Gordimer's earlier and later fiction.

By the time of *Livingstone's Companions* in 1972, failed friendships are the focus of much of her interest. One story in the collection, "Africa Emergent," raises the issue in its opening paragraph. The narrator states that shows of friendship for a man in prison are a luxury, not important and perhaps dangerous: "If I said, I was a friend of so-and-so, black man awaiting trial for treason, what good would it do him? And, who knows, it might draw just that decisive bit more attention to me."[8] Political danger, betrayal and imprisonment are elements of inter-racial friendship in the post-Sharpeville state that add new dimensions of uncertainty. The narrator of "Africa Emergent" continues: ". . . not that he really was such a friend. But that's something else you won't understand; everything is ambiguous, here. We hardly know, by now, what we can do and what we can't do; it's difficult to say, goaded in on oneself by laws and doubts and rebellion and caution and—not least—self-disgust, what is or is not a friendship. I'm talking about black and white, of course" (p. 369).

Maureen Smales is not a friend of her servant, July. The disintegration of her relationship with him, especially the pre-revolutionary view she had of its benign, liberated quality, is prefigured in earlier versions of this theme in Gordimer's fiction. Closest of all to the climactic final row in *July's People* is the crucial insulting match in *Burger's Daughter* between Rosa Burger and her childhood playmate, Baasie, now a black exile in London.

Infuriated by Rosa's easy reassertion of their childhood friendship, he insists on his new identity as Zwelinzima, not Baasie, and attacks her for posing as different from other whites because of her political commitment. She has told him that she took a fake pass to his father in the black underground before he was caught by the police. He replies:

> Whites are locking up blacks every day. You want to make the big confession?—why do you think you should be different from all the other whites who've been shitting on us ever since they came? He was able to go back home and get caught because you took the pass there . . . You think because you're telling me it makes it all right—for you . . . But he's dead, and what about all the others—who cares whose "fault"—they die because it's the whites killing them, black blood is the stuff to get rid of white shit.—[9]

Under this barrage Rosa strikes back with insults of her own, attacking Zwelinzima's safety in exile: "This kind of talk sounds better from people who are in the country than people like us" (p. 322). To which he replies: "You didn't even know my name. I don't have to tell you what I'm doing" (p. 322), and she delivers the classic riposte: "—What is it you want?—the insult thrilled her as she delivered herself of it—You want something. If it's money, I'm telling you there isn't any. Go and ask one of your white English liberals who'll pay but won't fight" (p. 322). This incident is shattering to Rosa. She describes herself as disintegrated and humiliated by it. That she should have adopted the position she did is far more distressing to her than the insults she endured herself: "Repelled by him. Hating him so much! Wanting to be *loved*!—how I disfigured myself. How filthy and ugly, in the bathroom mirror. Debauched . . . trotting out the holier-than-thou accusation—the final craven defence of the kind of people for whom there is going to be no future" (p. 329). To see herself—even momentarily—behaving in typical white South African fashion is to shake the foundations of her identity. Hence the cataclysmic nature of her reaction: she abandons her French lover and returns to South Africa and inevitable imprisonment.

Maureen Smales is not a political being like Rosa Burger. Her apolitical role in pre-revolutionary Johannesburg as liberal wife of liberal architect carries none of the responsibilities of Rosa's role as Lionel Burger's daughter. Nevertheless Maureen sees herself and the life of her family as largely untainted by the grotesque prejudices of the white master-race norm. This belief is what collapses in her final confrontation with July. She, and her past, are revealed in a new and, to her, damning light. Unlike Rosa, she has no commitment to return to. The material props of her life have already been stripped from her in the bush. Disintegrated like Rosa, she can only run like an animal away from the scene of her humiliation.

Relations with July are merely part of Maureen's crisis of identity. Her appearance, interests, sexuality have all changed substantially in her new existence as a white bourgeois peasant. Early in the book she recognizes: "She was already not what she was. No fiction could compete with what she was finding she did not know, could not have imagined or discovered through imagination" (p. 29). Discovering who they are in their elemental bush life is difficult for both adult Smales. Maureen ceases to recognise in Bam the traits of the suburban architect. At one point she has "a single throb of impulse" to "go over to the man and sink against, embrace him, touch someone recollected, not the one who persisted in his name, occasionally supplying meat, catching fish for people" (p. 93). And Bam finds himself thinking of his bush wife as "her," rather than Maureen: "Her, not 'Maureen.' Not 'his wife.' The presence in the mud hut, mute with an activity of being, of sense of self he could not follow because here there were no familiar areas in which it could be visualized moving, no familiar entities that could be shaping it. With 'her' there was no undersurface of recognition; only moments of finding each other out" (p. 105).

Problematic as their recognition of self is, one element of identity remains constant for the Smales, even in their village existence. They are white. They are seen as white and they are treated as white. Relations with all their new neighbours are affected by their alien whiteness and because of this Maureen begins to understand more about their earlier whiteness in Johannesburg. Near the beginning of the novel an authorial voice described the Smales' previous, ineffectual plans to escape their present predicament, while "there was still time":

> They sickened at the appalling thought that they might find they had lived out their whole lives as they were, born white pariah dogs in a black continent. They joined political parties and "contact" groups in willingness to slough privilege it was supposed to be their white dog nature to guard with Mirages and tanks; they were not believed. They had thought of leaving, then, while they were young

enough to cast off the blacks' rejection as well as white privilege,
to make a life in another country. They had stayed. (p. 8)

Recognition that she cannot escape being a white pariah dog, that
black rejection is a permanent fact of both her new and her old life
is what emerges in Maureen's battle with July. Just as the Smales
were "not believed" in their previous attempts to "slough privilege,"
so are they suspect now as friendly white peasants.

Although Maureen and Bam have difficulty recognising their
previous selves in each other, their white arrogance remains a constant
factor. Centuries of white dominance lie behind them. When July
returns after his first appropriation of their van, Maureen is appalled
to see Bam's assumption of his former role: "Maureen was unbelieving
to see on the white man's face the old, sardonic, controlled challenge of the patron.—And where were you yesterday? What's the
story?—" (p. 53). Even when shocked that the district chief wants
him to pass on his firearms and their mystique, Bam cannot refrain
from lecturing that cynical local boss about his obligations as a black
man: "You're not going to take guns and help the white government
kill blacks, are you? Are you? For this—this village and this empty
bush? And they'll kill you. You mustn't let the government make
you kill each other. The whole black nation is your nation" (p. 120).
Pathetically condescending as this political sermon is, it comes at the
very moment when the Smales discover another example of their
ethnocentric ignorance of July's real nature. The chief mentions his
true name, Mwawate: " 'July' was a name for whites to use; for fifteen
years they had not been told what the chief's subject really was
called" (p. 120).[10] Maureen's sense of hollowness as she listens to
Bam's speech reflects an awareness of past emptiness as well as the
present void: "she was hearing him say what he and she had always
said, it came lamenting, searching from their whole life across the
silent bush in which they had fallen from the fabric of that life as
loose buttons drop and are lost" (p. 120).

Even July's role as their saviour, hiding them in the bush, is
theoretically problematic to the Smales' white view of the black
freedom struggle. They know their urban concepts are irrelevant as
they try to discuss black self interest: "He struggled hopelessly for
words that were not phrases from back there, words that would make
the truth that must be forming here, out of the blacks, out of
themselves . . . But the words would not come. They were blocked
by an old vocabulary" (p. 127). What does come is Maureen's non-
political apprehension of the hopelessly entwined lives of their servant
and his overlords: "He's been mixed up with us for fifteen years. No
one will ever be able to disentangle that, so long as he's alive; is
that it? A fine answer to give the blacks who are getting killed to

set him free" (p. 128). It is the Smales' former code of evaluation that emerges even at the height of their present perplexity. Only when July and Maureen finally bare their teeth at each other does she understand the unthinking condescension of that code.

Not that the Smales are particularly obtuse or self-deceiving. They represent a norm of white decency, viciously compromised by their status as inevitable overlords. The surreptitious, underhand grip of their environment has been beautifully embodied in an incident remembered from Maureen's childhood. Like other female protagonists in Nadine Gordimer's fiction, she has grown up on a mine property outside Johannesburg. That typically enclosed, comfortable and cloistered white community living both in isolation and side-by-side with the tawdry, raw, exploited world of migrant black labourers in their "compound" has been used in *The Lying Days* and *Occasion For Loving* to locate the schizoid roots of white fairmindedness. In Maureen's case, the domestic cosiness of life in the white married quarters is real. Part of the cosiness involves an easy and affectionate relation with her black maid, Lydia. Meeting her mistress on her way home from school, Lydia enjoys gossip with acquaintances en route and shares Cokes and gum purchased by Maureen. Holding hands, they walk happily home while Lydia carries Maureen's schoolcase on her head. The pair are spotted by a photographer and years later Maureen discovers the photograph in a *Life* coffee-table book. It is used to illustrate white *herrenvolk* attitudes: young white schoolgirl and black woman carrying her schoolcase. Innocent as the warmth was between her and Lydia, Maureen has an inkling—in the bush— that the photograph captured a truth about their situation which left them its victims: "Why had Lydia carried her case? Did the photographer know what he saw, when they crossed the road like that, together? Did the book, placing the pair in its context, give the reason she and Lydia, in their affection and ignorance, didn't know?" (p. 33).

July's view of his relation to the Smales family is rooted in his status as servant. Speculating that he will probably be introduced to the chief as "the Master," Bamford Smales reflects: "How many times, back there, had Maureen and Bam tried to get him to drop the Simon Legree term, but he wouldn't, couldn't, as if there was no term to replace it, none that would express exactly what the relationship between Bam and him was, for him" (p. 111). The fallen condition of the Smales family has left them comparatively powerless but has not affected the only point of connection between them and July. However embarrassing the nature of their masterhood used to be to Bam and Maureen—and hence their insistence that it should be overlooked in words and manner—masterhood is all that July ultimately is prepared to accept from them. Their suggestion of a more appropriately relaxed relationship (both before and after) ignores July's own view of himself. He does not accept their right to define him as a man rather than as a servant.

Understanding this side of her previous arrogance is part of Maureen's final trauma. In her penultimate spat with July she tries to hurt him by suggesting that he has been less than honorable to both his village wife and his city mistress, now abandoned in the chaos of the urban fighting. Her "venom" expresses itself in a sneering question whether he is frightened that she may tell his wife "something." The fury in his reply, that there is nothing she *can* tell about him except that he has worked satisfactorily for her for fifteen years, reveals the inappropriateness of her concepts of what would be dignified or honourable for him. He is outside her code of values: "It [fear] spread from him; she was feeling no personal threat in him, not physical, anyway, but in herself. How was she to have known, until she came here, that the special consideration she had shown for his dignity as a man, while he was by definition a servant, would become his humiliation itself" (p. 98).

Revelation of this kind strikes at the very core of any concept of white decency and humanity within the apartheid state. For all its marvelously vivid evocation of what a future war could be like, *July's People* basically explores the wilderness of the present. Throughout the book Nadine Gordimer peels away the protective layers with which well-meaning whites who reject official South African mores try to distance themselves from their inevitably tainted roles. It is not white power that the author describes as crumbling in *July's People*, but the final illusion of white innocence.

The presumption of her western morality is at the heart of Maureen's last bitter insight. She has been troubled since her arrival in the village to discover in July's hut items pilfered from her past existence. With middle-class scorn and indignation she finally accuses him of stealing things. She is "stampeded by a wild rush of need to destroy everything between them" (p. 152) and when he denies her charge she counters with another middle-class concept: "I said nothing because I was ashamed to think you would do it" (p. 152). Only when July answers back angrily in his own language, for the first time refusing to accommodate her incomprehension, does she at last understand: "She understood although she knew no word. Understood everything: what he had had to be, how she had covered up to herself for him, in order for him to be her idea of him. But for himself—to be intelligent, honest, dignified for *her* was nothing; his measure as a man was taken elsewhere and by others" (p. 152). After such knowledge is forgiveness even desirable? The impasse is total and mere goodwill totally inadequate to cope with it.

Failure of communication between white and black within the

poisoned apartheid world is one of those fictional themes Nadine Gordimer constantly reworks. In *July's People* the collapse of white military power which the novel assumes is far less disturbing than the collapse of white moral power which it analyses. Part of the degradation of white suzerainty is shown to be white scruples themselves, even the scruples of humane, dissenting whites. The paradox which epitomizes the deadlock of the book's ending is that only when the black man refuses to talk the white woman's language is she able to understand "everything."

Notes

1. Nadine Gordimer, *Selected Stories* (London: Jonathan Cape, 1975), pp. 9–10.

2. Nadine Gordimer, *July's People* (Johannesburg: Ravan Press, 1981), p. 3.

3. Nadine Gordimer, "Is There Nowhere Else Where We Can Meet?", *Selected Stories*, pp. 17–18.

4. Nadine Gordimer, *The Conservationist* (London: Jonathan Cape, 1974), p. 250.

5. Nadine Gordimer, *The Late Bourgeois World* (London: Jonathan Cape, 1966), p. 160.

6. Nadine Gordimer, "Ah, Woe Is Me," *Selected Stories*, p. 30.

7. Nadine Gordimer, *Occasion For Loving* (New York: Viking, 1963), p. 308. The echoes of this fictional relationship hang over a sentence in Nadine Gordimer's recent article in *The New York Review of Books*. She is speaking of herself: "A black man I may surely call my friend because we have survived a time when he did not find it possible to accept a white's friendship, and a time when I didn't think I could accept that he should decide when that time was past, said to me this year, 'Whites have to learn to struggle.' " ("Living in the Interregnum," *The New York Review of Books*, January 20, 1983, p. 22.) The whole essay, based on the James Lecture at the New York Institute for the Humanities in October 1982, offers an analysis of the roles open to whites which is a non-fictional extension of the argument in *July's People*. The title of the essay draws on the quotation from Gramsci which is the epigraph for *July's People:* "The old is dying, and the new cannot be born; in this interregnum there arises a great diversity of morbid symptoms."

8. Nadine Gordimer, "Africa Emergent," *Selected Stories*, p. 369.

9. Nadine Gordimer, *Burger's Daughter* (London: Jonathan Cape, 1979), p. 322.

10. The whites' ignorance of a black acquaintance's real name recalls Baasie/Zwelinzima's insult to Rosa Burger that she does not even know his name.

What's a Poor White to Do?
White South African Option in
A Sport of Nature[1]   Richard Peck[°]

As the South African tragedy gains momentum daily, one looks in vain for a white role which might ease the transition to majority rule in South Africa and reduce the toll of life there.[2] Unfortunately, not even in the best of committed white fiction, where one might hope for influential visions to arise first, do we find a vision which is compelling.

Nadine Gordimer's most recent novel, *A Sport of Nature* (1987),[3] examines and rejects a variety of white South African roles—conservative, hedonist, and liberal—and offers a vision of a more revolutionary alternative. The vision, unfortunately, seems less than compelling, even to Gordimer herself. It seems to be an attempt to push beyond the revolutionary alternative endorsed in *Burger's Daughter* (1979).[4] There she rejected the approach of the South African Communist Party and proposed an alternative evidently intended to be more humane.[5] In *A Sport of Nature* she recognizes that the proposal offered in *Burger's Daughter* did not adequately come to terms with the power relationships so crucial to change in South Africa and proposes a new alternative which faces the demands of power more squarely. However, she seems less than pleased with the result. As if uncertain what to think, she so distances herself from the new approach that it is not clear whether she has endorsed it or condemned it. Her ambivalence may well arise from its sacrifice of humane means to ends that are at best uncertain and quite possibly unattractive.

In *A Sport of Nature* the female relatives of the protagonist, Hillela, represent the three least satisfactory white options. Her Aunt Olga is happy with the status quo; her mother, Ruthie, flees South Africa; and her Aunt Pauline is as committed a liberal as we have seen in Gordimer's works. Hillela herself at first unconsciously follows her mother's hedonistic escapism, but later develops through several more committed approaches.

In Olga, Gordimer continues her long-standing but muted criticism of conservative whites. Olga is kind to her servants and preserves strong family feeling and a respect for her Jewish traditions, but is preoccupied with material values and oblivious to politics. Olga and her husband "can't take pleasure in anything that hasn't a market value" (18). Pauline notes to Hillela that Olga's reaction to the Sharpeville massacre is that "I've no right to deprive you of a holiday. For reasons of my own. That was her phrase exactly: 'for reasons of

[°] From *Ariel* 19 (1988):75–93. Reprinted by permission of the author.

your own.' That's all Sharpeville and sixty-nine dead meant to her" (27). And Olga's reaction to politics "is always to be afraid of *trouble*!" (25). She is thankful for the police and the courts because they "lock away burglars, rapists, embezzlers, car thieves, murderers where they couldn't threaten decent people any longer" (327). Gordimer takes it as given that *apartheid* is indefensible,[6] and considers most who support it to be smugly ignorant and materialistic, faults worthy more of contempt than of great moral vehemence.[7]

Gordimer has shown more interest over the years in those who flee South Africa. These come in two varieties: those so overcome by the moral dilemmas of South Africa that they attempt to defect (as did Rosa Burger); and those oblivious to South African realities who flee on hedonistic journeys. Gordimer rejects both approaches, but with considerable understanding. Those who attempt to defect she uses to drive home the impossibility of escape and the necessity of commitment. And the hedonists she uses as a source of principles which humanize her committed protagonists.

Hedonistic flight figures as prominently in *A Sport of Nature* as it did in *Burger's Daughter*. Conrad's hedonism forms one of the theses in the dialectical argument of *Burger's Daughter*. Gordimer rejects the hedonism but uses Conrad's emphasis on emotion to criticize the excessive ideologization of the Communists and as a source of the emotional reaction to suffering which is central to Rosa's committed synthesis.[8] In *A Sport of Nature* the hedonism figures so strongly that Krauss has concluded (mistakenly) that it is Hillela's essence, making her nothing more than "a highly impressionable sexual object."[9] But here too Gordimer rejects the hedonism while valorizing some of its constituent elements.

Ruthie has fled "the Calvinism and koshering of this place" in search of "passion and tragedy" in the fado songs of Mozambique (46), abandoning her child Hillela, and leaving behind for her little more than drafts of letters to her Portuguese lover (48–50). She has rejected both Olga's materialism and Pauline's love of her fellow man to pursue the love of one man (49), and that expressed in joyously physical terms.

Neither in her youth (4; 47) nor when she meets Ruthie much later (289–99) does Hillela show any family feeling for the mother she has hardly known. But she does respond to the descriptions of physical love in Ruthie's letters, and unconsciously follows Ruthie in her sexual freedom, her scant attention to both Olga's materialism and Pauline's liberalism, and her flight from South Africa because of a man who subsequently abandons her. Hillela in her early years is oblivious to South African realities and bent on a rebellious pursuit of pleasure. In Pauline's words: "She's a-moral. I mean, in the sense of the morality of this country" (44).

Hillela is not a conservative accommodationist, since part of her amorality is an attractive unwillingness to pay attention to the categories that order life in South Africa: she is thrown out of her Rhodesian school for visiting a Coloured boy (12–13); she explodes in defence of her father's new wife Billie whom Olga thinks too "tarty" to be a fit mother (17); and she ignores the Afrikaner background of her musical friend Gert Prinsloo (54–6). When she meets Rey she pays no attention to his nationality: "categories were never relevant to her ordering of life" (108). Even in making love to her cousin Sasha she refuses to categorize people (32).

Nor is Hillela a liberal, since she is also amoral in her deliberate ignoring of politics in South Africa. To show this Gordimer frequently juxtaposes political events and discussions against indications that Hillela is totally oblivious to them. Two examples suffice to illustrate this pattern.[10] In one of the earliest occurrences of the pattern, Hillela greets Pauline and Carole as they protest the formation of the South African Republic, then returns to her coffee bar to sing folk songs, getting thrown out when the proprietor smells marijuana (52–3). The crudest such juxtaposition is the reference to torture in the observation that "while electric currents were passing through the reproductive organs of others, Hillela had an abortion" (114). When Hillela flees South Africa with Rey, the reader agrees with Pauline that "Smoking pot in a coffee bar, that was more in that little girl's line. . . . She has no political sense, no convictions, not the faintest idea" (121–2). Pauline's explanation for Hillela's flight is accurate and clearly establishes the parallel with Ruthie:

> Attached herself to some man—that's what it was all about, *He* was the one who had to go.
> Pauline and Olga were only two of three sisters, after all; still.
> Attached herself to some man.
> My poor Ruthie. (123)

Gordimer uses elements of Hillela's hedonistic youth as bases for her more committed later approaches. Hillela's refusal to use South African categories in her assessment of people is crucial, as is her sexuality and the love for an individual man. Gordimer valorizes Hillela's love for a black man[11] as the source both of her utopian vision and of the motivation for her search for means of realizing that vision. As in *Burger's Daughter*, hedonistic escapism is rejected, but used to humanize and motivate the protagonist in her commitment.

For the liberal approach Gordimer reserves a vitriol which has grown ever stronger over the years. As ex-communists are said to make the strongest anti-communists, Gordimer's own attempt to move beyond liberalism leads her to be increasingly unforgiving of liberals.[12] She increasingly finds the liberalism a hypocritical attitudinizing which salves the consciences of its adherents while contributing nothing to needed change in South Africa. In recent years Gordimer has evidently seen her political task as puncturing the delusions of South Africa's liberals and proposing more efficacious and more committed alternatives.

In *A Sport of Nature* the liberals, Pauline and Joe, are attacked as mercilessly as were the Smaleses of Gordimer's 1981 *July's People*,[13] of whom Hardwick concludes that "something is askew in the vehemence of the moral rebuke to the Smaleses, husband and wife."[14] The falseness of Pauline and Joe's position is treated no more kindly, despite the fact that they are more committed and active than most of Gordimer's liberals.

Pauline criticizes Joe's activities as a lawyer defending political cases, asking "What will you be at our Nuremberg? . . . The one who tried to serve justice through the rule of law, or the one who betrayed justice by trying to serve it through the rule of unjust laws?" (67). But Pauline's own activities are no more than meliorative: she defends a black waiter verbally abused by a schoolgirl (19–23); she organizes a Saturday school to compensate for the inadequacies of "Bantu Education" (22–23); she distributes leaflets against the Verwoerd republic, until she hears that liberals are being arrested and destroys the remaining leaflets (60–61); and she goes to protest meetings (52). She and Joe do give aid to a fleeing Black Consciousness activist (73–78). But when one of Rosa Burger's circle earlier asked Pauline to shelter an activist, Pauline refused, pleading that it would endanger Joe's "absolutely necessary" work as a lawyer (29). And Pauline feels caught out in her hypocrisy when Hillela looks at her in a knowing way (47). Sasha accuses them of being "careful not to let anything happen to you" (39). Hillela characterizes their approach as "hesitations and doubts, the shilly-shallying of what was more effective between this commitment or that, this second-hand protest or that" (209). It was, she says, nothing but talk: "Everybody talked and argued . . . And whenever I heard them again, they were still talking and arguing, living the same way in the same place" (222).

In *A Sport of Nature* Gordimer criticizes most strongly the liberals' inability to find a role in a South African history which is multiethnic and predominantly black. The relations of Pauline and Joe with other ethnic groups are presented as anything but easy and natural. Pauline suspects others of anti-semitism (36), and all members of her family are clearly prejudiced against Afrikaners (36, 54). But more serious are their strained relations with blacks. They are unable to criticize the unwise activities of one of their black protegés (58–9). Sasha concludes that Pauline's "blacks were like Aunt Olga's whatnots, they were handled with such care not to say or do anything that might chip the friendship they allowed her to claim" (317). Gordimer criticizes this by contrast with Sasha's more natural relationships with blacks (83, 317), and by contrast with Hillela's unwillingness to categorize people, and her later marriages with blacks. Hillela has an honest and innocent recognition of the importance of racial differences (177), but sees beyond them. When she marries the black revolutionary Whaila she "had what [Pauline and Joe] couldn't find: a sign in her marriage, a sure and certain instruction to which one could attach oneself and feel the tug of history" (199).[15] Hillela has "given up being white" but reports that Pauline and Joe "wanted to but they didn't seem to know how" (186).

Nor do Pauline and Joe have any vision of the future or of the means for attaining it. Sasha criticizes their rationality at the expense of a utopian vision, noting that *"Without Utopia . . . there's a failure of the imagination—and that's a failure to know how to go on living"* (187).[16] He says he hated them because he "expected them to have solutions but they only had questions" (317). When Sasha later returns to revolutionary activity, we are told that "nothing in the advantages of his youth had prepared him for" his circumstances (335).

If Gordimer demolishes the conservative, hedonist, and liberal pre-revolutionary white stances, she has considerably less success moving beyond them. She has been searching for an alternative to liberalism which would be more efficacious in promoting change, but which would preserve the humanistic elements that have given liberalism its appeal. Yet she has failed in her search, once on each side of the equation. Rosa Burger's post-liberal alternative preserved humane values but seemed unlikely to be efficacious in contributing to needed change. Hillela's alternative is efficacious, but may not preserve humane values.

Hillela is drawn to participation in the South African cause because of her love for Whaila. She moves through love for one man to love for a people and eventually to the cause as a way to express that love. In the end she finds an efficacious means of promoting change. But Gordimer's ambivalent and often sardonic treatment of Hillela suggests that Gordimer is apprehensive about the sacrifice of humane values inherent in Hillela's approach.

Hillela's love for Whaila transforms her from her old hedonism. Whaila asks himself "What am I to you, that you transform yourself" (181)? And after his death Hillela asks herself *"What am I without him? And if, without him, I am nothing, what was I?"* (215). Hillela reads the revolutionary doctrine she had earlier ignored (180). She participates in political discussions which before left her daydreaming (183–6). She comes to terms with the necessity for violence, including the possibility that "innocent" people may be killed (207). And she worries about the role of whites in the revolution, maintaining that she herself has "given up being white" (186). When she has their black child she is delighted *not* to have reproduced herself with all the advantages of her whiteness (195).[17]

Much of Hillela's transformation is derivative, a deference to the ideas of others. She defers to the exiles: "teach me, she said" (180). When Nkrumah dies, she "assum[es] instinctively from observance of those with whom she lived the appropriate attitude" (190–91). And when she tells Whaila that she cannot imagine the deaths of innocents "he was aware of her waiting for him to tell her what she should be feeling about the unimaginable" (207). "The ideas of others worked in Hillela's blood like alcohol" (183).

But Hillela's most important change is not derivative: it involves the utopian vision which her love for Whaila gives her. The vision is of a time when love between white and black can be free and natural, a time in which it will make sense for a black and a white to say that their child is "our colour" (178–9), a time in which a "rainbow family" (207) will be possible. Hillela's vision arises from her refusal to pay attention to categories among people, the most attractive characteristic of her hedonistic youth. In naïve innocence which echoes the delusions of liberalism, she lives in the utopia as if it were the reality, at least until Whaila's assassination awakens her from her delusion. Although Whaila finds it an attractive vision, it does not originate with him. When Hillela first announces that she wants their child to be "our colour," Whaila's reaction is one of "dolour" about this "creature made of love, without a label; that's a freak" (178–9). And it certainly does not originate with Pauline. When she hears that Hillela has married Whaila, her reaction is that "it solves nothing . . . Feeling free to sleep with a black man doesn't set him free" (187).

Gordimer celebrates Hillela's vision. When Pauline denigrates Hillela's marriage, Sasha (perhaps the only character who has Gordimer's complete confidence) writes in reply: *"Instinct is utopian. Emotion is utopian . . . Without utopia . . . there's a failure of the imagination—and that's a failure to know how to go on living. It will take another kind of being to stay on, here. A new white person. Not us. The chance is a wild chance—like falling in love"* (187). We hear of Hillela's "sign in her marriage" (199). Whaila too "saw their own closeness as a sign; the human cause, the human identity that should be possible, once the race and class struggle were won. With her, it was already one world; what could be" (208).

Hillela's love for Whaila leads her to identify with his cause, symbolized by their handclasp when he tells her about a raid into South Africa: "He was lover and brother to her in the great family of a cause" (210). But her identification has hardly begun before Whaila is assassinated.

The shortcoming of Hillela's approach, of course, is that she is living in a " *'time that hasn't yet come'* " (233). She has deluded herself by ignoring the realities of power, symbolized by the assassination of Whaila. Her love for her rainbow family, she realizes, *"can't be got away with, it's cornered, it's easily done away with in two shots"* (232). She now expresses her love in terms of revenge for Whaila's death, in an identification with the rainbow family defined in broader terms, and in an attempt to carry on the cause symbolized by the handclasp. She understands that *"the handclasp belongs to tragedy, not grief . . . A tragedy . . . is when a human being is destroyed engaging himself with events greater than personal relationships . . . tragedy is a sign that the struggle must go on"* (215).

Hillela's dedication to the cause goes through stages broadly paralleling the foreign policies of the regions in which she finds (or places) herself. In Eastern Europe she attempts to dedicate herself to the weapons for liberation; in the United States she seeks humanitarian aid for those harmed by the liberation wars; and in Africa she searches for African levers of power.

Hillela's first reaction to Whaila's death is a fanatical dedication. Her old friend and lover Arnold notes both the change and the fanaticism, thinking that "she was part of the preoccupation she once had disrupted so naturally" (218) and telling others later that "she was the type to have become a terrorist, a hijacker. . . . It wasn't that she was undisciplined; no discipline was demanding enough for her" (219). She so submerges herself in the cause that "no history of her really can be personal history, then; its ends were all apparently outside herself" (225). She reflects that "the handclasp is the only love made flesh. Learn that. Read the handclasp, learning the kind of love in the calibre and striking power of hardware" (233).

Why Hillela abandons this phase is left unclear, and even deliberately confused, by Gordimer. But it seems likely that it is because the activities she is allowed do not satisfy her fanaticism. For all her dedication to "the calibre and striking power of hardware" her activities hardly go beyond typing, translation, and giving occasional speeches. She condemns herself as she once condemned Pauline and Joe: "now I'm getting like them . . . I'm talking, talking" (223). And her Russian friend Pavel comments that she is too much the individualist to be merely a functionary: "You got your own talent" (230).

In the U.S. she turns her talent to an able use of bureaucracy and academia to benefit the liberation movements and the Africans damaged by the liberation wars, which she now sees as her real rainbow family (251). She tells her old friend Udi "I am not a bureaucrat, I have to use bureaucracy," and says she is using it "looking for ways to free Whaila" (249). She says later "I wanted to get rid of the people who came to the flat and shot Whaila, . . .

[all South African whites] because all of them, *they let it happen"* (267). But she gets sidetracked into a preoccupation with the suffering caused by the wars: "now it's soup powder I've been doling out. When you see everything reduced to hunger . . . [y]ou only want to find something to stuff in those mouths. You lose all sense of what you wanted to do" (268).

But Hillela rejects this approach as well, and in having Hillela do so Gordimer emphasizes the weakness of the position in which she left Rosa Burger. Although Hillela never gives reasons for "moving on" once again, it is not hard to find them in comments made by her old friend Udi and by the General. Of her work with the bureaucracy Udi asks: "what can that sort of thing achieve. It will be the big powers who'll decide what happens to blacks. And the power of other black heads of state influencing the big powers. A waste, yes . . . it's *this* that's a waste of your life—" (249). And Reuel (the General) comments of her "doling out soup powder" that "that's not *getting rid*" (268). He has earlier explained "they send us guns and soup powder, êh. Some get the guns. That's the important thing, to be the side that gets the guns. You will never come to power on soup powder" (267).

In the General, soon to be President, Hillela recognizes a means of placing herself on the side that gets the guns, a means of obtaining influence through a black head of state. "She must have had a pretty good inkling he was sure of getting back into power" (269). She sees in him one who will not die, one who knows how to use weapons in the cause, one whose handclasp "is on recognition, irresistible" (281). And, in fact, when the General becomes President he and Hillela help the South African liberation movement:[18] "safe houses were provided and the experienced lobbying ability and growing prestige of the President were brought into play in the world to obtain increasing support for those who temporarily occupied the safe houses . . . [Hillela] was always present at these negotiations" (332). When the South African revolution arrives the President (now Chairman of the OAU as well) "was part of the negotiations that continued outside the country concurrently with undeclared civil war there," and he later is "an extremely useful adviser to the black liberation leaders" in their negotiations with the corporations. "So, in many ways, he can be regarded as a brother who has been part of the South African liberation struggle in accordance with the old Pan-African ideal" (337).

By attaching herself to Reuel, Hillela has found a way beyond the dead end of Rosa Burger's compassionate wait-and-see, a way to exert leverage in the South African power equation while leaving it to blacks to make the revolution and define the South African future. If her contribution is marginal, it is as large as any South African white in the opposition could hope to make. In fact, it is certainly larger than any but a handful of whites could hope to make, given the limited number of African heads of state and the minuscule number willing to marry white South Africans however dedicated and however sexually imaginative.

If Gordimer intends *A Sport of Nature* to be "inspirational," clearly her message is more about strategy than about tactical details. The point is that love and compassion and the utopian vision they create are necessary but not sufficient in the South African setting, that committed whites must find leverage in the power equation. Such tactical details as are generalizable suggest that the search for levers of power requires a certain rootlessness and ruthlessness, adaptability and survival skill, coupled with a willingness to take advantage of whatever sources of power one may have. Gordimer strongly emphasizes these characteristics in Hillela, although it is less clear that she endorses them.

The novel opens with a signal of Hillela's rootlessness as she changes her name from the "Kim" used at school to the "Hillela" used with her family, with both names equally meaningless to her (3). Both early and late in the novel we hear of her lack of feeling for her mother; and throughout the novel Hillela is either "somewhere about" or "moving on," dropping parents, relatives, old friends, acquaintances, and lovers as she goes.[19] When the President gives her an Igbo version of his name (303), her rootlessness is complete: Olga recognizes her in the newspaper only by her face, there being nothing familiar left of her name (304). Gordimer suggests that such rootlessness is a requisite to being able to "give up being white" and seek out levers of power wherever they may present themselves. But it is not to be celebrated. Whaila finds that "sometimes [Hillela's] lack of any identification with her own people dismayed him . . . there was something missing in her . . . like a limb or an organ" (208). And the President has stronger feeling for the importance of Hillela's kinship to her mother than has Hillela herself (296).

Ruthlessness too may be necessary but is not to be celebrated. Hillela has no difficulty imposing on people. As she flees South Africa "friends who had offered her 'something to wear' had not failed to notice she took the best garments" (119), and she endangers her uncle Joe and his work by asking him to contravene exchange control restrictions for her (122). Later she so overstays her welcome with London liberals (198) that when she reappears several years later they hope she is not planning to stay with them again (288). Hillela treats people as means to an end as she moves through them, dropping them as they lose their usefulness. We hear a number of snide comments that "Hillela has never lost her instinct for avoiding losers" (209). The worst example may well be her casual dropping of her

American fiancé Brad to "move on" with Reuel. The commentary virtually links this to military necessity: "she told him with true kindness, the impulse with which her guerrillas cared for some of the homeless and starving in their war" (263). And earlier on the same page Hillela has said "what else is war? You're a victim, or you fight and make victims" (263).

Gordimer also stresses Hillela's adaptability and survival instincts. They are necessary because of the variety of settings into which the cause takes her, from testifying before the US Congress to drinking contaminated water with guerrillas in the African bush. She makes use of everything in her background, serving tea or African food to visitors as the occasion demands; "there hasn't been anything she hasn't profited by, at one period or another" (205). She is a survivor: Pavel notes "you are too clever for anything to happen to you, Hillela" (231, 232–3). Gordimer's considerable emphasis on Hillela's Jewish background underlines these themes, through a dual evocation of the wandering Jew and the Holocaust survivors. Certainly Gordimer has rarely in the past placed such emphasis on Jewishness in her writing about South Africa.[20] The evocation of the Holocaust and its connection with South Africa is explicit when Karel shows Hillela the can of Zyklon B on his bookshelf in memory of the treatment of death as "some ordinary . . . commodity," and Hillela cries—not for Whaila's recent death but for her own lost innocence as she faces "the necessity to deal in death . . . meeting death with death, not flowers and memorials" (227–8).

Hillela is certainly skilled at the manipulation of such limited sources of power as have been given to her. She trades on the death of Whaila as a source of credentials (217; see also 239). Her sexuality passes from being merely a source of pleasure and of truth to being something that can be manipulated: "something new has been learned . . . One can offer, without giving. It's a form of power" (198). Her sexual attractiveness helps get aid for Africa: "lust is the best aid raiser" (245). Later it is instrumental in establishing her connection with the General (275, 283); his son notes that "this one not only knew the need to move on, but also what she would not reveal to his father: what it was necessary to do, to bring this about" (286), which we understand to mean her trading on her sexuality. Moreover, she is perfectly aware of what she is doing. One of the attractions of her planned marriage to Brad, she thinks, is that there would be "no need to watch for what can be traded—searching pockets for attributes: martyr's wife, expressive Latin eyes and large breasts" (260).

But if these characteristics are necessary to Hillela's pursuit of power, it is far from clear that Gordimer endorses them.

Doubt about what Gordimer endorses arises from the extreme

distance which she establishes from her protagonist. Much of the narration is in shifting third-person voices, frequently that of a biographer largely hostile to Hillela. The biographer often suggests how little is known of her, and casts doubts on her worthiness. Gordimer creates a double distance from her creation, then, by interposing another person, and by having that other person profess ignorance and doubt.

The epitome of this distancing and disapproving may well be the biographer's comment that little is known about Hillela during one period of her life, followed by the observation that "[i]n the lives of the greatest, there are such lacunae—Christ and Shakespeare disappear from and then reappear in the chronicles that documentation and human memory provide" (100). Gordimer distances herself by interposing the biographer; the biographer creates further distance by telling us how little is known; and the absurd comparison with Christ and Shakespeare creates further distance through its disapproving irony. Neither then nor by the end of the novel does the comparison seem apt.

Nor does the disapproving tone apply only to Hillela's hedonistic youth when a liberal (or post-liberal) author might well disapprove of her creation. The recurring phrase "trust her" and variations on it serve as a litmus. It carries a tone of disapproval which increases over the course of the novel, starting as a comment on her innocence but ending as thoroughly snide. It first appears applied to Rey when he is with a distrusting group of blacks and Hillela thinks innocently "*Trust him!* Trust him!" (115). But we learn that Rey is eminently untrustworthy, abandoning Hillela (129), playing the ANC against the PAC (138), and probably acting as an informer as well (318). For a while the phrase seems a genuine comment on Hillela's trustworthiness, as in the exiles' assessment that they can trust Hillela (135), and Udi's assessment that she can be trusted not to make mistakes by dancing her life away (152). But it takes on snide tones in the biographer's report that Hillela did well in distancing herself from her white relatives by having a black child and in naming her daughter after Winnie Mandela: "Trust her, as her enemies would remark" (195). Later the phrase becomes increasingly snide as it refers to her success at social climbing and her callousness, to her getting into a position where she can dispense grants (241), to her protecting herself from knowing the pain her letters cause to Brad (301), and to her choosing as husband a president who manages his country well (331).

Other signs of the biographer's disapproval are common. The biographer frequently points out Hillela's callousness in dumping people as she "moves on." The voice also suggests that she lies about her past: the biographer reports Hillela's usual story of how she met

Whaila, says "Well, it's not impossible," and then sets about de-molishing the account by noting other versions Hillela has told and by citing reasons that the usual version is most unlikely (170–71). The biographer also raises doubts about Hillela's maturity and ded-ication. When she disappears from Eastern Europe, the biographer offers explanations drawn from the politics of the liberation movement, but ends by suggesting that she may well have left merely on a whim: "Maybe she left as she had hitched a lift to Durban one afternoon after school. That is a judgment that has to be considered. A harsh one" (236).

Why all of this distance between Gordimer and Hillela? There is some small possibility that Gordimer intends the biographer to embody Pauline's lesson to Carole: "When you do what's right, here . . . You have to accept that you won't be popular—with some people" (21). But the disapproval is too unrelenting to bear no more than that as its point. And the point is dulled by the fact that Gordimer establishes no distance between herself and the biographer's point of view. Gordimer herself seems at least ambivalent about her creation and perhaps even disapproving.[21]

Much of what Hillela has to do to achieve her success may well be distasteful to Gordimer. One may well imagine that Gordimer bemoans the diminishment of Hillela's humanity in using people as means to an end and in her glib acceptance of the need to make victims, however necessary that is to the seizure of power. The distasteful means must be yet less attractive if Gordimer feels there is no guarantee of the end that Hillela achieves through them. Indeed, in a number of Gordimer's recent works we see a sense that the future often betrays one's best hopes for it.

With the partial exception of the overly facile and unconvincing triumph of the South African liberation movement in *A Sport of Nature*, Gordimer's vision of the future has become increasingly pessimistic in recent years. In *Burger's Daughter* Rosa capitulates to agnosticism about the future which will be designed by the children of Soweto. But her agnosticism is optimistic in a way that has dis-appeared in Gordimer's later works. When the future that the Smaleses have been waiting for arrives in *July's People*, its reality is so fright-ening that they flee to a haven in which they destroy both their present and their past, running in the end to rejoin an unknown but almost certainly distasteful future. The collection *Something Out There* (1984)[22] is full of tales of "diminishment"[23] and betrayal in which the future turns out to be worse than imagined. The township house-wife in "A City of the Dead, a City of the Living" (*SOT* 9–26) betrays the fugitive she and her husband have been sheltering. The holocaust survivors of "Sins of the Third Age" (*SOT* 65–77) remake their lives and plan their future, only to discover when it arrives that it has been emptied by the husband's infidelity. The wife in "Terminal" (*SOT* 97–101) arrives at a future she had tried to avoid when her husband revives her despite their pact to help each other commit suicide in case of terminal illness. The physicist and the writer in "Rags and Bones" (*SOT* 89–96) whose letters show they thought each other Nobel Prize material turn out to have been non-entities. General Giant in "At the Rendezvous of Victory" (*SOT* 27–38) creates a liberated future for his people, only to discover that it is a future in which he has no place.[24] Even in *A Sport of Nature* the liberated South African future of "Whaila's Country" seems little likely to become Hillela's utopia. The President who is giving such useful advice to the new rulers and whose country is so widely praised still has "a prison where individuals designated Enemies of the People are held," still sees "the occasional expulsion of a miscreant foreign journalist" and still has a son "feared and known by the designated Enemies of the People as the President's hit man" (331). And Gordimer indicates that white conservatives and industrialists will do very well, thank you, under the new South African regime (339, 340).

We cannot be surprised if Gordimer is less than enthusiastic about advocating distasteful means justified by ends to be found in an uncertain and probably distasteful future. It is a measure of the horror of the South African past and present that she has brought herself to such advocacy; but that does not mean that she has to like what she advocates. But where then is the influential vision of a role for whites to come from?

Notes

1. For comments on earlier drafts I am grateful to Susan Kirschner and to the editor of this issue. Remaining errors and weaknesses are my own responsibility.

2. The point is not a "narcissistic focus . . . on the importance of white involvement . . . [in a] paternalistic posturing [which] . . . downplay[s] the role of black South Africans in the achievement of their own independence," as Jennifer Krauss has it in her "Activism 101," rev. of *A Sport of Nature, The New Republic* 18 May 1987: 33. Rather the point is to recognize both that blacks will make the revolution in South Africa and that whites now have the power there. To hope for a white role which shortens the struggle need not be narcissistic or paternalistic, nor need it downplay the role of blacks. See, for example, the role envisioned for whites by Steve Biko in "White Racism and Black Consciousness" in Hendrik W. van der Merwe and David Welsh, eds. *Student Perspectives on South Africa* (Cape Town: David Philip, 1972), reprinted in Steve Biko, *I Write What I Like* (New York: Harper & Row, 1978) 65–66:

> Most white dissident groups are aware of the power wielded by the white power structure. . . . Why then do they persist in talking to the blacks? Since they are aware that the problem in this country is white racism, who do they not address themselves to the white world? . . . The liberal must fight on his own and for himself. . . . They must realise that they themselves are oppressed, and that they must fight for their own

freedom and not that of the nebulous "they" with whom they can hardly claim identification.

3. Nadine Gordimer, *A Sport of Nature* (New York: Alfred A. Knopf, 1987). Further references to this novel will be incorporated in the text.

4. Nadine Gordimer, *Burger's Daughter* (New York: Penguin Books, 1980). Further references to this novel will be abbreviated as *BD* and incorporated in the text.

5. For a further development of this argument, see Richard Peck, "One Foot before the Other into an Unknown Future: The Dialectic in Nadine Gordimer's *Burger's Daughter*," *WLWE*. Forthcoming.

6. This saves her work from the weakness suggested by Diane Johnson: "since there is no defense on [sic] apartheid, it can seem that something obvious is being advanced with great righteousness." "Living Legends," rev. of *A Sport of Nature, New York Review of Books* 16 July 1987: 8. Gordimer is less interested in delineating the nature of the problem of *apartheid* than she is in searching for solutions to it, condemning false solutions as she goes.

7. More worthy of Gordimer's moral vehemence are those who know better but line up on the wrong side. Thus, the only conservative in her recent fiction who receives Gordimer's full vitriol is the slick apologist for *apartheid*, Brandt Vermeulen, in *Burger's Daughter*. On the "merciless dissection" which Gordimer gives to Rosa's encounters with Vermeulen, see Robert Boyers, "Public and Private: On *Burger's Daughter*," *Salmagundi* 62 (1984): 77.

8. Peck, "One Foot before the Other."

9. Krauss, "Activism 101": 34.

10. Other examples include those on pages 52–3, 65–70, 89–91, 101, 107, 112, and 114.

11. Gordimer's emphasis on Hillela's physical love throughout the novel seems meant to suggest the bankruptcy of ideologies in the South African setting by giving value to the most elemental emotions stripped of the baggage of ideology. Certainly there is much emphasis throughout the novel on the "truthfulness" which Hillela finds in the act of love, a truthfulness greater than that to be found in merely verbal expressions of love. See, for example, 141. On variations of the miscegenation theme in Gordimer's earlier fiction, see Susan M. Greenstein, "Miranda's Story: Nadine Gordimer and the Literature of Empire," *Novel* 18 (1985): 227–42.

12. For a discussion of Gordimer's place in the South African liberal movement and the examination of the crisis of South African liberalism in her fiction, see Irene Wettenhall, "Liberalism and Radicalism in South Africa Since 1948: Nadine Gordimer's Fiction," *New Literature Review* 8 (1980): 36–44.

13. Nadine Gordimer, *July's People* (New York: Penguin, 1981).

14. Elizabeth Hardwick, "Somebody Out There" rev. of *Something Out There* by Nadine Gordimer, *The New York Review of Books* 16 August 1984: 6.

15. Compare this with page 66, where we are told that Pauline and Joe lack such a sign and cannot feel the tug of history.

16. Compare this with Rosa Burger's defence of the utopia, *BD* 296.

17. This is an old theme in Gordimer's fiction, appearing as early as her *The Lying Days* of 1953. See Rose Moss, "Hand in Glove, Nadine Gordimer: South African Writer," *Moana: Pacific Quarterly* 6.3–4: (1981): 111, on that novel's vision of the future represented in an unborn child whose mother wants not to reproduce herself. Contrast this with Krauss' misreading that "Hillela is happy to have merely 'reproduced herself,' " in her "Activism 101": 36.

18. Krauss is unfair in suggesting that Hillela plays no role during this time other

than becoming "involved in preserving and decorating the imperial palace." "Activism 101": 35.

19. She drops Olga (96), Sasha (99), Pauline (131, 199), her political refugee friends (161), her Embassy family (174), her father (202), a committee she was working with when she ran off with the General (276), and her fiancé Brad (300).

20. Note, however, the importance of Joel's Jewishness in *The Lying Days*. Abdul R. JanMohamed argues that he serves as "a critical mirror" for the gentile protagonist, and that "their own internalization of ethnic barriers" between gentile and Jew prevents the consummation of their relationship. *Manichean Aesthetics; The Politics of Literature in Colonial Africa* (Amherst, Mass.: U of Massachusetts P, 1983) 91.

21. Mark Uhlig reports that Gordimer said "I am completely different from Hillela," and added "that the path chosen by her heroine 'would be quite shocking to moralistic people—including myself.' " Reported in "Shocked by Her Own Heroine" [interview with Nadine Gordimer], *New York Times Book Review* 3 May 1987: 20. For an excellent discussion of irony in Gordimer's treatment of Hillela, see Rowland Smith, "Leisure, Law, and Loathing: Matrons, Mistresses, Mothers in the Fiction of Nadine Gordimer and Jillian Becker," *WLWE* 28.1 (1988): 41–51.

22. Nadine Gordimer, *Something Out There* (New York: Viking, 1984). Further references to this collection of stories will be abbreviated as *SOT* and incorporated in the text.

23. Merle Rubin, "Gordimer's Stories: A Stark, Harsh View of South African Life" rev. of *Something Out There* by Nadine Gordimer, *The Christian Science Monitor* 9 August 1984: 24.

24. That the title comes from Aimé Cesaire's statement only makes the point more poignant: "No race possesses the monopoly of beauty, / of intelligence, of force, and there is / a place for all at the rendezvous of victory." *Return to My Native Land* (Harmondsworth: Penguin, 1969) 85.

Nadine Gordimer's "Family of Women"

Sheila Roberts[*]

> What he had seen for the first time was woman's nakedness, all stages of change and deterioration, of abuse and attrition by pain, loving and unloving use . . . What he was feeling was deep distasteful awe at the knowledge of their beauty and its decay.
> —*A Soldier's Embrace*

Nadine Gordimer is distinctive among women writers in that her work has as its central concern an examination of the events and processes that have shaped and still shape a political reality. Had she not been a South African writer and one who possesses a highly informed political sense, she might well have written novels that allowed her to be classed among contemporary feminist writers. There

[*] From *Theoria* 9 (May 1983):45–57. Reprinted by permission.

is certainly a penetrating awareness of the condition of women—black and white—in her work, an awareness that sometimes informs single short stories to the exclusion of the politics of government, for example, "Siblings" and "Time Did" in *A Soldier's Embrace*.[1] But, to generalize, I would say that the female characters in her novels are all more troubled about their moral position as citizens in a racist country than they are about their position as women relating to men. Not that these two positions do not interlock at times: they do. Nevertheless, in those novels with female protagonists the strongest focus is not on their status as women but on the moral validity of action as women in various circumstances in an overall political ambience.

Of Nadine Gordimer's eight published novels, the four that I wish to discuss here all have female protagonists: *The Lying Days* (1953), *Occasion for Loving* (1960), *The Late Bourgeois World* (1966), and *Burger's Daughter* (1979).[2] What immediately strikes the reader as the strongest similarity between these protagonists is that their ideological commitments or political convictions are frequently in conflict with their personal needs and their place in the family.

Helen Shaw in *The Lying Days* achieves political awareness and sophistication slowly and painfully. In the process she is estranged from her conservative parents and even, conversely, from her politically concerned lover. The book constitutes in effect Helen Shaw's quest for self-education as a political human being and wholeness as a woman, a quest that like Rosa Burger's in *Burger's Daughter* will involve a journey overseas. Both Helen Shaw and Rosa Burger are in their twenties when their stories end. Helen Shaw leaving South Africa and Rosa Burger returning to it.

In a study of Nadine Gordimer's work published in 1974, Robert Haugh claimed that *The Lying Days*, Gordimer's first novel, was her best partly because, although Helen Shaw does "wither into the truth," she does not assume "the dry harshness, the weary passivity and the scepticism which approaches misanthropy" evident in the characters of later novels.[3] When Haugh wrote this, *Burger's Daughter* had not yet been published but I doubt whether he would have wanted to alter his contention in light of this recent work. Although Rosa Burger is close in age to Helen Shaw, she does possess a certain harshness, passivity, and scepticism evident in the personalities of Gordimer's older protagonists, Jessie Stilwell and Elizabeth van den Sandt, and arguably for good reason.

When we are first introduced to Jessie Stilwell in *Occasion for Loving* and Elizabeth van den Sandt in *The Late Bourgeois World*, these women are in their thirties. They are experienced, self-actualizing, and politically educated. But their ability to act warmly or even tolerantly towards those who are closest to them has been inhibited or frozen by their experiences as young girls and by their disenchantment with society, politics, and ordinary human relations. It is in these books that "the dry harshness, the weary passivity, and the scepticism" are most strongly in evidence. For instance, even though Helen Shaw quarrels bitterly with her mother over social and racial issues, she herself suffers cruelly from the disaffection, especially in the knowledge that both parents love her. Unlike Jessie Stilwell and Elizabeth van den Sandt, she eventually succeeds in accepting her parents for what they are. She learns (as Rosa Burger does after her) that she can only free herself of her parents by acknowledging their presence in her. As Joel Aaron so astutely advises her:

> Making them over would be getting rid of them as they are. Well, you can't do it. You can't do it by going to live somewhere else, either. You can't even do it by never seeing them again for the rest of your life. There is that in you that is them, and it's that unkillable fibre of you that will hurt you and pull you off balance wherever you run to—unless you accept it. Accept them in you, accept them as they are, even if you choose to live differently, and you'll be all right. Funnily enough, that's the only way to be free of them. . . .[4]

More importantly, Helen Shaw learns in her teens to oppose her mother when her own legitimate emotional and intellectual needs are at stake, and out of her opposition grows her sense of identity and her capacity for tolerance. In contrast, Jessie Stilwell in *Occasion for Living* allows her mother to dominate her until the day when, herself a young widow with a baby, she realizes bitterly that

> she had been handed from mother to husband to being a mother herself without ever having had the freedom that does not belong to any other time of life but extreme youth . . . Her husband was dead, but she was alive to the knowledge that, in the name of love, her mother had sucked from her the delicious nectar she had never known she had—the half-shaped years, the inconsequence without fingerprint, of the time from fifteen to twenty.[5]

The consequence of this realization is that Jessie becomes suspicious of and repelled by the demonstrativeness of love: "Love appalled her with its hammering demands, love clamoured and dunned, love would throw down and tear to pieces its object."[6] About her fifteen-year-old son Morgan she decides, without any evidence except her own discomfort in his presence, that no love exists between them. She treats her aged mother with quiet consideration but no affection, and her husband hears with bewilderment her step-father complain that Jessie had never been much like a daughter to him.

What redeems Jessie Stilwell is her uneasiness with her own inability to be spontaneously loving, and her sharp self-analysis. She also tries to act in a morally valid way, particularly in response to the love affair between the Englishwoman, Ann Davis, and the black man, Gideon Shibalo. The reader finishes *Occasion for Loving* with the intimation that Jessie will strive for wisdom, gentleness, and the capacity to stretch to meet new demands. Even if she and her husband Tom will never break out of the moral dilemma of political liberalism in which they are entrenched, they will at least contemplate action that will be effective as well as morally valid. Towards the end of the book, Jessie says to Gideon Shibalo, "Well, if you want to live like a human being you've got to keep on proving it. It's not a state automatically conferred upon you because you walk upright on two legs, any more than because you've got a white skin."[7]

Elizabeth van den Sandt in *The Late Bourgeois World* shows no such potential for mental expansion and emotional growth at the end of the book. She arouses the reader's dislike from the first paragraphs of the narration by her egocentric response to news of her former husband's suicide. When Graham Mill, her lover, asks why Max van den Sandt would have done such a thing, she replies, feeling "immense irritation break out like cold sweat . . . 'Because of me!' "[8] When the reader learns that Elizabeth and Max have been divorced for over six years, this motive for suicide becomes unconvincing, increasingly so as Elizabeth mentally reconstructs for the reader the political events of the twelve years since she first met Max.

The novel, which covers one day in the life of the protagonist, is narrated in the first person so the reader has only Elizabeth's memories, thoughts, and opinions on which to base his understanding. But Elizabeth is hardly reliable: her cool, critical, and self-satisfied voice itself creates "an immense irritation," and the reader is left wondering whether Gordimer intends to convey the all-pervasive influence of the late bourgeois world by providing us with a narrator as unequal to the demands life makes on her as the bourgeois world is to increasing social disintegration and change.

Elizabeth is complacently irrational and self-deluding. She congratulates herself on the fact that her son Bobo was *not* conceived in one of the middle-class white suburbs of Johannesburg but instead in the back of a car out in the veld, and she is proud that neither she nor Graham "makes money out of cheap labour or performs a service confined to people of a particular colour."[9] Graham, a lawyer, sometimes defends people on political charges, and she spends working hours in a laboratory analysing stools, urine, and blood. She fails to realize that holding such professional jobs on "white" salaries does not exonerate either Graham or herself from their guilty participation in a whites-only hegemony.

Of her parents, Elizabeth has some passing thoughts to the effect that they "were extremely gratified to have [her] 'marry into' the

Van den Sandts" because not many families in her small town could boast of a daughter married to the son of a wealthy Member of Parliament. But she also assumes that her parents would be "equally gratified, now, to know that he is dead."[10] The reader cannot take such a reaction on trust even if he accepts that Max's political activities had been an embarrassment to Elizabeth's parents, as they were to his own. Yet embarrassed or not, Max's parents never did disown him: Elizabeth states that when Max was arrested on a charge of sabotage, he "died" for his parents but the facts are that his father paid for his defence and his mother attended his trial several times. The reader simply cannot believe Elizabeth; she is too harsh, too dry, too sceptical.

The reader also loses faith in the durability of Elizabeth's relationship with Graham. Later in the day when she wishes she could have lunch with him, she decides not to do anything about it "because we make a point of not living in each other's pocket, and if I were to start it, I'd have to expect him to make the same sort of use of me at some time when it might not be convenient."[11] That evening Graham asks suddenly, "How would you say things are with us?" Elizabeth chooses to misinterpret his question and successfully hedges it. At this point the reader must assume that things are not well with them and can never be well with Elizabeth, certainly not in the sense of her ability to love. Michael Wade's interpretation of Elizabeth's behaviour is that, having learnt to reject liberalism because the preconditions for its existence are not available in South Africa, she must perforce reject the traditions of romantic love as well and merely "bide her time": ". . . Unfortunately, mature liberalism of all ideologies can least afford—or is least able—to live in a vacuum; it needs the nourishment of an established romantic tradition, in art and in life. So Graham's (and to an extent Elizabeth's) life is reduced in stature by the necessity of having to learn to 'sit still' in South Africa."[12]

In composing *Burger's Daughter*, Gordimer returned to the form of the *bildungsroman* which she was so successful with in *The Lying Days*. Although the structure of *Burger's Daughter* is non-linear and the story is built up unchronologically by means of the interwoven narrative voices of the implied author and of Rosa Burger, Gordimer has here reverted full circle to the matter of her first novel—the life and growth towards maturity of a young girl. But *Burger's Daughter* has this fundamental difference from *The Lying Days:* Rosa Burger achieves an astute political awareness very early in life through the influence of her activist parents. The crisis of her own personal needs in conflict with the political commitment that has been thrust upon her, surfaces partly when her parents force her to pretend to be engaged to a detainee so that she can have visiting rights to him, and then comes to a head in her twenty-fifth year. But the conflict is resolved within the space of ten months. Yet for all her closeness in age to Helen Shaw, Rosa Burger seems closer in personality to Jessie Stilwell and Elizabeth van den Sandt. Like them, Rosa communicates to the reader an emotional distance or detachment from the crucial events of her life, and possesses a drily critical attitude, a cool evaluating vision, towards her family, her lovers, and even towards those on the periphery of her life.

The richly imagined and finely constructed portrayal of the mental and emotional life of a young woman in *The Lying Days* demonstrates that Nadine Gordimer could have presented her entire "family" of women in as warm and complexly human a way as the most exacting (perhaps romantically liberal) reader would have desired. The reasons why she did not choose to do so in later books must be sought in the fluctuating situations of freedom and subordinacy from which her protagonists try to extricate themselves.

Before continuing this discussion, I think it would be useful to digress briefly and refer to the remarkable parallels between *The Lying Days,* published in 1953 and Marilyn French's best-selling novel *The Women's Room,* published more than twenty years later. Helen Shaw, like Mira in *The Women's Room,* is the only child of careful, conservative, middle-class parents. Both daughters have mothers who express strong distaste at any manifestation of female sexuality; both achieve a measure of self-sufficiency through education and exposure to political liberalism; and both for a time submerge their own intellectual needs in the interests of those of "the man." Both authors take pains to illuminate not only the mental and emotional lives of young women but also "the carefully-contrived pattern of reversal of appearance and reality that constitutes the design"[13] of the novels.

However, Helen Shaw—unlike Mira—has loving and reasonably happily married parents who will ultimately allow her to have her way. Her mother's expressed distaste for sexuality—she refers to women who live with men to whom they are not married as "filthy beasts"—has no real crippling power over Helen's own passionate nature. Helen, moreover, has a stubborn courage that Mira only acquires in middle-age.

Perhaps these differences between Helen and Mira's personalities constitute important clues not only to why Helen Shaw might be viewed by critics as Gordimer's most successful female protagonist but also to why there is, if at all, merely a thin strand of feminism in Gordimer's work. Having started her novelistic career with the successful depiction of a free woman and one who is conceivably autobiographic to some extent, it is understandable that Gordimer would have continued in this fashion. In relation to the Miras of contemporary feminist fiction, Gordimer's protagonists all enjoy a large measure of personal freedom. Even those like Jessie and Elizabeth who are emotionally inhibited are capable of deeply satisfying sexual lives. They all shun political conservatism: in fact, their active political lives are both cause and effect of their prevailing over the oppressive dependency of the women of their generation. They exhibit no lack of self-esteem in the presence of men; they make their own decisions; and they all enjoy professions out of the home.

While admitting these similarities between Helen, Jessie, Elizabeth, and Rosa, I still contend that Helen's is the happiest situation. However narrow and misguided her parents may be, they certainly love Helen and express deep concern about her well-being. Their early indulgence gives Helen the confidence to assert herself. In contrast, as I have pointed out, Jessie Stilwell's youth is paralysed by her mother's unhealthy possessiveness. The woman pretends to Jessie for years that she, her daughter, has a "heart condition" which prevents her from leading the normal, active life of a school girl. Whereas Helen Shaw chooses capriciously *not* to go to university, then chooses to go; decides to live with her boyfriend, then leaves him and heads for Europe, both Jessie and Elizabeth marry young and become pregnant. And Rosa Burger, while obviously loved by her parents, has her own individual needs, even her desire for romantic and sexual love, subjugated to the greater demands of the communist party to which her parents owe undeviating allegiance. Thus, of the four women—all only daughters of their parents—only Helen Shaw has multiple options available to her in her youth, including the tacit support of well-meaning if uncomprehending parents. Because Helen has physical freedom, she can live at will in an environment of students and intellectuals and consequently arrive at some understanding of the reality behind the appearance of white middle-class life in a racist South Africa. Because she has freedom of movement at an age when Jessie Stilwell and Elizabeth van den Sandt are in early marriages and Rosa Burger is denied a passport, she is able to act on her assessment of the authenticity of her own life, of the significance of her intimacy with men like Joel Aaron and Paul Clark, and of the necessity to leave South Africa to gain a wider perspective of the demands of the self against those of society. Although Rosa Burger ultimately achieves her own wide perspective, her initial impulse in leaving South Africa is purely that of escape.

Helen's age is perhaps the crux of the matter. She truly "escapes" very young and the reader may assume that she has had no time in which to grow drily harsh, wearily passive, or sceptical. And it is only with the publication of *Burger's Daughter* that Gordimer forces the reader to question what it was that Helen escaped to and what it might be that she would return to.

What emerges from Gordimer's novels after *The Lying Days* is that life in a monolithic Nationalist South Africa succeeds in disillusioning and hardening those frustrated in their work for social and political change, especially work based on an inadequate European tradition of liberalism. Whether work based on some other foundation would be more effective is doubtful from the evidence of *Burger's Daughter:* that does not reduce the moral validity of such work— even ineffectual work is justifiable as a form of "witnessing." But when the novel opens, Lionel Burger is in prison. He dies in the course of the narrative, and the book ends with Rosa Burger herself in jail, a matter of months after she has been told by a black man that his people don't need the help of a Lionel Burger and that her father's personal sacrifice was insignificant in the face of *his* people's constant persecution.

Even Helen Shaw does not evade some of the effects of the two years (1948 to 1950) during which she lives under the Nationalist Government. Her relationship with Paul Clark, while remaining actively sexual, becomes one of vigilance, tensions, and evasions. She watches her own and Paul's reactions constantly and is totally absorbed in the importance, as she sees it, of his social work among Africans. She eventually becomes conscious of a sense of loss:

> as if there is discovered to be another person in you who mysteriously wrests you from yourself and takes over, thrusting you back to yourself in confusion when the fancy takes it—the thought of it made me sick with dismay. I had the instinct to clutch, searching at my life, like a woman suddenly conscious of some infinitesimal lack of weight about her person that warns her that something has gone. . . .[14]

Rosa Burger is, of course, the most tragically affected of all Gordimer's female protagonists, although the reader only accepts intellectually that Rosa's life is a tragedy. Rosa herself does not convey an extent of personal pain, fear, or terror sufficient to wrench at the reader's emotions.[15] I would argue, however, that had she done so, had her suffering been desperate, she could not convincingly have been the trained daughter of Lionel Burger, the loyal communist who devoted his life to the cause. During his trial, Lionel Burger had said: "If I have ever been certain of anything in my life, it is that I acted according to my conscience on all counts. I would be guilty only if I were innocent of working to destroy racism in my country."[16] Rosa, who all her life has witnessed the comings and going of party members—black and white—in her home, and who even as a young child learnt to live with the threat and the actuality of her parents spending time in jail, does temporarily lose conviction in the usefulness of continuing to fight racism in South Africa. Her growing scepticism and her drily critical vision of all facets of life in South

Africa and, later, in Europe make her seem to the reader much older than her twenty-five years. Secretly she visits an influential Afrikaner and succeeds in obtaining a passport valid for one year's travel. In joy and trepidation at her chance to "know somewhere else,"[17] she leaves the country. In the south of France she joins her father's first wife, Katya, a former ballet dancer who had found herself unequal to the task of being married to a devoted communist. There Rosa enjoys life in all its easy sensuality, amorality, and physical freedom. She has an affair with a married Frenchman and plans to join him permanently in Paris after her expected visit to London. She will ignore the conditions of the passport granted her by the South African government.

Yet, paradoxically, it is in the sensuous paradise of the French south coast that Rosa becomes distressingly aware of the inevitability of old age, senility, and death. Her experience here is similar to, but more intense than, the moments that both Jessie Stilwell and Elizabeth van den Sandt endure confronted by the fact of ageing. Rosa sees the signs of physical disintegration in Katya and her friends, listens to their talk of diets, menopause, and mastectomies, and is accosted one day in the street by a very old, disoriented woman standing in her night dress. The woman asks her urgently, "What time is it?", a question of similar import to the one Elizabeth van den Sandt's grandmother asks, "What happened?". Elizabeth's silent response is:

> There is nothing to say.
> She asks now only the questions that are never answered. I can't tell her, you are going to die, that's all. She's had all the things that have been devised to soften life but there doesn't seem to have been anything done to make death more bearable.[18]

And so, in the midst of pleasure, leisure, and freedom, Rosa achieves new certainties, not those handed to her by her father, but her own. She must acknowledge the unavoidability of decay and death and recognize that life as the Frenchman's mistress in France would be "un paradis inventé," like a Bonnard landscape of the unicorn tapestry she sees at Cluny. In such a life, self-indulgent and useless, the thought of old age and death would become obsessive and terrible.

While she is in London, Rosa receives a midnight call from Baasie, a black man who as a child lived in the Burger household. What she learns in this bitter conversation with Baasie is that, just as her father's beliefs could not be bequeathed to her unquestioningly, her father's achievement could not be laid at her door without her own continued, independent action. Moreover, she sees that only by accepting that which in herself derives from her father, can she act as a fully free person. These truths are the final goads that send Rosa back to South Africa, determined to prove each day over again that she wants to live like a human being.

In her decision to act "according to [her] conscience on all counts," Rosa goes several steps further towards a life of personal austerity, reduced freedom, and danger than Jessie Stilwell ever contemplates or than Elizabeth van den Sandt considers when she decides at the end of *The Late Bourgeois World* (while thinking the words "afraid, alive, afraid, alive, afraid, alive . . ."[19]) to use her grandmother's banking account for depositing sums sent from overseas to anti-government groups.

Thus Rosa decides consciously to deny herself personal, romantic affiliations, freedoms, and pleasures in the commitment to fight racial oppression. Her conscious actions are more rational, more humanly creditable than the dry, pessimistic responses of Jessie and Elizabeth, poorly understood even by themselves and obviously arising out of the infectious scepticism of life in South Africa. Rosa hoped for a full life of the body, the senses, and the intelligence, but sees that such a life, exclusive of commitment to others, is not justifiable, particularly not for a South African who does not want to be "just like the others."

I have mentioned Ann Davis, the young Englishwoman who lightly enters a sexual relationship with a black South African, Gideon Shibalo, in *Occasion for Loving*. Ann is a secondary and not very interesting character. The reader has difficulty believing that Gideon could love her to the extent that he is prepared to give up his political work, his family and friends, and leave South Africa with her. (The reader has comparable difficulty believing that Rosa Burger does indeed love the Frenchman, Bernard Chabalier, and is therefore not greatly disturbed when Rosa rejects him and returns to South Africa.) It seems to me that Gordimer's intention in drawing Ann Davis's frivolous, entertainment-loving character, with its lack of any real sense of the vulnerability of others, was to demonstrate how dangerous such a person can be in a country like South Africa. When Lionel and Rosa Burger break the country's laws it is with full awareness of the possible consequences or the expected gains: their behaviour is knowledgeably planned. Ann, however, has neither the political interest nor the self-discipline to analyse the effects of her actions on people like the Stilwells, on her husband Boaz, and particularly on men like Gideon. Rather grandly, she simply ignores apartheid when it suits her, her bright spontaneity being part of her attractiveness for Gideon. But when the full significance of her helpless position as consort to a black man in South Africa finally strikes her, she summarily abandons Gideon—as she can so easily, being a white Englishwoman—and leaves the country with her husband for an extended tour of the islands in the Indian Ocean.

Ann's lack of substance, of seriousness, is emphasized in the language used by the other characters in reference to her. She is called "the pretty little dear" and Boaz's "little wife." Her husband describes her affair with Gideon like that of "a child picking daisies," and she is always called a "girl," never a woman. This is not to say that Ann, in her way, does not love Gideon but simply that in a country like South Africa love without responsibility is not enough. The reader remembers Ann Davis when he reads Part Two of *Burger's Daughter:* Ann belongs in the richly personal but trivial world of the Côte d'Azur with Katya Bagnelli, Didier, Manolis, Pierre, Gaby, and all the others who survive leisurely without ambitions, professions, or political commitments.

For me Gordimer's portraits of women are generally much more vital and memorable than those of men with the possible exception of that of Gideon Shibalo. Max van den Sandt, Graham Mill, Tom Stilwell, Bernard Chabalier, and even Mehring in *The Conservationist,* retain shadowy edges: their physicality is not created with the solidity and immediacy granted to Helen Shaw, Jessie Stilwell, Rosa Burger, Clare Terblanche, the black woman, Marisa, and Katya Bagnelli. Even the number of old women in Gordimer's novels, although mostly minor characters, are drawn very sharply, perhaps too sharply, their corporality conveyed with a detectable element of disgust. Jessie Stilwell's mother, for instance

> scarcely existed in the moment. Her carefully powdered face was a mummification of such moments as the girl's [i.e. Ann's] eager experiences; layer on layer, bitumen on bandage, she held the dead shape of passion and vitality in the stretch of thick white flesh falling from cheekbone to jaw, the sallow eyes and straggling but still black eyebrows holding up the lifeless skin round them, and the incision of the mouth. The lips showed only when she spoke, shining pale under a lick of saliva.[20]

When Elizabeth van den Sandt visits her grandmother in a nursing home, she stares at the other patients one of whom "has a reckless drinker's face that diabetics sometimes have, and looks as if she had once been good-looking—like a finished whore," another is a "monster with the enormous belly . . . sitting on a chair with her legs splayed out, like a dead frog swollen on a pond."[21] Elizabeth focuses on the "painted mouth" of her grandmother as she did on that of Max's mother, and as Rosa Burger does in her scrutiny of the lives of Katya Bagnelli and her friends: it is almost as if there is something shameful in an old woman putting on make-up.

I have already referred to Elizabeth van den Sandt's unlikeable egocentricity and coldness. She and her husband Max further repel the reader by their treatment of Felicity Hare, the naïvely obliging young Englishwoman. They both call her "Sunbun" and concentrate unflatteringly on her physical attributes. Elizabeth sees her legs as "enormous, marbled . . . doubled up in a great fleshy pedestal," and remarks at one point that "she needs a man, our Sunbun" and derides "her bloody great tits."[22]

Rosa Burger's cool evaluating vision of others can also seem harsh. She assesses Clare Terblanche, her contemporary, in the following way:

> She's something sad rather than ugly, a woman without sexual pride—as a female she has no vision of herself to divert others from her physical defects. The way she stood—it irritated me. Clare Terblanche has always stood like that, as if someone plonked down a tripod, without the flow of her movement behind her or projected ahead of her! There's an ordinary explanation: knock-kneed . . . The dandruff, and the eczema it caused, they were of nervous origin. Why did we pretend not to notice this affliction? It was "unimportant." She knew I was seeing her clumsy stance, the tormenting patches of inflamed and shedding skin, stripped of familiar context. Poor thing; and she knew I thought: poor thing.[23]

At this point Rosa wants to escape the apparent repetitive uselessness of subversive activity and is angered because Clare, unquestioningly following in her parents' footsteps, wants Rosa to assist in copying some political documents. But the reader remembers how Rosa's mother herself was "a woman without sexual pride" or vanity. The difference—one out of Clare's control, however—is that Rosa Burger's mother was beautiful.

It is probably unfair to lay at Gordimer's door the sexist attitudes of her characters, yet it is noticeable that the less attractive aspects of men's bodies are not frequently emphasized. It is also surprising that Gordimer allows Rosa Burger no indignant reaction when Bernard Chabalier calls Baasie "a cunt" for making an upsetting telephone call to Rosa.

In their resemblance to one another, Gordimer's female characters form for the reader a recognizable kinship; they become members of a "family" or "families." In this they are comparable to Faulkner's or Patrick White's characters. And Gordimer, like Faulkner and White, has recorded the ethos of a nation and established a twentieth-century historiography for a country. In the relatedness of theme, character, and preoccupation with moral issues, her books like theirs form a unified canon. It is to Gordimer's great credit that she, more than Faulkner and White, depicts both men and women, black and white, equally significantly involved in the processes and events of politics and equally caught in the dilemma of the moral validity of action. Her women characters can think as well as her men do, work as well as they do, manifest an equal physical courage, and are by no means "second-class" citizens. In her fiction Gordimer has, it would seem, by-passed the decades of the feminist movement's greatest literary activity, and has since the fifties established female protagonists whose lives must be taken seriously.

Notes

1. New York: Viking, 1980.

2. All page references are to the following editions: *The Lying Days*, New York: Simon and Schuster, 1953; *Occasion for Loving*, New York: Viking, 1960; *The Late Bourgeois World*, New York: Viking, 1966; *Burger's Daughter*, Harmondsworth: Penguin, 1980.

3. *Nadine Gordimer*, New York: Twayne, 1974, p. 94.

4. *The Lying Days*, op. cit. p. 109.

5. *Occasion for Loving*, op. cit. p. 42.

6. Ibid. p. 62.

7. Ibid. p. 257.

8. *The Late Bourgeois World*, op. cit. p. 6.

9. Ibid. p. 44.

10. Ibid. p. 75.

11. Ibid. p. 40.

12. *Nadine Gordimer*, Modern African Writers. London: Evans Brothers, 1978, p. 131.

13. Michael Wade, *Nadine Gordimer*, ibid. p. 6.

14. *The Lying Days*, ibid. p. 258.

15. There is, however, a mood of humour, defiance, and gaiety infusing the final chapters dealing with Rosa and Marisa's incarceration. The reader is reminded of the lines in Yeats's poem 'Lapis Lazuli':

> All perform their tragic play.
> There struts Hamlet, there is Lear.
> That's Ophelia, that Cordelia;
> Yet they, should the last scene be there.
> The great stage curtain about to drop.
> If worthy their prominent part in the play.
> Do not break up their lines to weep.
> They know that Hamlet and Lear are gay;
> Gaiety transfiguring all that dread.

16. *Burger's Daughter*, op. cit. p. 27.

17. Ibid. p. 185.

18. *The Late Bourgeois World*, op. cit. p. 77.

19. Ibid. p. 120.

20. *Occasion for Loving*, op. cit. pp. 106–7.

21. *The Late Bourgeois World*, op. cit. p. 71.

22. Ibid. pp. 61–4.

23. *Burger's Daughter*, op. cit. pp. 123–4.

Nadine Gordimer:
The Politicisation of Women   Dorothy Driver[*]

Throughout both her fiction and her other writings and statements, Nadine Gordimer has been committed to getting away from what T. T. Moyana calls "one-eyed literature," a literature that views the world with a (in her case, white) racial perspective.[1] In basic agreement with Marxist critics, who recognise, in the words of Terry Eagleton, that literary works "have a relation to that dominant way of seeing the world which is the 'social mentality' or ideology of an age,"[2] Gordimer has at various times noted the extraordinary difficulty that a writer may have in subverting or transcending that dominant ideology. Speaking for whites, she has said, "we actually *see* blacks differently, which includes *not seeing*,"[3] and proceeds in her fiction to document these blinkered perceptions, to show the hesitant and often inarticulate shifts into awareness of white South Africans towards black, and, on one occasion at least, to present quite explicitly the perspective of a white South African who has developed "eyes the colour of the lining of black mussel shells" (BD, p. 308).[4] Her major literary effort seems to be geared towards freeing herself from her white consciousness ("my consciousness has the same tint as my face"[5]) and freeing white consciousness from the colonial strictures which trap whites into roles of capitalist exploiters, landlords and employers, whether in towns or on farms, whether male or female, always in some way perpetrators and perpetuators of apartheid, that final and most inhuman entrenchment of colonialism, "the ugliest creation of man" (Gordimer, 1983, p. 21).

Gordimer has repeatedly been referred to as a writer "remarkable for her ability to reflect changing moods and issues in the South African society she describes,"[6] as a writer who "responds with immediacy to important social and historical developments" and who constructs "fictional 'types' . . . representative of social and historical movements."[7] She has herself noted the strong relation between her fiction and society. In the Introduction to her *Selected Stories*, for example, she refers to the historical sense that the chronological order of the stories lays bare: "The change in social attitudes unconsciously reflected in the stories represents both that of the people in my society—that is to say, history—and my apprehension of it; in the writing, I am acting upon my society, and in the manner of my apprehension, all the time history is acting upon me."[8] She has spoken of the immediate effects on work in progress of external events—of the Soweto children's uprising in 1976 on *Burger's Daughter*, for

[*] From *English in Africa* 10 (October 1983):29–54. Reprinted by permission.

instance[9]—and has even composed one of her public lectures as a *mimesis* of that continual impingement.[10]

Critics generally identify her various novels and short story collections as specific stages in the social psychology of a white South African who shifts from a position of uneasy liberalism to a recognition of the marginality of liberalism and of its inherent hypocrisies, and finally into a "revolutionary" attitude, which accepts as both inevitable and welcome the take-over of power in the country by a "liberating African consciousness that will eventually transcend white cultural and political domination."[11] (Her last four novels, published between 1970 and 1982, would all qualify for such a "revolutionary" position.) This sort of development is as clear in her non-fictional statements as in her fictional ones, and it is therefore probably no surprise to those who have read her recent novels to discover that in her recent James Lecture, presented at the New York Institute for the Humanities on 14 October 1982, she acknowledges the justness of Bishop Tutu's statement that blacks must have "a primacy in determining the course and goal of the struggle. Whites must learn to follow."[12] *How* whites follow is crucial: "Since skills, technical and intellectual, can be bought in markets other than those of the vanquished colonial power, although they are important as a commodity ready to hand, they do not constitute a claim on the future. That claim rests on something else: how to offer *one's self*" (1983, pp. 21–22).

Gordimer urges the fictional selves of her characters, male, female, black as well as white, into a state of preparedness for the "new era" with a dedication so fierce that it almost dispels the tones of disillusionment and near-cynicism that characterise her voice. Her novels usually end with the characters facing forward, looking ahead, existing now in something akin to a state of grace,[13] whether a moment of confession—as in *Occasion for Loving*, where Jessie Stilwell hangs her head in shame at Ann's betrayal of Gideon, herself (guilty by gender) standing "drawn up" before her husband "as before a tribunal" (p. 288)—or a moment of commitment—as in *Burger's Daughter*, where Rosa stands in the prison cell, blessed by the same ray of light that fell on her father. Never clearer than this are Gordimer's affinities with Graham Greene, whom she finds "unique" for that "questing lucidity that no other writer in the English language can come near."[14]

Gordimer has always felt a strong sense of political duty as a writer, and her fiction has a marked didactic thrust, sometimes emerging, as it does early in her career, in the form of less irony and more authorial explication, or, as it does later, in the form of more irony and obliquity. Even in her first novel we see an effort to document the kind of South African life in literature that has not been documented before as a political act, an anti-colonial and anti-racist act:

"I had never [says her heroine] read a book in which I myself was recognisable, in which there was a 'girl' like Anna who did the housework and the cooking and called the mother and father Missus and Baas" (LD, p. 20). By 1966 Gordimer had published a book that she called "subversive"[15] and which was indeed banned, and had consciously striven to create a fictional world as "part of the African continent"[16] rather than as a colony of Europe, with the attendant cultural and political implications. Ten years later she concluded *The Conservationist* with an allusion to the ANC slogan, "Afrika! Mayibuye!"—"Africa! May it come back!": "They had put him away to rest, at last; he had come back. He took possession of this earth, theirs; one of them."

Until recently, however, Gordimer has felt the need to insist that she is not primarily or essentially a political writer; that she has no "message," just writes about what she sees. In 1965 she said, "I don't suppose, if I had lived elsewhere, my writing would have reflected politics much. If at all."[17] This sort of comment appears again and again. But last year she admitted that she would cross out the final phrase, "if at all": "Obviously if I had lived elsewhere, even in apparently 'happy' countries, like Sweden and Canada, shall we say, there are always particular trends in society, particular problems, that would again affect people's lives, that would have come into my work, so that there would have been perhaps directly or indirectly some kind of political concern."[18]

It may be that Gordimer would have been a different kind of writer in a country in which she was not constantly faced with the fact of apartheid; whether she would have revealed an interest in class or gender rather more than an interest in the abiding dishonesties, hypocrisies and ironies of human life is open to debate. Her early emphasis on short fiction and her preoccupation with Mansfield-like "slices of life" and moments of revelation suggest an apolitical interest that was gradually overtaken: witness the growing concern with what she calls not "the how, but the why" (Ravenscroft, 1965, p. 28); witness, too, the changing proportion of story to novel.[19] Nor is she a political writer in the sense that she has made an original contribution to a political philosophy; she has, on the whole, translated existing political philosophies into fictional form, and, but for the transcending function of her irony, has toed a straightforward political line, though not necessarily party-political. Nevertheless, not only was she the first major South African writer to provide a critique of liberalism, she was also the first to illustrate the psychological repressions implied by colonialism. She has explored in the most thorough-going fashion the relation between the private and political self in a country with legislation and social habits that continually impinge on the sense of individual privacy; she has re-evaluated the kind of political commitment that leaves far behind E M Forster's dictum that personal loyalty is more important than patriotism;[20] she has examined the psychological unfitness for revolutionary change that characterises even those whites who yearn for revolution and also the majority of blacks, who have lived too long in dependency to whites.

All these statements are intended to pay tribute to a writer who has as one of her major purposes the redefinition of political consciousnesses and political roles. Her voice has been directed not simply towards Britain but towards the Western world in general so that they may see their responsibility to "the West's formerly subject peoples" (Gordimer, 1983, p. 29), people of the so-called Third World who have long served to support the "developed" world. In different ways, both her literary and her geographical allusions help to universalise the issue of colonialism, to spread the blame: she draws from and therefore looks to a wider literary and geographical world than other South African writers of her generation. Although the structure of the South African publishing world has until recently made it necessary for her to publish her works outside the country and to make the corresponding adjustments in her narrative process (a glossary, the inclusion of information that a South African readership would not normally need[21]), and although she has said that she does not write for a specific audience[22] and that South Africans seem incapable of coping with as modern a style as she uses, she has nevertheless hoped that her fiction will be seen as "liberating" for her South African readers.[23] Her scrupulous attention to black participation in South African society and culture as well as what seems to be a constant need to assure blacks of the presence of at least some whites who take account of their struggle for freedom would make of black South Africans what Stephen Clingman calls, after Jean-Paul Sartre, a "virtual public,"[24] if not an actual one. More directly than this, Gordimer's fiction is also addressed towards white South African women in a way that draws them into the circle of blame and responsibility. It is only when we understand this incorporation that we can understand her particular narrative stance towards and her treatment of women; it is initially only within these terms, within the terms that Gordimer has created her fiction, that we can understand her presentation of the political issues of race and sex.

Given Gordimer's recognition of ideological controls over perception as well as her felt relation to the current socio-political climate, it is perhaps disappointing that she has been reluctant to think of herself as a feminist writer. Indeed, many of her comments may even initially be taken as reactionary in feminist terms. Susan Gardner notes that Gordimer is on record as saying, presumably defiantly, that she is simply "a writer who happens to be a woman,"[25] thus refusing, at least publicly and officially, to assume what a feminist critic assumes to be the duty of a woman writer. One might note, too, as hopelessly out of touch with the current social situation, Gordimer's statement that "All writers are androgynous beings,"[26] for she must know as well as anyone else what Kate Millett shows in her *Sexual Politics* (1971): that not all writers are androgynous nor even attempt to be. Gordimer surely means that all writers (like all people) *ought to be* androgynous, and that she strives to be so to make up for a society which is not androgynous. She recognizes, for instance, that women comprise a generally disadvantaged working group,[27] and are in a legally subordinate position, "being honorary children."[28] She has Bernard Chabalier say to Rosa Burger that having a child on her own is "no easier than it ever was" for a woman (BD, p. 303). In fact, throughout her fiction she makes enough statements for us to acknowledge her interest in the debased status of women in society, and her recent admission that she has become "much more radical" both "as a woman and a citizen" (Gray, 1981, p. 271) reminds us of that correction regarding her political function cited earlier, and authorizes us not simply to look for a recent development of feminist thought but to doubt that this feminist impulse had ever been absent.

Relationships between men and women in Gordimer's fiction are generally characterized by inequality. Many of her white women define themselves in terms of how males wish to see them; wearing the masks of make-up so that they look "two-dimensional," as in "The Smell of Death and Flowers" (NPL, p. 124), and speaking, also in this story, in a "small, unassertive feminine voice, a voice gently toned for the utterance of banal pleasantries" (p. 128). But Gordimer also records the exceptions; like Lerice in "Six Feet of the Country," whose enthusiastic managing of the farm clearly threatens her husband, as does her untidy, "unfeminine" appearance; like Rita Cunningham in "Friday's Footprint," who has to wait until her husband's death to find out that she is a good businesswoman; like Barbara in "The Life of the Imagination," who recognizes in herself mothering an ill child the "image of the mother that men have often chosen to perpetuate, the autobiographers, the Prousts" (NPL, p. 423).

Gordimer often gives particular polemical force to her documentation of inequality in male-female relationships by employing it to define female growth. Helen Shaw's development in *The Lying Days* is imaged partly in terms of her noting the extent to which John Marcus dominates Jenny Marcus; another part in terms of her perceiving the domestic trap that she's walking into—" 'Hell, Helen,' " says her lover Paul to her, " 'you're becoming a rotten wife. You might have put food on' " (p. 285)—and finally knowing that she must move out of its reach: "Here I was, back where they [the women like her mother] were, cooking a man's breakfast and keeping my mouth shut" (p. 314). In *Burger's Daughter* Rosa Burger chooses to be in a prison cell as a political prisoner rather than in a Paris apartment as a sexual one: her recognition of the French prostitute as a "poor thing, a hamster turning her female treadmill" that makes Rosa's "sense of sorority" suddenly appallingly clear, her decoding of Bernard Chabalier's invitation—

> I want first to show you *la dame à la licorne* in the Cluny.—
> —You will arrange treats for me.—
> —What is that?—
> —When you take children out to amuse them.—(p. 288)

and her vision of the unicorn's Lady, "bedecked, coaxed, secured at last by a caress" (p. 341) with the attendant images of a "pet monkey tethered by a chain" (p. 340), the mirror that the Lady holds to give the unicorn back the image of himself, the plaits on her head "imitating the modelling of his horn" (p. 340), and the reminder of "the age of the thumbscrew and dungeon" (p. 341), all these moments explain Rosa's choice.[29] The paradoxes set up here are tantalising ones: the taken-for-granted personal freedom of the life of a mistress is only an apparent one; it is only in prison that Rosa becomes free.

Obviously, Gordimer's women become more politically involved in the struggle against apartheid during the course of her fiction—against Elizabeth Van Den Sandt of *The Late Bourgeois World*, with her tentative agreement to open her grandmother's bank account to PAC funds, one measures Antonia of *The Conservationist*, arrested and deported for subversive activities; and against her, Rosa Burger, actively at the service of black revolutionaries (Maureen Smales, though "yearning for there to be no time left at all" (JP, p. 8) until the black take-over, and an admirer of Castro, "the bourgeois white who succeeded in turning revolutionary" (p. 37), is probably a regressive step; history has not moved fast enough for Gordimer's reflecting artistic consciousness). Whether these women become politicized in feminist terms is debatable: there are no self-defined feminists as heroines. If there is at least a shift (one that Gordimer herself suggests[30]) towards the portrayal of women who show more independence and self-sufficiency either within their marriages or, more important, while deciding to remain unmarried, Gordimer's endowment of independence even to these later heroines is, except in the case of Rosa Burger, noticeably grudging. Antonia seems continually to need to show herself off against Mehring, to use his conservative politics as a foil for her revolutionary image.[31] The relationship between Maureen and Bam Smales is an uneasy balance of power and Maureen's position not always sympathetically depicted:

she has "a will that twisted itself around [her husband], he was split and at the same time held together by it" (JP, p. 44). And the repeated references in this novel to the "master bedroom," both as generalized concept (p. 65) and as the particular place where Maureen and Bam used to sleep, signal irony: unlike Maureen, the rural black women sleep in their own houses. This contrast reminds us of the contrast Gordimer sets up in the novel between the black women's role regarding food and the white woman's: it is not given to Maureen, never before responsible for the family's food, to be responsible now—the author withholds from her that right, thus refusing her that state of grace referred to earlier.

Gordimer's continuing concern with the position of white women in a colonial, racist society is particularly evident both in the ways that she explores women's sexuality and in the ways that she exploits sexual development in her presentation of political development. Even as early as *The Lying Days* she refuses to explore experience "only through sexuality," which, as Carolyn Heilbrun suggests,[32] is one of the commonest traps into which a non-feminist writer falls. For Helen Shaw, sexual intercourse comes to mean both copulation and communication: new political experience is accessible to a young woman primarily through participation in a male world, and to this world she can have access most easily through sexual communion. Yet Helen strives to dissociate herself from the men who teach her and she also takes pride in being ahead of them: her reference to being better-read than Ludi acts as a significant comment, albeit unwitting,[33] on Doris Lessing's Martha Quest, who, like other heroines before her,[34] gets her reading matter from men. In *Occasion for Loving* Gordimer has Jessie Stilwell say, "You know, Boaz, I sometimes get afraid that everything we think of as love—even sex—is nearly always power instead" (p. 154) and suggests, through Jessie's husband, that Ann's affair with Gideon is her only way of living the "serious" life that the intelligent Jessie naturally lives (p. 282).

Sexuality is important in Gordimer's fiction, both as a concept and as a device. Her general aim, to speak first of sexuality as a concept, seems to be to retain for women the right to be sexually attractive and vital beings, without being therefore classified as "merely" feminine. While her views on sexuality are controversial,[35] they should not be taken as simplistic or accidental. Her discussion of the popular feminist concept "sex object" will serve my purpose here. In *The Lying Days* Helen Shaw is looked at by Joel with "that deeply desired, faintly insulting recognition of the pure female, discounting me, making of me a creature of no name" (p. 201), and, at least for the moment, assumes the right to do the same: "and I saw him then for a moment not as Joel, but a young man alive and strange beside me" (p. 201). But, lest one take as absolute her assertion that one may take an impersonal sexual pleasure without necessarily harming the other or oneself, Gordimer must also present the ironic obverse: Mehring in *The Conservationist* is severely characterized through his de-personalizing treatment of the Portuguese girl on the plane, as is Brandt Vermeulen in *Burger's Daughter* through the plastic female torso in his house. This latter image, taken from the "permissive" society, both validates Rosa's bid for a private life through sexuality, by compelling us to see her as different from the plastic torso, *and* foreshadows her subsequent discovery about sexual "freedom."

There are a variety of other occasions where Gordimer shows a deep and explicit interest in feminist issues. To keep still to *The Lying Days* and *Burger's Daughter*, one thinks of her ironic portrayal, in the first novel, of Isa, "the ardent feminist" (LD, p. 218), and, in the second, of the two different songs, the "private" love song that the Creole singer Josette Arnys sings in the bar (BD, p. 270) and the "public" love song that the black revolutionary Marisa Kgosana sings in prison (BD, pp. 354–55). But the point to be made here is that Gordimer frees herself to use sexuality as a device through which to give her female characters social mobility, as suggested above; and also to reveal to them the "fullness of life, the revealed and the hidden" (LD, p. 183) but particularly the life under the surface of things. If she draws on sexuality as a common bond between men and women, she draws on gender identity as a common bond between women; she also explores through sexuality the notion of a private life, so complex a concept in South African society, and she is able to set up a reverberating metaphorical relation between sexism and racism that has important implications regarding her political stance. Above all, the device of sexuality is a crucial component of her didactic voice and also of her ironic mode.

Early in her fiction Gordimer opens up the general area of racism and sexism in terms of chaotic, pre-rational responses. The first chapter of *The Lying Days* presents Helen Shaw's first move out along the road of independence as she disobeys the parental injunction that comes from racial/sexual fear: "a little girl must not be left alone because there were native boys about" (p. 14). Her journey is textured with sexual and sex-related imagery: the "hard and cool" tree trunk, the "tough little seal of dried blood" (p. 17) of the scab that Helen lifts off, feeling "the pleasure of the break with the thin tissue" (p. 17), the blood in the butchery, the reptilian images, the smell of urine that "had soured the earth with a crude animal foulness" (p. 23). Her subsequent retreat is precipitated by knowledge of that very complexity of race and sex that she had tried to discard:

I passed a Mine boy standing with his back to me and his legs apart. I had vaguely noticed them standing in that curious way before, as I whisked past in the car. But as I passed this one . . . I saw a little stream of water curving from him. Not shock but a sudden press of knowledge, hot and unwanted, came upon me. A question that had waited inside me but had never risen into words or thoughts because there were no words for it—no words with myself, my mother, with Olwen even. (p. 24)

She knows now the answer to that earlier question: "A curious feeling prickled round my shoulders. Was there something to be afraid of?" (p. 18).

The topic is picked up again in Gordimer's next novel, *Occasion for Loving*, where Jessie Stilwell talks to Gideon Shibalo of the irrational truth about race and sex:

"I remember the young black man with a bare chest, mowing the lawn. The bare legs and the strong arms that carried things for us, moved furniture. The black man that I must never be left alone with in the house. No one explained why, but it didn't matter. I used to feel, at night, when I turned my back to the dark passage and bent to wash my face in the bathroom, that someone was coming up behind me. Who was it, do you think? And how many more little white girls are there for whom the very first man was a black man? The very first man, the man of the sex phantasies. . . ." (p. 253)

Gordimer now makes explicit the sexual nature of the hot, unwanted knowledge of *The Lying Days*. And at the end of the novel Jessie Stilwell stands in shame on behalf of all white women, not for Ann's sexual love of Gideon but for her final betrayal of him. Gordimer thus throws into clearer focus the complex links between race and sex, and women's part in the complexity, by stressing both the pre-rational attraction against which the white man, the colonial Prospero, reacts, and woman's obedience to his strictures. Interestingly, Gordimer exposes an area that Shulamith Firestone seems to shy from, despite her attempt to go deeper into the connection between sex and racism "than anyone has cared to go."[36] Firestone discusses the connection between white women and black men primarily in terms of "a clear-cut polarization of feelings in white women" between "a vicarious identification with the black man [and] a hysterical (but inauthentic) racism" (p. 110), the latter stemming from "the precariousness of her own class(less) situation" (p. 110), being an attempt to "merge completely into the powerful egos of their [white] men" (p. 109). She spends less time on "the white woman's frequent identification with the black man personally" (p. 109), and does not expand into the sexual.

While something of the same guilt as expressed by Jessie Stilwell may be expressed by Mary Turner in Doris Lessing's *The Grass is Singing,* where she tempts the black "houseboy" to "rape" her *and* kill her in one final act, this attraction and betrayal between white woman and black man seems to be an area unexplored in South African fiction. The sex act between white female and black male is rare enough: Jillian Becker's presentation of it in *The Virgins* (1976), a pleasurable, trivial moment between two adolescents trying out sex for the first time together, without much guilt, without much moral fanfare (beyond the hint that Annie is making use of an "inferior") was sufficient to get the book banned. More common in South African literature is sex between white male and black female, the recurrence of which theme seems partly explicable in terms of the need to explore the equation between sexual and racial oppression. The husband in Olive Schreiner's *From Man to Man,* to take an early example, is the more negatively viewed for his "colonization" of the body of one of the domestic servants; his wife tries to repair this wrong by adopting the offspring and bringing her up, within the terms of the mental set of the time, as "one of the family." Her duty is to expiate the sin of the white man. Various writers have tried to cure this aspect of colonial sin by having their male characters fall in love with women of colour—William Plomer's Turbott Wolfe "simply" falls in love with Nhliziyombi.

After *Occasion for Loving* Gordimer too diverts her attention to the male oppressor's act of "love" with the female oppressed: in *A World of Strangers* she provides an oblique comment on the apparent innocence of such an act. Much like Turbott Wolfe, Toby Hood first declaims, "I want to live! I want to see people who interest me and amuse me, black, white, or any colour. I want to take care of my own relationships with men and women who come into my life, and let the abstractions of race and politics go hang" (p. 36). Later, after she has him discover—through Anna Louw, through Steven Sithole, through Cecil Rowe—that politics inevitably intrudes into personal relationships, Gordimer cannot have him act upon the suggestion by his friend Steven that he "interest him[self] in a nice African girl" (p. 215) and thereby consummate, as it were, his Africanist sympathies, for he would, one assumes, then become the self that he has lately begun to reject, the colonial figure mistakenly reflected in the eyes of an old man in the township who says, with a concupiscent grin, "Morning, baas', for what could I have come for but sex?" (p. 162).

By the 1960s Gordimer had apparently decided to channel her discussion of the connection between racism and sexism into what is for her and for other South African writers a fairly well-trodden area, the metaphorical link, on the ground of "oppression," of the two concepts. (The concepts are referred to here in their most generalized sense as umbrella concepts, incorporating, besides oppression, such things as exploitation, patronisation, and so on.) The image of woman, to which clings the implications of oppression, is of course used in a variety of metaphors by a variety of writers. In "Rain-Queen," which Gordimer has said is "about corruption. Of a child by grown-ups,"[37] Gordimer uses a female child as the available image. Woman is as easily used as a sign of racial oppression. A man's domination over women is quite congruent with his domination over blacks, and illustrates the thesis, popularized by Frantz Fanon, that in "Europe and in every country characterized as civilizing or civilized, the family is a miniature of the nation. . . . There is no disproportion between the life of the family and the life of the nation."[38]

In *The Conservationist* Mehring's attitude towards women is returned to again and again as a means of characterizing him as racially exploitative and as incapable of seeing other (black) human beings in other than functional terms: "what's the reason we go after [women]—she was pretty. She had a smashing figure.—" (p. 71), he says to his son about his mother; "there's a special pleasure in having a woman you've paid" (p. 71), he says to Antonia. Through Mehring's relationship with Antonia, Gordimer highlights another "special pleasure" that males feel, and thus puts power into sex and, by implication, sex into power. As the intelligent Mehring himself records, "It is in opposition (the disputed territory of argument, the battle for self definition that goes on beneath the words) that attraction lies, with a woman like that. It's there . . . that intimacy takes place" (p. 95); and, the thoughts given more brutally now, though with an uneasy hesitancy: "The flirtatious sneer in her voice unexpectedly gave him an erection. (Even then, perhaps? . . . the beginning of these—inappropriate—reactions now, being pecked on the cheek by some child he's known since she was in napkins)" (p. 64). Pauline Smith makes the same connections in *The Beadle* and "The Miller"—Mintje's tears fill the miller with exultation, as does "the quick rise and fall of her bosom"—implicitly though not explicitly in service of a racial theme.[39]

Gordimer's analysis of colonial domination in sexual terms involves the utilization of female images also in relation to the land, again quite a standard literary practice, in order to illustrate control and ownership; "underfoot [the lucerne leaves] give out now and then a sweetish whiff of summer—breath from the mouth of a cow, or the mouth of a warm sleepy woman turned to in the morning" (C, p. 9). Indeed, the extremely close connection between racial and sexual domination is emphasized in one of the concluding images of the novel. When Mehring has sex with the woman that he's picked up at the side of the road, it is now the turn of the subsidiary subject of the metaphor to become the principal subject.[40] "The grain of the skin is gigantic, muddy and coarse. A moon surface. Grey-brown with layers of muck that don't cover the blemishes" (p. 246).

Whereas one might simply suggest that Gordimer is using the images available to her as a realist writer who accepts that women are oppressed, the transposition of principal and subsidiary subjects in her metaphor indicates that she is reasserting, for polemical purposes, the image of woman as oppressed being; putting it before our eyes as a literal, crucial and unpleasant fact. Besides the number of occasions in her fiction in which sexual oppression stands for racial oppression, there are also a number in which the primary purpose of the story seems to be to document sexual oppression, to assert sexism as the principal subject. The marital direction of "Six Feet of the Country" and "The Train from Rhodesia" is of particular interest, since in both these stories it is through awareness of the husband's racially dubious behaviour that the women come to a realization about the nature of their marriages: in "The Train from Rhodesia" the young woman's vision is cleared; she comes to see the wooden lion that is the object of her husband's bargaining as "something different" now (NPL, p. 54) and at the end of the story will turn her back on her husband, thus identifying with the exploited black man: "a weariness, a tastelessness, the discovery of a void made her hands slacken their grip, atrophy emptily, as if the hour was not worth their grasp. She was feeling like this again. *She had thought it was something to do with singleness, with being alone and belonging too much to herself*" (p. 55, my emphasis).

Perception also changes for the farmer's wife in "Six Feet of the Country." The story deals with a man who stands in a paternalistic relation to his black labourers and who is the only recourse they have against a hostile white world; his refusal to assume responsibility for them stuns Lerice, his wife, into "standing in the middle of a room as people do when they are shortly to leave on a journey, looking searchingly about her at the most familiar objects as if she had never seen them before" (NPL, p. 73). In this story such moments are habitual, reminding us of Gordimer's phrase, quoted earlier in this paper, "females on a treadmill."

"Six Feet of the Country" has made absolutely clear the comparable position of women and blacks: there is a common bond between them, and thus between racism and sexism. When the farmer complains about how much time he has to spend trying to help Petrus get back the corpse from the police, he notices that Lerice and Petrus "both kept their eyes turned on me as I spoke, and, oddly, for those moments they looked exactly alike, though it sounds impossible . . ." (p. 77). "The Bridegroom" also deals with the metaphorical link between racial and sexual exploitation. The story presents an evening in the life of a young white Afrikaner at a road camp, the white "boss" among a group of labourers and entirely dependent on them for his physical needs, for luxuries, for emotional needs. His attitude towards Piet, who cooks his food and generally looks after him, is, as the title suggests, a pointer to his attitude towards his future wife, but if there is any uneasiness in him and in his fiancée's family about the marriage it is placed squarely on the other people among whom the newly-weds must live: "He had had a hard time, trying to overcome the prejudice of the girl's parents against the sort of life he could offer her . . . alone with him in a road camp, 'surrounded by a gang of kaffirs all day,' as her mother had said" (NPL, p. 184). Interestingly, Gordimer does not dramatize the relationship between white male and female in any way other than this: that is, she presents only the racism half of the metaphor (which acts, as the title suggests, as subsidiary subject, "organizing" our perception, as Max Black would say): the other half is as clear to us as readers of Gordimer as the other half of the carpe diem theme was clear to readers of Herrick's "To Dianeme," to use an example from a very different culture. This story comes after "Six Feet of the Country" and "The Train from Rhodesia," which have prepared us for the psychological link between sexism and racism, making the racism half of the metaphor explicit, and asserting from it something about the relationship between man and wife.

"An Intruder" can stand as the final illustration of Gordimer's exploration of the metaphorical relation between racial and sexual oppression. The story focuses primarily on the courtship and marriage between a young woman, Marie, and her several-times-divorced husband, James. James is initially characterized by his patronizing behaviour towards his fiancée, his "little marmoset, [his] rabbit-nose, little teenage doll" (NPL, p. 380), quite clearly a preliminary signal of his essentially vicious character. The only hint that this sexist relationship stands in metaphorical relation to other social relations is Marie's distaste for the "thick mesh burglar-proofing over the windows" (p. 381), an image which creates the link between the racial situation "outside" and the corresponding situation "inside." The story provides an answer to Marie's question, " 'What are all these people afraid of?' " (p. 381). As in "The Life of the Imagination," the answer is that they are afraid of what they themselves create, images with a terrible truth that emerge out of repression.

Gordimer's interest here is on the relations between men and women, the "inside" (sexual) psychology that matches in some way the "outside" (racial) reality. Possibly there is a suggestion here that the "inside" creates or determines the "outside," as seems to occur more obviously in *The Conservationist,* where the author's use of image and narrative situation speaks of how psychology controls reality. Through Mehring's dominating point of view much of the "reality" is remembered rather than given "objective" reality via an authorial medium; it is presented as already acted upon by Mehring's dominating consciousness, his skewed perceptions. His repression of the image from the world in which he is *not* in absolute control destroys him: its final mocking surfacing cued by the body of the woman he would normally have paid for, would normally have controlled.

Once one speaks of sexism *determining* racism, one accepts that the connection between the two is no longer simply a metaphorical one, but reaches the level of the literal: racism as a consequence of sexism. That Gordimer would subscribe to such a view is supported also by her presentation of Mehring's son: the "androgynous" adolescent, free from gender, free from racism. Clearly such a view places a significance on sexism that we have not up till now acknowledged, though it has been hinted at, and takes one into a feminist domain, where Gordimer would assert, along with a social critic like Firestone, that "racism is sexism extended" (1971, p. 108).

But what is particularly remarkable about "An Intruder" in these terms is that Gordimer, quite explicitly, suddenly draws back from the final feminist assertion that the story has progressively moved towards, and that is initially signalled by the characterization of James as an extremely unpleasant male chauvinist. From the beginning of the story Gordimer invites us to see Marie's innocence as sexual frustration or repression: the "small slow smile that men brought to her face without her knowing why" (NPL, p. 378) is very soon explained as a sign of "appalling sexual desire" which Marie has to repress "like a child bottling up tears" (p. 379) and which is not satisfied by "all the strange things" that James teaches her to do and that "she would not have guessed were lovemaking at all" (p. 380). Just as Marie's body becomes the vehicle for James's obscenities, so does her mind:

> "What do you think you'd call me if we were divorced?" [she asks, suddenly fearful of the insults he piles on the past wives he once presumably loved.]
> "You . . ." He took Marie's head between his hands and smoothed back the hair from her temples, kissing her as if trying with his lips the feel of a piece of velvet. "What could anyone say about you." When he released her she said, going deep pink from the ledges of her small collar-bones to her black eyes, all pupil: "That sugar-tit tart." The vocabulary was his all right, coming out in her soft, slow voice. He was enchanted, picked her up, carried her round the room. "Teenage-doll! Marmoset-angel! I'll have to wash your mouth out with soap and water!" (p. 382)

Because Gordimer sets up so close a connection between husband and wife, and because of the various reminders of Marie's oppression and repression, the reader has developed two expectations, not mutually exclusive, by the time of the story's climax: one, that Marie will continue to be the agent for James's violence and ugliness, and, two, that there will have developed in her a strong need to express rage, not on behalf of James but against him. The climax of the story negates neither of these two possibilities. Marie goes into the kitchen early one Sunday morning to see it in disarray, as if vandals had been there. Even the white muslin curtains "were ripped to shreds" (p. 384). In the bathroom her cosmetics are spilt, and her underwear "arranged in an obscene collage with intimate objects of toilet" (p. 385); the living room mess is even more significant:

> On each of the three divisions of the sofa cushions there was a little pile, an offering. One was a slime of contraceptive jelly with hair-combings—hers—that must have been taken from the waste-paper basket in the bedroom; the other was toothpaste and razor blades; the third was a mucous of half-rotted vegetable matter— peelings, tea leaves, dregs—the intestines of the dustbin. (p. 385)

Largely because of the nature of the imagery, any reader familiar with the pattern in literature written by women in which a maddened self emerges on behalf of the "feminine" docile self would immediately slot this story into that tradition, a tradition created by such diverse pieces of fiction as Charlotte Brontë's *Jane Eyre* and Emily Dickinson's "The Soul has Bandaged moments—,"[41] and which, to come closer to home, generates the violence in Doris Lessing's *The Grass is Singing* and, perhaps, Pauline Smith's "The Schoolmaster," where the male acts of violence may be read as surrogate enactments of woman's rage. Yet Gordimer, who has up till now encouraged such a reading of "An Intruder," suddenly dismisses the feminist possibility:

> "Did either of us go into the living room before we went to bed?" [James asks Marie]—For of course he didn't remember a thing until he woke and found she had flung herself on him terrified.
> "No, I told you. I went into the living room to get a bottle of lime juice, I went into all the rooms," she repeated in her soft, slow, reasonable voice; and this time, while she was speaking, she began to know what else he would never *remember*, something so simple that she had missed it. (p. 386, my emphasis)

Had Gordimer used a word other than "remember" or had she located that word in a passage of free indirect style, it would be possible to keep reading the story as being about the enactment of a woman's suppressed rage. But now, finally, the feminist "intruder" is kept out, repressed; the story settles back into the Gordimer canon of stories about dual responsibilities, male and female, for violence. Gordimer very firmly presents the couple as a unit: James generates ugliness and Marie hides it, just as she hides the hideous burglar bars with white, frilly curtains. In her is manifest the "frilly mind" function that Gordimer introduced in *The Late Bourgeois World*, whereby Mrs. Van Den Sandt puts a "frilly cover over everything; the lavatory seat, her mind—" (p. 33).

Gordimer's withdrawal comes as a surprise given the apparent run of her feminist sympathies: the creation of a context in which sexism is presented as a social fact and is even seen as a source of racism; the representation of the texture of women's lives; the polemical use of metaphor as a validation of ordinary domestic experience ("the warmth of body that brought out the smell of khaki as the warmth of the iron brings up the odour of a fabric" (LD, p. 42)); a concern with issues such as women's sexuality; the sympathetic presentation of women as open to new awareness, as intuitive beings. "An Intruder" functions for us as an objectification of Gordimer's own statements that she is not a feminist; what remains to be answered is why she has chosen to speak of herself and to create herself in these terms.

The answer has already been hinted at in the fiction. Gordimer's non-feminist stance stems clearly from its South African context, from her lack of ease at being a woman who is also a white South African. When a Johannesburg newspaper offered her the title "Woman of the Year" in 1976 she declined, saying that "The only candidates are surely Winnie Mandela, who came out of house arrest to stand between the police and the schoolchildren and be imprisoned, or any one of the black township women who have walked beside their marching children, carrying water to wash the tear gas from their eyes."[42] The previous year she had refused an invitation to a Woman's Conference in Grahamstown because "all the women in the country do not enjoy the same rights."[43] What she is talking about is not simply the superior claim of black women to feminist struggles, but the insignificance of feminism in South Africa: "the woman issue withers in comparison with the issue of the voteless, powerless state of South African blacks, irrespective of sex. It was bizarre then . . . as now . . . to regard a campaign for women's rights—black or white—as relevant,"[44] she says in 1980 of Olive Schreiner's feminism, and the following year adds, "I am not a feminist, except insofar as I carry, still, the tattered banner of full human rights for all human beings" (1981, p. 1).

Her attitude towards white South African women emerges particularly clearly and severely in a comment that she made last year, during the time when there was discussion in parliament about the conscription of women. Gordimer went on record as saying that white women should be treated no differently from white men in this respect: "South African women helped to bring into power a white minority government which has brought the country into a state of war. Women have got what they deserve—what they asked for."[45] While the intent of such a statement might well have been to jolt women into public dissociation from inter-racial warfare—she has also recently raised a question regarding the submission of liberal whites to army call-up (1983, p. 24)—the statement also reminds us of her severe treatment of white women in some of her fiction. "Happy Event" contrasts the "right" of a white South African woman to have an abortion so that she can enjoy a luxury holiday, with the "criminal act" of the black woman who gets rid of a baby for her own economic survival, a baby who may or may not have died on its own. The white woman could not be more harshly judged: the gentle voice that she on one occasion assumes towards Lena, the domestic servant, is drowned by her irritation at getting her feet wet when she has to go out to her room; the "gift" of the cheap blue satin nightgown is seen exactly for what it is—Ella Plaistow getting rid of the garment that she wore in the nursing home and "somehow felt she didn't want to wear again" (p. 110). "Happy Event" stands in testimony to the overriding effect of racist vision on an attempt by one (white) woman to empathize with another (black), and on the attempt by one (black) woman to call upon another (white) for help (a call that is symbolized by the use of the nightgown as protective wrap for the baby), and stands in ironic contrast to the moments elsewhere in Gordimer's fiction where a white female like Helen Shaw recognizes a gender-commonality with a black female like Mary Setswayo. Racism is stronger than the reaction against sexism.

If one is to accept, with Adrienne Rich, that women are not responsible for the power that men have asserted over slaves but "have been impressed into its service, not only as the marriage-property and creature-objects of white men, but as their active and passive instruments,"[46] one should note that "Happy Event" stresses this instrumentality to such an extent that one loses sight of the *source* of racism. So, although Gordimer has quite clearly accepted the comparable position of women and blacks, identifying and even validating the sympathetic bond caused by the commonality of oppression, she also treats the notion with irony at other moments in her fiction. Moreover, there are also occasions when she seems to subvert this particular commonality. First of all, she asserts the metaphorical relation between sexism and racism but makes the apparent common ground dependency rather than oppression, and thus is somewhat less sympathetic towards white women. This dependency-connection is briefly hinted at in *July's People,* for instance, where Maureen's mother's husband is referred to as "My Jim" and her servant as "Our Jim" (p. 31), and is made clearer in such a story as "Enemies" where Alfred, "houseboy" to the white woman, Clara Hansen, does many of the sort of things for her that a husband does for a woman, so that when an elderly woman dies on the train that Mrs. Hansen is travelling on she sends Alfred the kind of telegram she would send to a husband—" 'It was not me' " (NPL, p. 106)—imagining that the bond of sympathy that dependency is usually based on is there for Alfred too.

Secondly, Gordimer invalidates the metaphorical connection between racism and sexism on the very grounds on which she has at other times seemed to validate it. At various points in her fiction the identity of the oppression suffered by blacks and that suffered by white women is vehemently rejected by the black male characters. The sympathetic attitude that the "progressive young woman in disguise" adopts towards Steven Sithole in A World of Strangers is suddenly abhorrent to him when he sees it become nothing beyond the charm of a beautiful woman, appealing to him on those very terms that bind her to him: "he saw the girl, saw the feathers of her charm all spread out in complacent display" (p. 173), and publicly, if subtly, insults her by refusing her the reciprocal male response. In other words, he rejects that system of ideas in which racism and sexism stand in some sort of analogy to each other, an analogy that would be felt as of spiritual benefit to the white woman.

The same sort of moment is differently detailed in the short story "Which New Era Would That Be?" (Various critics have mentioned that Gordimer seems to practice in a short story what she will later present in a novel; the relation between this story and A World of Strangers suggests a more complicated relationship than that.[47]) Jake Alexander's response to Jennifer Tetzel's insistence on equality takes this form:

> But these women—oh, Christ!—these women felt as *you* did. They were sure of it. They thought they understood the humiliation of the black man walking the streets only by the permission of a pass written out by a white *person*, and the guilt and swagger of the coloured man light-faced enough to slink, fugitive from his own skin, into the preserves—the cinemas, bars, libraries—marked 'EUROPEANS ONLY'. Yes, breathless with stout sensitivity, they insisted on walking the whole teeter-totter of the colour line. There was no escaping their understanding. They even insisted on feeling the resentment *you* must feel at their identifying themselves with your feelings. . . . (NPL, p. 83, second emphasis mine)

In contrast to Steven Sithole, the (presumably) less intelligent and less articulate Jake Alexander demands mere sexuality as the link between him and Jennifer, "Who the hell wants a woman to look at you honestly, anyway? What has all this to do with a *woman*—with what men and women have for each other in their eyes?" (p. 83), and when Jennifer refuses to grant him that easy sexual response, though with "her beauty, her strong provocativeness, full on" (p. 86), insisting on shaking hands, speaking in the "clear" voice that invariably alerts one to the women with whom Gordimer seems most in sympathy, and above all going to the length of rejecting the black victim's viewpoint, Maxie's story, "to the length of calling [Maxie] a liar to show by frankness how much she respected him" (p. 94), Jake Alexander reacts with male rage and violence:

> His eye encountered the chair that he had cleared for Jennifer Tetzel to sit on. Suddenly he kicked it, hard, so that it went flying on to its side. Then, rubbing his big hands together and bursting into loud whistling to accompany an impromptu series of dance steps, he said, "Now, boys!" and as they stirred, he planked the pan down on the ring and turned the gas up till it roared beneath it. (pp. 94–5)

Like Steven Sithole, though in a very different manner, and in one more harshly evaluated by the author, Jake Alexander holds on to the sexist world, holds on to the world from which the women wish to embark in their desire to establish common ground. And the two women are treated as much as *white* women as July insists on treating Maureen Smales in *July's People*, to her dismay. It is significant, too, that since he does not find Maureen sexually attractive, sexuality can be no weapon for her; she turns instead to blackmail.

As Gardner notes (1982, p. 66), no one doubts white women's complicity in racism in this country. Yet Gordimer *is* to be commended for illustrating various ways in which South African women participate and benefit by racial oppression, for losing that Eurocentric vision against which a black feminist like Gloria Joseph rails,[48] and for insisting, not on women's passivity, but on their responsibility.

But the relationship that Gordimer draws between racism and sexism becomes more complicated than this. As already suggested, Gordimer employs the two concepts in metaphorical relation to each other, and her transposition of principal and subsidiary subject is one of the strongest ways in which her fiction belies the minimising of the issue of sexism that occurs in her nonfictional statements. Her occasional fictional hint that the connection between the two ideological systems is a literal and even a casual one, with sexism sometimes as the originator, is more radical than one would expect. The sexism metaphor "organizes" (to use Black's terminology again) our view of racism, and, because of Gordimer's transposition, so that racism is not invariably the principal subject, the racism metaphor organizes our view of sexism. Yet even the metaphorical relation between the two concepts seems occasionally to disturb Gordimer, and some of her fictional moments stand as reminders that the metaphor is *not* a

logical proposition. We are warned that only certain similarities between the two concepts obtain: racism is seen to be like sexism only
as long as one is able to evoke what Black calls "a system of associated
commonplaces" (p. 40). Black's thesis is that a metaphor depends
upon a set of cultural assumptions about the nature of the concepts
employed, "a set of standard beliefs . . . (current platitudes) that
are the common possession of the members of some speech community
. . . part of a system of ideas, not sharply delineated, and yet
sufficiently definite to admit of detailed enumeration" (pp. 40–41).
Gordimer draws attention to the *absence* of such cultural unanimity
in South Africa in this respect and thus withdraws sympathy from
white women.

So keen, in fact, does Gordimer seem to be to correct any
tendency in her towards agreement with the Firestone/Millet/Rich
thesis that racism stems from sexism that she writes in 1982 a story
that subverts this proposition, and at the same time corrects her
earlier statements regarding the sexist behaviour of black men, which
had been so necessary a fictional device for her at certain points. In
"A City of the Dead, A City of the Living"[49] Samson and Nanike
Moreke are asked to hide a foreign revolutionary, Shisonka, for a
few days until he can get out of the country: he has blown up a
police station and the police are searching for him. Nanike is depicted
as a house-proud, bourgeois woman, and Shisonka's entry into her
world is disturbing: he wears one earring, not like "the men who
came to work on the mines who had earrings, but in both ears—
country people. He's a town person; another one who reads newspapers" (p. 45); he has no children although "everyone has children"
(p. 48); he helps her with the washing up, "scrapes the pot and dried
everything . . . [though] it's not man's work" (p. 49); he "picks up
the baby as if it belongs to him" (p. 50). The story ends with Nanike
betraying him. She doesn't know why:

> I get ready to say that to anyone who is going to ask me, but nobody
> in this house asks. The baby laughs at me while I wash her, stares
> up while we're alone in the house and she's feeding at the breast,
> and to her I say out loud: I don't know why. (p. 52, emphasis in
> original)

But Gordimer knows why: the man has offered Nanike a non-sexist
future, and she doesn't want it, just as July can't accept the future
offered him. Perhaps the author reasserts the close bond between
racism and sexism but now reverses the Firestone thesis, saying,
sexism is racism extended; eradicate racism, and sexism goes; perhaps
she is simply and finally invalidating that metaphorical relation altogether, the metaphor that issues from the woman's faulty perceptions. It is significant that the woman who spits in judgement at

Nanike Moreke is a prostitute, someone who has most to gain and least to lose from a non-sexist future.

This story is one of the few in which Gordimer focuses exclusively on a black consciousness engaged with itself rather than with a white world (though of course the white world stands in the wings); the first in which she focuses on the political consciousness of a black woman; the first in which she denies that sexism is as inherent in black male culture as in white.[50] In her 1982 James Lecture she made a plea to black South African writers to move beyond "the representation of conditions" that has been so necessary a literary mode for them, and to start detailing "the torturous inner qualities of prescience and perceptions" (1983, p. 25), to use "the thematic life-material that underlines and motivates" (p. 26) the actions of blacks; perhaps Gordimer is writing this story *for* black writers, showing them how they should do for black consciousness what she has tried to do for white. But she has then been less than fair to herself, and to them. The artificiality of the occasion may account for some of the story's atypical features: the different focus, the glorification of a black male revolutionary, the simplification of her normal techniques of presentation of consciousness. But what one misses above all, despite one's memory of occasional unease in the hall of mirrors of Gordimer's fiction, amidst the sets of images that perfidiously reflect one another's obverse, is her characteristic chiaroscuro of irony and didacticism. In this story her "message" leaps finally out of the shadows, and her irony creeps back into the dark.

Notes

1. T. T. Moyana. "Problems of a Creative Writer in South Africa," in Christopher Heywood, ed., *Aspects of South African Literature* (London: Heinemann Educational, 1976), p. 86. Gordimer said in 1963: "First . . . you leave your mother's house, and later you leave the house of the white race. Since then the fact that I am a white person has strongly affected my writing." John Barkham, "South African: Perplexities, Brutalities, Absurdities," *The Saturday Review*, 46, (12 January 1963).

2. Terry Eagleton, *Marxism and Literary Criticism* (Berkeley: University of California Press, 1976), p. 6.

3. Nadine Gordimer, "Living in the Interregnum," *The New York Review*, 20 January 1983, p. 21.

4. The novels by Nadine Gordimer referred to are: *The Lying Days* (1953; rpt. London: Cape, 1978) abbreviated as LD; *A World of Strangers* (1958; rpt. Harmondsworth, Essex: Penguin, 1962), abbreviated as WS; *Occasion for Loving* (1963; rpt. London: Cape, 1978), abbreviated as OL; *The Late Bourgeois World* (London: Gollancz, 1966), abbreviated as LBW; *A Guest of Honour* (New York, 1970; rpt. Harmondsworth, Essex: Penguin, 1973), abbreviated as GH; *The Conservationist* (London: Cape, 1974), abbreviated as C; *Burger's Daughter* (London: Cape, 1979), abbreviated as BD; and *July's People* (Johannesburg: Ravan/Taurus, 1981), abbreviated as JP.

5. Nadine Gordimer, "Relevance and Commitment," a paper delivered at a conference on The State of Art in South Africa, Cape Town, July 1979.

6. Rowland Smith, "Living for the Future: Nadine Gordimer's *Burger's Daughter*," *WLWE*, 29, 2 (1980), 1.

7. Stephen Clingman, "History from the Inside: The Novels of Nadine Gordimer." *Journal of Southern African Studies*, 7, 2 (April 1981), 166. Clingman notes her indebtedness to Lukacs' concept "critical realism."

8. Nadine Gordimer, *Selected Stories* (1975; rpt. under title *No Place Like: Selected Stories*, Harmondsworth, Essex: Penguin, 1978), p. 13. All further references in the text are to the Penguin edition, abbreviated as NPL.

9. She says: "There would have been a different ending . . . without the Soweto riots." Stephen Gray, "An Interview with Nadine Gordimer," *Contemporary Literature*, 22, 3 (1981), 269.

10. The James Lecture, published as "Living in the Interregnum," 1983.

11. Paul Rich, "Tradition and Revolt in South African Fiction: The Novels of André Brink, Nadine Gordimer and J M Coetzee," *Journal of Southern African Studies*, 9, 1 (April 1982), 60.

12. Nadine Gordimer quoting Desmond Tutu in *Frontline*, 12, 5 (April 1982); Gordimer, 1983, p. 22.

13. See Susan Gardner, " 'A Story for this Place and Time': An Interview with Nadine Gordimer about *Burger's Daughter*," *Kunapipi*, 3, 1 (1981), 111, where Gordimer accepts Conor Cruise O'Brien's use of religious terminology to describe *Burger's Daughter* even though Gordimer is an atheist.

14. Nadine Gordimer in Johannes Riis, "Interview with Nadine Gordimer," *Kunapipi*, 2, 1 (1980), 25.

15. Nadine Gordimer in Marshall Lee, "Nadine Gordimer: The Integrity of a Writer," *The Star (Literary Review)*, 26 June 1971. See also Nadine Gordimer, "South Africa: Towards a Desk-Drawer Literature," *The Classic*, 2, 4 (1968), 66–74.

16. Gordimer speaks of the feeling "that began to be strong in me about 15 years ago that we are part of the continent first. We should see ourselves as part of the African continent rather than in relation to Europe and the United States." Pat Schwartz, "Gordimer Still Clings to a Sense of Wonder," *Rand Daily Mail*, 24 July 1981.

17. Nadine Gordimer in Arthur Ravenscroft, "A Writer in South Africa: Nadine Gordimer," *The London Magazine*, 5, 2 (May 1965), 23.

18. Nadine Gordimer in Diana Cooper-Clark, "The Clash: An Interview with Nadine Gordimer," *The London Magazine*, New Series, 22, 11 (February 1983), 46–47. The 1965 comment is also quoted here.

19. Michael King suggests some of the ways in which Gordimer's political horizons stretch after 1966 and notes that since then "she has had five novels published and only two collections of short stories." "Race and History in the Stories of Nadine Gordimer," unpublished paper, p. 11.

20. E M Forster, "What I Believe," in *Two Cheers for Democracy* (London: Arnold, 1951), p. 78. The various (and generally gently ironic) allusions to E M Forster in Gordimer's early work suggest that this was a consciously argued point. Gordimer herself says that "E M Forster influenced my handling of human relationships, and indeed my conception of them" (Ravenscroft, 1965, p. 24). For an analysis of some affinities between Gordimer and Forster see Dorian Haarhoff, "Two Cheers for Socialism: Nadine Gordimer and E. M. Forster," *English in Africa* 9, 1 (1982), 55–64.

21. To take *The Conservationist* as just one example, there are a variety of details

woven into the text that are necessary only for non-South Africans, from "the palms of the small black hands" (p. 8), to "Afrikaans, with all its homely turns of phrase and its diminutives comfortingly formed by rounding off a word with a suffix instead of preceding it with an adjective such as 'tiny' or 'little' " (p. 44).

22. This is implicit in Gordimer's comment: "A writer shouldn't be pressed into any kind of orthodoxy—a critics' orthodoxy, a political orthodoxy, a regime's orthodoxy, even the orthodoxy of friendship and loyalty imposed upon him/her by family and friends. The taking of this freedom is both the bravest and the monstrous side of what a writer *is*. You must give yourself the freedom to write as if you were dead." Diana Cooper-Clark, 1983, p. 58.

23. See the following extract in Gray, 1981: Nadine Gordimer: "The South African public, normally speaking, doesn't read much modern fiction, never mind contemporary fiction that breaks with the mode of direct narrative. In *The Conservationist* I completely ignored the difficulties of the reader. I've had some complaints" . . . Stephen Gray: "Do you feel that this method [stylistic and rhetorical contrasts in *Burger's Daughter*] is ultimately more liberating for your reader in South Africa. . . .? Nadine Gordimer: "Yes, I think so. It should be. That's what one is trying for" (p. 266).

24. Stephen Clingman, "Writing in a Fractured Society: The case of Nadine Gordimer," unpublished paper delivered at a Conference on the History and Ideology of Anglo-Saxon Racial Attitudes, c1870–1970. Research Unit on Ethnic Relations, University of Aston in Birmingham, 13–15 September 1982, p. 17; quoting Jean-Paul Sartre, *What is Literature* (London: Methuen, 1950), Chapter 3, who suggests that this listening public is felt as sitting in implicit judgement on the author.

25. Susan Gardner, "Still Waiting for the Great Feminist Novel: Nadine Gordimer's *Burger's Daughter*," Hecate, 8, 1 (1982), 66, quoting Gordimer's talk to Women in Publishing, Johannesburg, 8 May 1981, entitled "A Note on Women and Literature in South Africa," and published in shortened form as "Women Who Took the Literary Lead." *Rand Daily Mail*, 14 May 1981.

26. Nadine Gordimer, Introduction to *Selected Stories* (1975); reprinted in the Penguin edition, *No Place Like* (1978), p. 11.

27. Nadine Gordimer, "A Note on Women and Literature in South Africa," 1981, full unpublished text, p. 2.

28. Nadine Gordimer, "What Being a South African Means to Me," *South African Outlook* (June 1979), 88.

29. The importance of the French prostitute is substantiated by Gordimer:

One thing I think lots of people have missed—the reason why Rosa goes back to South Africa and, ultimately, to prison. It's not just because she has that terrible midnight telephone call with her former black stepbrother, Baasie, and that really brings her nose to nose with reality. It started long before, it started in France, in that village, when she met that woman in the street in her dressing gown, who doesn't know where she is. And it really hits Rosa that you get old, lonely, dotty. That you suffer. That Katya, running from political suffering, has simply postponed what is coming. . . . The alternatives have some horrible sides to them, too. (Gardner, 1981, p. 111)

Here Gordimer subordinates the feminist point that is stressed in the novel.

30. Gordimer is quoted as saying that although she does not see her women characters as moving towards "liberated" status, she thinks they "would now feel

more confident, more sure of themselves." June Vigor, "The Controversialist," *The Argus*, 16 September 1975, p. 7.

31. Interpretation of Antonia's character is difficult since we perceive her through Mehring's faulty perceptions. Elisabeth Gerver sees Antonia simply as a self-determining revolutionary woman who finds for herself "a personal vitality in political action which does not need close attachment to a man," and (unconvincingly) explains her affair with Mehring as evidence that she is able to separate physical attraction from revolutionary activity, while "*he* is finally unable to free himself from response to African rights that she represents" and thus treats her with contempt. "Women Revolutionaries in the Novels of Nadine Gordimer and Doris Lessing," *WLWE*, 17, 1 (1978), 43–44. Gordimer, however, suggests that we are not to take Antonia so unequivocally, speaking of "the pretences" that she has (Gray, 1981, p. 267).

32. Carolyn Heilbrun, quoted by Tillie Olson, *Silences* (New York: Delacorte Press/Seymour Lawrence, 1978), p. 255.

33. Gordimer had not read Doris Lessing at this stage: "The first part of *Children of Violence, Martha Quest*, has some very striking similarities with my first novel, *The Lying Days*, which I wrote at the same time. Not because we influenced each other— I don't suppose we'd heard of each other, the similarities had to arise. . . . " (Riis, 1980, p. 25).

34. For another heroine who gets her reading matter from men: see Christina Stead, *For Love Alone* (1944). Helen Shaw does take books from Joel, but she has already started reading Donne, Eliot, Auden; Pepys, Smollett, Chekov, Lawrence, Hemingway.

35. Susan Gardner objects to the uncritical presentation of sexual attractiveness and sexual development in Rosa, and the negative treatment of Clara: Gordimer "offers little threat to patriarchal norms and images" (Gardner, 1982, p. 70); "combatting [sexist clichés] was not her primary concern in *Burger's Daughter*" (p. 71).

36. Shulamith Firestone, *The Dialectic of Sex: The Case for Feminist Revolution* (1970; rpt. New York: Bantam, 1971), p. 107. See Judie Newman, "Prospero's Complex: Race and Sex in *Burger's Daughter*," paper delivered at a Conference on the History and Ideology of Anglo-Saxon Racial Attitudes, c1870–1970, Research Unit on Ethnic Relations, University of Aston in Birmingham, 13–15 September 1982. Newman reads *Burger's Daughter* in terms of theses promulgated by Mannoni, Fanon, Kovel, among others, about the psychological relation between sexism and racism.

37. Gordimer in Stephen Gray, "Landmark in Fiction," *Contrast*, 8, 2 (1973), 83. Not surprisingly, the image comes first:

> And the whole story came to me from a tiny thing, a saying somebody told me of in the Congo, about eight years before I wrote that story. They told me that when it rained in the afternoons a Congolese would say: Little shower, just time for a girl. And then go off and find some little girl, and the affair lasted just for the hour the rain lasted. And it's from that germ that that story came. (p. 83)

38. Frantz Fanon, *Black Skin White Masks*, translated by Charles Lam Markmann (1967; rpt. London: Paladin, 1970), p. 100–101.

39. Pauline Smith, *The Little Karoo* (1930; rpt. Cape Town: Balkema, 1981), p. 57. For an argument that such insights regarding sex and power are ultimately and implicitly used in service of a racial theme, see my paper, "Pauline Smith: A Feminist Map," delivered at annual conference of AUETSA, University of Natal, Pietermaritzburg, July 1982.

40. For these terms and those that follow during the course of this paper

concerning metaphor, I am indebted to Max Black, *Models and Metaphors* (Ithaca, N.Y.: Cornell University Press, 1962), Chapter 3.

41. See Sandra M. Gilbert and Susan Gubar, *The Madwoman in the Attic: The Woman Writer and the Nineteenth-Century Literary Imagination* (New Haven, Conn.: Yale University Press, 1979).

42. Nadine Gordimer, "Letter from South Africa," *The New York Review*, 23, 20 (9 December 1976), 10.

43. Nadine Gordimer, quoted by June Vigot, 1975. It's interesting to note that many of the occasions on which Gordimer is drawn to make aggressive statements about South African women are when she is being interviewed by women. During the course of her interviews with men she often reminds them that she is a woman writer.

44. Nadine Gordimer, "The Prison-House of Colonialism" [Review of Ruth First and Ann Scott's biography of Olive Schreiner], *The Times Literary Supplement*, 15 August 1980, p. 918.

45. Nadine Gordimer quoted in an anonymous article, "Nadine's View," *Daily Despatch*, 30 March 1982.

46. Adrienne Rich, "Disloyal to Civilization: Feminism, Racism, Gynephobia (1978)" in *On Lies, Secrets and Silences: Selected Prose, 1966–1978* (New York: Norton, 1979), p. 282.

47. See Michael Wade, Nadine Gordimer, *Modern African Writers* (London: Evans, 1978), pp. 101–107. Clingman, 1982, explores the relation between short story and novel in a more sophisticated way, suggesting that the short story is a "genetic blueprint" for what follows, "not in the sense that it *generates* her future work, but only in that it is the first to embody her more deeply generated compulsion" (p. 16). It would probably be productive to explore the relation between the two in terms of Gordimer's constant need to examine basic situations from different angles, one "solution" an ironic comment upon another, creating something like the effect created in a hall of mirrors.

48. "The feminist question has never truly embraced Black women," Gloria Joseph, "The Incompatible Ménage à Trois: Marxism, Feminism, and Racism" in Lydia Sargent, ed., *Women and Revolution: The Unhappy Marriage of Marxism and Feminism* (London: Pluto, 1 81), p. 93.

49. Nadine Gordimer, "A City of the Dead, A City of the Living," *New Yorker*, 5 April 1982, 44–52.

50. There is the hint of such a thesis in *A Guest of Honour* (1970): James Bray refers to the sexist authoritarianism of colonial Africa, which "according to [Wilhelm Reich's] theory, simply doesn't exist in African societies, their sexual life has always been ordered in a way that makes satisfaction available to everyone the moment he's [sic] physically ready. . . . " (pp. 437–38); and Shinza protests, among other things, Mweta's sexist and apparently unAfrican treatment of the female members of PIP (p. 361).

Deep History

Stephen Clingman°

> . . . it was an absence somehow always present. *A Guest of Honour*
> . . . one is never talking to oneself, always one is addressed to
> someone . . . even dreams are performed before an audience.
>
> *Burger's Daughter*

In drawing an example from geology, Lévi-Strauss suggests that
it is through structural oppositions that knowledge becomes available.
For it is precisely in the geological "fault," where two opposed strata
come together, that the "master-meaning" of a landscape, as he puts
it, becomes clear. Here the "space and time" of the past are suddenly
juxtaposed and become one; here the entire history of a previous
era is laid out for inspection.[1] We may follow up Lévi-Strauss's
analogy. If space and time become "one" in the geological fault,
they are also, in a sense, split apart. Were it not for this basic
fissure—or contradiction—past history might well be an undifferentiated continuum. The surface patterns of the evidence at hand,
through analytic deconstruction and then reconstruction, come to
reveal another "narrative": of the collisions and juxtapositions of the
past whose effect has been to produce that ambivalence, opposition,
or split.

Viewed in this light the unlikely subject of geology has some
relevance for this study. Here too the concepts of structural "faults"
or "contradictions" have been of central importance; in a sense our
whole investigation has developed from such juxtapositions. To begin
with, there has been the primary juxtaposition of the subjectivity of
Gordimer as a writer and the objective, external world around her;
out of the engagement of the former with the latter a "consciousness
of history" itself has been generated, inseparable in this case from
its condensation in fictional writing. Contradictions and "faults" *internal* to Gordimer's work have also been vital, for these have frequently been the key to her historical consciousness, its range and
limits and hence perceptible "shape." Through the deconstruction
of such faults, and their reconstruction in alternative form, by re-
enacting the original engagement between subjective and objective
that underlies them, the present narrative—a "history of consciousness"—has been written. In so far as these contradictions in Gordimer's work have been most useful to this study, they have also
been of greatest "value." This is paradoxical from the point of view

° From *The Novels of Nadine Gordimer: History from the Inside* (London: Allen and
Unwin: 1986), 205–22. Reprinted by permission.

of conventional aesthetic theory, since internal fractures are usually held to be a fictional work's greatest "fault."

Yet this history so far has been a distinctly localized and linear one; there has been no attempt to survey the overall "landscape" of Gordimer's situation, as it were. In quantum fashion we have moved from one set of four or five years to the next, tracing the responses of Gordimer's novels to their respective historical moments. Patterns have been traced through these moments, and this is then the diachronic development of Gordimer's consciousness of history. But what we have not really dealt with so far are its *synchronic* features, or what we may think of as the "deep history" of her writing. It seems this "deep history" might be considered in two ways. On the one hand, it would refer to those overall circumstances and determinations that affect Gordimer's fiction in general, and the general patterns of her response; in this sense they are the determinations and patterns affecting and characterizing Gordimer's writing as a whole in this period. On the other hand, it appears a "deep history" may be thought of nearly literally; what we have yet to assess is what goes on at the deeper levels of a consciousness of history itself.

These are, then, the areas of inquiry in this final chapter. First we shall investigate the possibility—perhaps paradoxically for a study of historical consciousness—that there is an "historical unconscious" in Gordimer's work, underlying its overall responses. Following this, we shall examine the feature with which it is associated, and from which in a sense it proceeds: the degree to which Gordimer writes from a "split position" in South Africa. This may be the fundamental historical "fault" of her situation, and certain patterns of her work will be set out in terms of this split.

2

If one is searching for a deep history one cannot go much deeper than the idea of an "historical unconscious."[2] In South Africa this idea proceeds from the fact of systematic social fracture maintained in the dual interests of white profit and power. This fragmentation, as suggested in the Introduction, has to do not only with the basic division of South African society between black and white along class and race lines, but also with the numerous subdivisions within these groups. Its basic effects for writing have been noted time and again, not least by South African writers. Nadine Gordimer puts it in the following way: "living in a society that has been as deeply and calculatedly compartmentalised as South Africa's has been under the colour bar, the writer's potential has unscalable limitations."[3] Others are in broad agreement with her views. Focusing on questions of characterization and social understanding, Alex La Guma states: "The problem is living in one set compartment and knowing only of your own life, and then trying to project yourself into the life or the environment of another part, of another party."[4]

Ezekiel Mphahlele deals with the problem of social fragmentation in relation to South African culture as a whole. In conditions that isolate whole communities and make social intercourse difficult or impossible, he argues, there can hardly be a healthy common culture: "And the problem of a national culture is *per se* the problem of a national literature. It must remain sectional and sterile as long as such conditions remain."[5] Nat Nakasa indicates that his cultural identity is intrinsically bound up with his class and social situation. He is meant to be a Pondo, he writes, but he doesn't even know the language. He was brought up in a Zulu-speaking home, but he no longer thinks in Zulu because it cannot cope with the demands he has to face. He concludes: "I am just not a tribesman, whether I like it or not. I am, inescapably, a part of the city slums, the factory machines and our beloved shebeens."[6]

Elsewhere Nadine Gordimer has suggested a further dimension of the effects of social fracture in South Africa. At the widest level of the social formation itself, she writes, external forces enter the very "breast and brain" of the artist, determining the nature and state of art in South Africa. She carries on to say that as a writer she is fully aware that "my consciousness inevitably has the same tint as my face."[7]

Whether it be characterization, culture, class, or consciousness, explicit or implicit in each of these views is a certain aspect of *limitation* for writing in South Africa, consequent on the effects of social fracture. This question was also raised in the Introduction, but there it was suggested that it should not be interpreted too rigorously. Nadine Gordimer, it was anticipated, would not be entirely confined by the general limitations that affect her; and, indeed, the evidence of this study indicates that the writers themselves are perhaps too pessimistic in their assessment of the consequences of social fracture for their work. At different stages, we have seen how Gordimer has been closely involved in a black social world; and even at the height of Black Consciousness exclusivism she was at least able to present its tone and tenor with great accuracy. Moreover, in terms of what her novels represent, we have seen that at different times they have crossed boundaries of both colour and class; in both *A World of Strangers* and *The Conservationist* the degree to which these novels respond to an overall historical moment is the same as that to which they escape any strict limitation by their social position—even though that position may none the less be clear. Ideologically Gordimer's work has ranged both within and beyond her "class" situation.

Nevertheless, at a deep level the fact of limitation still applies.

Nadine Gordimer may write about blacks in South Africa; she may mix with them as well as have close black friends. But there is still a crucial sense in which she is divided from the black world, even at those moments of her closest approach. Gordimer, quite simply, is not "of" the black South African world, nor could she be under present circumstances. This basic social limitation is also, in a deep sense, an historical one; an historical gap stands between Gordimer and the black world. Like Jessie and Gideon in *Occasion for Loving*, or Rosa and Zwelinzima in *Burger's Daughter*, there is a certain history that must pass before they can really stand together on the same ground. And even then it might be problematic, for the question would arise as to which part of the black world Gordimer wished to stand with.

From this deeper, dual aspect of limitation the idea of an historical unconscious develops. In one sense, and perhaps on one level, the idea of an "unconscious" is already familiar to us here. It is this that has marked out the structural "silences," "gaps," or contradictions of Gordimer's work, where it reaches the boundaries of its vision due to an aspect of ideological, social, or historical limitation, or more usually an uneven, superimposed combination of all three. This has been our use of Macherey's concept of the "not-said," but what it seems to refer to primarily is not so much an unconscious as a "non-conscious"—it suggests those areas of which Gordimer's work is not or cannot be aware.

Noticeably on occasion Gordimer's work invokes a concept of the unconscious in a classic psychoanalytic sense. In *A World of Strangers* the collective "nightmare" that the white hunters experience represents, internally at least, an emanation from their subconscious, a projection of their own social and political malevolence rising in the weird surroundings of the blighted hunting landscape to haunt them. In *Burger's Daughter* Gordimer undertakes a psychoanalytic investigation into the deeper compulsions and distortions of a white political response to apartheid. In her latest novella, "Something out there," she deals again with the political fears and obsessions of a white unconscious, associated analogically in the text with a marauding and threatening wild animal.[8]

The Conservationist is perhaps the most suggestive of Gordimer's works from this point of view. From our discussion of the novel three main features seem relevant. First, as we saw earlier, it is a major theme of *The Conservationist* that the raising of the black body simultaneously represents a "return of the repressed" on both political and psychological levels; just as the body represents a return of the black world in political terms, equally, internal to Mehring's psyche, it signifies that a site of repression is bound to return to consciousness in threatening and subversive ways. The second point concerns the

question of "address." Whether consciously or unconsciously, Mehring feels compelled to "address" himself to the black body as a
representative of the oppressed black world; it is precisely as such
a representative that the body stands as an ultimate arbiter over the
meaning of his own existence. A linked aspect is that this is also
address to the future, for it is as an incarnation of a future destiny
that the body stands in judgement on Mehring's present. The third
point is of basic importance. For the reason there can be this "return
of the repressed"—and the reason there is a compulsion of "address"
for Mehring—is because there is, in the first place, a state of political
repression in South Africa. Mehring does not just live in a fractured
society. He lives in a state of *oppressive* fracture, or fracture geared
to oppression and exploitation. The fundamental political disequili-
brium this involves sets up the dynamic of its own reversal in his
psyche.

These conjunctions between the political and the psychological,
between "conscious" discourse and subconscious compulsion, seem
very suggestive for Gordimer's fiction as a whole. One might normally
be wary of leaping from fictional themes to authors as if no difference
existed. Nevertheless, it is by no means clear that the themes of a
fictional text do not include, whether consciously or unconsciously,
the situation of their "authors." And the three points that have been
isolated in relation to *The Conservationist* can, it appears, be extended
to include the situation of Nadine Gordimer herself as a writer, and
to some degree to characterize her fictional response to it.

There is one obvious difference between Gordimer and Mehring.
Whereas he is a fundamental pillar of the oppressive system in South
Africa, she is essentially an opponent. Perhaps we should then not
expect anything very similar between the writer and her character,
either by way of repression or else by way of "return." Yet the two
do have something in common; both—in Gordimer's case despite
herself—are situated in a fractured society and, moreover, one in
which fracture and oppression are linked. For Gordimer as well as
for her character there is a domain of social repression that objectively
applies to her situation whether she desires it subjectively or not.
On a deep level, therefore, a whole domain of South African life
belongs to the "unconscious" of her fiction—the repressed black
world that her writing cannot really be part *of* and from which (much
like the individual unconscious) it cannot directly speak. Indeed,
there is good reason to believe that the "unconscious" as it is apparent
here, implies more than simply Macherey's definition of the "non-
conscious." For in Gordimer's work it seems that this state of objective
social repression lays the ground for the action of those other two
phenomena noted in relation to Mehring: the persistent "return" of
this repressed world in compulsive ways in her fiction; and the way

her work repeatedly "addresses" itself to this world and the future it represents.

One of Gordimer's earliest short stories, already mentioned, again becomes of relevance. Entitled "Is there nowhere else we can meet?"[9] the story was first published in 1947 when Gordimer was 23. At this stage, if we remember her first unfinished novel with its incidental inclusion of racist rhetoric, in ideological terms Gordimer's work had, at the least, by no means "settled down" even into the kind of pre-liberal stance to be found in *The Lying Days*. But because the story occurs in such an unsettled and formative period, it is perhaps all the more interesting. Concerning an attack on a young white girl by a derelict black tramp, "Is there nowhere else we can meet?" is a symbolic allegory on numerous levels at once. Here again the concept of repression is important, for just as the tramp belongs to a world of political and economic repression, so too he belongs to a domain of psychic and sexual repression on the part of the young girl; again, on all counts the attack is a "return of the repressed." Most disturbing to the young girl is a personal inevitability she feels in advancing towards the attack; a strong strain of sexual symbolism indicates her fearful yet irresistible compulsion in this regard.

This feeling of inescapable necessity lends a mood of destiny to the encounter, and so the entire episode is raised to the level of an historical allegory, of an inevitable violent confrontation between black and white in South Africa. At the same time only an irony eventuates in the story, for nothing is consummated between the two figures except the futile theft of a handbag and parcel; paradoxically, considering her narrow escape, the young girl is left with a feeling of emptiness and loneliness. Thus the story is at once a prophecy of a future historic encounter promising an ultimate release, and an exploration of the agony of its present foreclosure on the part of the white figure, who at some level desperately needs that release. But also, it intimates, that release will entail a mauling, physical or emotional.

As such "Is there nowhere else we can meet?" seems to have anticipated the characteristic field explored by much of Gordimer's later work. The experience and expectation it depicts apply in varying degrees of intensity to the central characters of all of Gordimer's novels. Helen Shaw in *The Lying Days*; Toby Hood in *A World of Strangers*; Elizabeth Van Den Sandt in *The Late Bourgeois World*; Colonel Bray in *A Guest of Honour*; even, paradoxically, Mehring in *The Conservationist*; and Rosa Burger in *Burger's Daughter*: all are confronted by the black world; all at some level desire some release from their historical impasse; and all are to varying degrees contained by the ironies of its postponement. The story also anticipates the experience of Maureen Smales in *July's People*, who undergoes her mauling and release at the moment of revolution that the early work projects. This remarkable anticipation in "Is there nowhere else we can meet?," combined with the facts that it occurs in such condensed and symbolic form, and that it is produced in a work of formative and early youth, might then justify the claim that the short story is a genetic blueprint for all of Gordimer's future historically responsive work.[10]

The story may set up the characteristic field that Gordimer's future work is to investigate, but it does not determine the future forms nor the future implications assumed by that investigation. This, as we have traced, is something that changes from novel to novel. Further, in so far as the story *is* a genetic structure, it is symbolic in a sense beyond which it uses symbolism as a fictional technique. For example, Gordimer may have been able to choose the over-conscious Lawrentian imagery that characterizes the story's sexual symbolism, but what she evidently could *not* choose was the compulsion to represent this theme as part of a fictional complex—a complex which thereby in part becomes symbolic of that compulsion. This is even more significant in that the complex as a whole represents the fictional field to which Gordimer again and again returns. Thus we can say that the story is genetic not in the sense that it *generates* her future work, but only in that it is the first to embody this more deeply generated compulsion. And it is this phenomenon that we are then seeking. For this is, in a general sense, the "return of the repressed" in Gordimer's fiction: the persistent reappearance in her work of that politically repressed world separated from her at a deep level in the domain of her fictional "unconscious." In Gordimer's writing at least, fiction appears to be that "other place" where oppressive and oppressed worlds can, and perhaps must, meet.

A word of caution: one would not wish to argue in any abstract or deterministic fashion and say that the return of the repressed in Gordimer's fiction is an inevitable and necessary effect of an oppressive social fracture in South Africa. At the very least it might be expected that a certain subjective responsiveness on the part of the writer was a minimal condition for it to take place. Also, it is not entirely clear how far this phenomenon in Gordimer's work should be interpreted in, say, strictly Freudian terms. The Freudian analogy is highly suggestive; in Gordimer's case the "unconscious" of her world as a writer enters the condensation and displacement not of dreams, but of fiction.[11] On the other hand this "unconscious" is as much a social as an individual phenomenon; and it might apply to the fiction and the processes of its writing as much as it does to the author.[12]

Nevertheless there *is* a return of the repressed in Gordimer's writing; further, it is a psycho-fictional effect attendant upon a state of oppressive social fracture in South Africa. It is precisely those areas of which Gordimer's work is "not-conscious," which for her make up a world of objective social repression, that provoke the basic responses of her novels. And this may not be all that unrepresentative, even beyond the domain of her fiction *per se*. Anyone who has lived in South Africa would suspect that the "return of the repressed," as the psychic equivalent of a political threat, might well affect many white South Africans in the form of dream, wish-fulfilment, or, as in the case of Mehring or Gordimer's hunters, nightmare.

Other writers in other times and places have also been caught up in a situation of intense social and historical division. What common elements, by way of an "historical unconscious," might apply? In style, mood, and subject matter Gordimer's fiction has often been compared to that of prerevolutionary writing in Russia.[13] And in this context one does immediately think of the two "classic" historical revolutions, the French in 1789 and the Russian in 1917; for in both cases, confronting an impending social upheaval, writers were faced with an "overwhelming question."

As far as the French Revolution is concerned, Jean-Paul Sartre has analysed the predicament of its writers in a most interesting way.[14] For the first half of the eighteenth century, he argues, there was in a sense no historical "problem" for the writer. Typically bourgeois by birth, yet privileged on account of his function, the writer wrote for the readers who commissioned him—royalty and the aristocracy. In these circumstances there was an ideological hom-ogeneity between writer and reader, evinced, says Sartre, as matters of form, content, value and style; writing in this context was, in his words, "a ceremony of recognition analogous to the bow of saluta-tion."[15] Yet at about the time of the Revolution the writer experienced a rupture, and it was a rupture in terms of his audience. For now there was an alternative class on the rise, the bourgeoisie itself, and the writer fell into a divided position because he had a foot, as it were, in both class camps. This class became for the writer what Sartre terms a "virtual public." By this he does not mean that it was a reading public, or even a *potential* reading public. Rather this class was a kind of *listening* public, a self-projected gallery for the writer, waiting in implicit silent judgement on everything he wrote. It was a hitherto repressed class against whose significance, cause and values the significance, cause and values of all writing now had to be measured. Thus the "virtual public" makes silent, historic demands on the writer, becoming a presence and a problem he cannot ignore. It becomes a presence and a problem to which he must address himself in his writing.

The example from Sartre, in so far as it gives an "existential" account of the compulsion of an historical response, reminds us that there may well be a sliding scale in the phenomenon of the writer's "address," from an "unconscious" return of the repressed on the one hand to conscious feelings of existential accountability on the other, and probably incorporating aspects of conscience and commitment as well. In addition, with appropriate modifications, Sartre's model would seem to fit Nadine Gordimer perfectly. For the bourgeoisie of eighteenth-century France we need only substitute the oppressed black classes of twentieth-century South Africa as her own "virtual public." In her case, however, there is an added intensity to this relationship. For if socially speaking Gordimer is more decisively alienated from her virtual public than the eighteenth-century French writer, then in terms of the cause she supports she is to be located firmly on the side of an oppressed black world. Thus for Gordimer there is a very acute way in which she responds to her virtual public. She must write from her own situation, and of this she is well aware. But if for this reason she cannot write directly *for* her virtual public, she can at least write *towards* it, addressing the question of its oppression, the justice of its cause and the eventuality of its triumph. Implicitly this is also an address to the future, for this represents the moment in which that triumph will be realized.

Here we see just how important for Gordimer's fiction is that phenomenon noted earlier in relation to Mehring: the degree to which there is an "address" to the black world and to the future. Something else also becomes apparent. The address of Gordimer's work to the black world is at some level a writing *in favour* of that world, for this domain then becomes the arbiter of significance, value and action on Gordimer's side of the social dividing line. Simultaneously the future becomes the arbiter of meaning and action in the present. This dual address, therefore, in part seems to be responsible for the historical commitment of each of Gordimer's novels. In weighing up, against the realities of the present, the implicit demands made by both an oppressed black world and the future, in each given instance for Gordimer the appropriate form of her commitment in fiction is produced.

What we have seen so far bears this out. In the case of virtually every one of Gordimer's novels the question of commitment is highlighted by the fact that there is a central character who has to undertake it. When Toby commits himself to Sam in *A World of Strangers* it is an address to the black world and to the implicit demands of the future that to a large degree underlies it. Similarly, when Jessie attempts some form of solidarity with Gideon in *Occasion for Loving*, in part this dual address engenders the attempt. With slight variation much the same could be said of nearly all the other novels. Mehring does not commit himself either to the black world or to the future—he is not that sort of character. But then his novel in a sense makes his commitment for him. Maureen in *July's People* is not ultimately "addressed" to the black world. Indeed, in that she undergoes a revolutionary transformation as a matter of necessity and survival for *herself*, the novel seems to mark an important new departure for Gordimer's fiction. But we have also seen just how fundamentally *July's People* is addressed to the future; nothing less than a sense of the future is responsible for the positions it takes up in the present. All in all, then, if we are thinking in terms of a "deeper history" in Gordimer's fiction, this dual address is an intriguing phenomenon. For, to varying degrees in every case, it seems to be an "absent" world, considered both socially and temporally, that underlies the response of Gordimer's consciousness of history. The oppressed black world and the absent future together pose a "deep historic question" to which each novel is an attempted solution. Each attempts to answer the question of where it stands in relation to the oppressed and "absent" world.

If this "deep historic question" is a nearly invariable presence underlying the response of Gordimer's novels, then what is not invariable are the kinds of answer that are given. These, we have seen, change markedly from novel to novel, ranging in their ideological implications from the liberal variants of *The Lying Days* and *A World of Strangers*, to the socialist affirmations of *A Guest of Honour*, to the revolutionary alignment of *Burger's Daughter*.

A striking pattern is noticeable in this change: that as a condition of social fracture in South Africa has become more emphatic, and as oppression has intensified, so too has Nadine Gordimer, in response to a black world increasingly divided from her and a future ever more radical in its implications, become ever more radically attuned to the demands that these embody. Thus another layer of significance is added to the fact that in *Occasion for Loving* at the same moment that Gordimer is cut off from the inter-racial world of the 1950s, she discovers the failure of liberal humanism—the ideology that had sustained her when she was a part of that world. In *Burger's Daughter*, in a situation of acute social and historical marginality—induced not only by the structures of apartheid, but by the response of the black world itself, in the form of Black Consciousness and the Soweto Revolt—Gordimer turns to the legacy of a revolutionary tradition to negotiate the demands of a now deeply "absent" world and a problematic future. As for *July's People*, it is set in the "absent" moment itself: the moment of revolution in South Africa.

Overall, the picture arising from Gordimer's novels is one of inverse proportion on two fronts. The narrower her access to an oppressed black world—in terms of the underlying assumptions that might identify her in any simple fashion with that world—the more radical is her response to its implicit demands. And the less accommodating and simple the prospect of the future becomes, the more insistent is Gordimer's address towards its ultimate resolution. Earlier it was noted that at a deep level Gordimer's objective limits as a writer had two aspects, being both social and historical in nature. Here we see that even *at* a deep level their effects are by no means simple, indeed that they are at least paradoxical and contradictory. For in both social and historical terms these limits seem only to have invited their own transgression in Gordimer's fiction in inverse proportion to their limiting effects. This in perhaps its most dramatic form is the "return of the repressed" in Gordimer's work. What on one level belongs increasingly to the social and historical "unconscious" of her fiction, on another returns ever more strongly to her historical consciousness, prompting the deepest engagement and commitments of her work, and the ideological shifts these include.

One last point may be made before leaving the idea of an "historical unconscious," and this is where we might return to the Russian Revolution. There may be a sense in which what is concealed beneath the surface of Gordimer's work is identical with what lurks in the "unconscious" of South African history. For the prerevolutionary Russian writers, too, like those of eighteenth-century France, were active in the shadow of a looming social upheaval. They too could not ignore a new historical presence on their doorstep, often falling into a position divided between the class they belonged to materially and that to which they may have been responsive in varying degrees ideologically. Turgenev, Chernyshevsky, Dostoevsky, Chekhov, Tolstoy: all fall into this pattern.

There is a sub-text in nineteenth-century Russian writing; it is that sub-text of a coming revolution that, even if it was impossible to foresee exactly, is perhaps the controlling force, the real "subject," of this fiction in so far as it determines its deepest address, or on the other hand what it tries to avoid. Much like Mehring's unburied body in *The Conservationist* it tells of a repressed world that is "coming back" inevitably from the future. In the sense that the Russian Revolution did not exist before it occurred, it belonged to the "unconscious" of history. Yet it was predicated by every moment of what existed, fashioning by the magnetism of its absence all that occurred in the present: an "unconscious" reality, which so governed a history that it could not but occur.

3

The social and historical limits of Gordimer's situation are paradoxical and contradictory; they nevertheless set up the basic framework within which she writes. If they are in some sense "transgressed" in her fiction then these limits still determine what it is that has to be transgressed. A basic contradiction then remains for Gordimer's work;

the limits that are partially overcome in her novels are yet to be overcome in real life. Gordimer identifies with the disprivileged in South Africa, yet she does so from a position of privilege. She supports the oppressed and exploited classes; yet she does so from a position within the ruling class. There may be a "return of the repressed" in her work and an "address" to the black world and the future it represents. But by and large it is an overseas and local white élite that reads Gordimer's novels; and she is ultimately caught up by the confinements of the present. To modify Antonio Gramsci's phrase, Gordimer may be thought of as a "non-organic intellectual"—linked mentally to the oppressed classes but not physically or materially.[16] If we are thinking of the deep structural determinations of her writing, this is then perhaps the deepest, that Gordimer occupies what can be termed a "split historical position." This split has been responsible for the "historical unconscious" of her work, but it has also generated other broad patterns in her novels, which may be set out in terms of this "fault."

Unsurprisingly, given that they are organized around a division, these patterns take the form of oppositions. Thus, one recurrent pairing in Gordimer's work is that between a sense of "history" on the one hand and a sense of "existence" on the other. This pairing makes up a basic thematic polarity in *Occasion for Loving* as Jessie— and the novel as a whole—oscillate between one and the other. In *The Late Bourgeois World,* as Elizabeth makes her historical commitment she celebrates it on an existential plane. Bray, in *A Guest of Honour,* finds a way of accepting the conditions of history and of existence in the same instant. There is a definite logic to this pairing if we think of it in terms of Gordimer's split position. The sense of history is understandable enough in South African circumstances, and in terms of Gordimer's basic attitudes. But where feelings of social engagement are counterposed by the reality of social marginality, it is by no means surprising that a sense of solitary "existence" should vie so strongly with a sense of history. Also, where the effective results of a mental or practical commitment are likely to be all but invisible, it is understandable that a feeling of existential accountability—or even, on occasion, something approaching a sense of the "absurd"—comes to partner an historical approach and provide the basis for a philosophy of responsibility and endurance.

Gordimer has a personal empathy for existentialism—we remember her fondness for Sartre and Camus; but seen in terms of her split position this empathy takes on an historical intelligibility. This division then explains a further feature of Gordimer's novels: the degree to which they are fundamentally "meditational." If we have not asked what her novels "do," in the sense of what political effect they might have, or might be intended to have, this is because there is really nothing for them *to* do except reflect on the situation from which they emerge and construct essentially meditational hypotheses towards its eventual transformation. For this reason also, in contrast, say, to recent black South African fiction, which tends to present a whole spectrum of black society as a collective resource of historical agency,[17] the ultimate subject of Gordimer's novels is subjectivity itself, and a marginalized white subjectivity at that. In other words, there is something of the soliloquy about Gordimer, and it is an historical effect related to her "split position."

One of the central patterns of Gordimer's work has to do with another pair of counterparts: that of romance and realism. Gordimer has described herself as "a romantic struggling with reality,"[18] and something has been made of this by critics, though not from an historical point of view.[19] From this point of view, however, the pairing provides some central insights. For in Gordimer's work romanticism is the mode that overcomes real limitations; romance, for her, begins at the limits of the possible. In *A World of Strangers* we first saw the conjunction between romance and optimism: a romantic mode that carried deep historical truths to Toby. The ending of the novel was, despite its self-probationary procedures, still residually "romantic." In *The Late Bourgeois World* it was a vast and transcendent romanticism that overcame the limits of the possible. Most powerfully we saw this function fulfilled in *The Conservationist*, where its prophetic, symbolic mode produced what seemed impossible to achieve realistically. On the other hand, where Gordimer's work has primarily been concerned to estimate what is actually available, historically considered, realism has prevailed over romanticism. We saw this in *Occasion for Loving, A Guest of Honour* and *Burger's Daughter.*

There is an implicit dialectic between romanticism and realism in Gordimer's work, therefore, both between the novels and within them, and it clearly corresponds to the basic "fault" of her split position. Realism represents what is possible within the boundaries of her social and historical limits, romanticism what is desired beyond them. More lately, however, it seems there is a declining romanticism in Gordimer's work, especially in so far as it concerns what may be achieved historically by the white subject. To this degree Gordimer has perhaps internalized the realities of her split position, which is itself a development of some significance.

Romanticism and realism may be examined independently in Gordimer's work as manifestations of a basic contradiction. To take her romanticism first, probably the most important feature we have seen within it is its turn to nature, the land, and an attendant mythology. This, once again, appeared most strongly in *The Conservationist*, but was present in *A World of Strangers* and *A Guest of Honour* as well. In "Something out there" the wild animal that is linked with the white unconscious is also, by definition, part of an untameable "nature." In general this procedure in Gordimer's fiction is itself evidence of a "split position." For in her work nature has acted as a locus of symbolic displacement; it represents the world from which she is divided both socially and historically. In *The Conservationist*, as we saw, nature is deeply linked with the people, and vice versa. At the same time it represents the future as it raises its unburied "child," the black body, to life, and then receives it back into its own. Once again the attractions of this displacement make sense if we consider them from the point of view of Gordimer's position. For the white writer, cut off both from the people and from a desired alternative future, there is a fundamental consolation in nature. As a sign in the very "nature of things" of eternal revolution and cycle it represents the assurance of a political "return." Also, where the limits of the possible seem to be measured out by irony— another recurrent feature of Gordimer's novels—nature represents its overthrow by nothing less than irony itself, in its ever succeeding patterns of succession. In this guise nature easily bears the message of what Terry Eagleton has called the "ironic wit of history," that oppressors rise only to fall;[20] and this, if we think of Mehring, is exactly how Gordimer has used it. Perhaps most important of all, however, is that where a white political culture has its historical roots in a colonial or *settler* culture, the land "naturally" becomes a sign of the people. This from the black point of view is the logic of the political slogan "Afrika! Mayibuye!"—"Africa! May it come back!" And this too is the logic of Gordimer's use of it in *The Conservationist*.

More generally, Gordimer's symbolic use of nature may have a wider resonance. Stephen Gray has pointed out that, in the original colonial "romance" hunting novel, the subjection of nature in Africa also came to represent the subjection of its people and the putative "dark forces" with which they were identified.[21] What we may be witnessing now in one form in southern and South African white fiction is the reverse of this phenomenon, as nature "romantically" promises to return. It was Doris Lessing's *The Grass is Singing* that first presented a tale of the "return of the repressed" in political, psychological and environmental terms. André Brink writes of his "rumours of rain." There is Gordimer's *The Conservationist*. In J. M. Coetzee's *Waiting for the Barbarians* the demise of the allegoric imperial outpost is connected with natural cycles. To the extent that the return of nature represents the return of the people this fiction seems to be telling us that we are entering the last act—an act of peripeteia or reversal—of a drama that began a long time ago. This does not, however, affect the degree to which it is written from a "split position." For the turn to nature in white South African fiction is still an index of a residual alienation as much as it is of a new affiliation; it is a symbolic registration at the same time of identification and distance in social and historical terms.

Finally, there is Gordimer's realism. We have seen realism in her novels as a matter of their "perspective"—the way in which they link private and social destiny. We have seen it as a question of mode; for instance, in the classical realism of A World of Strangers. There is yet another kind of realism in her work, which in one version was understood very well by Bertolt Brecht: "The demand for a realistic style of writing can . . . no longer be so easily dismissed today. . . . The ruling classes use lies oftener than before—and bigger ones. To tell the truth is clearly an ever more urgent task."[22] This is not exactly Gordimer's realism—it is much more politically motivated. Yet it does capture something of what her writing is about. For at base Gordimer's novels are engaged in "truth-telling"; hers is a realism of naming and showing, of being witness to the times she has lived through; and a corollary of her realism is that it has undermined many of the "lies" of apartheid. Yet if to some degree she stands at one with Brecht on this issue, then in the rider he draws to his proposition she must, in a fundamental way, part company. For where the suffering of the masses is so great, remarks Brecht, concern with the difficulties of small groups in society "has come to be felt as ridiculous, contemptible."[23] On the contrary, there is only one ally against a growing barbarism, and that is the people. Consequently: "it is obvious that one must turn to the people, and [it is] now more necessary than ever to speak their language. Thus the terms popular art and realism become natural allies."[24]

It is the import of virtually everything that has been said in this chapter that such a "natural" alliance has necessarily been beyond Gordimer. To take only the issue of language mentioned by Brecht: it would be possible for Gordimer to learn a black language, or more than one, and attempt to write directly for a black audience; to the degree that most black readers are literate in English, there is in fact no need to trade languages at all. But to learn to write authentically in the popular codes these languages speak—whether in English, Zulu, Xhosa, Sotho, or a new "workers" language"—this in present circumstances is an issue of a different order altogether. The white South African poet Jeremy Cronin has written of the need "To learn how to speak/With the voices of this land."[25] But in a wider dimension, unless he means simply using local or dialect words, Cronin's prescription is altogether more demanding and problematic, for all its real value as an objective. As far as Gordimer is concerned, we have seen that the deep limitations of her situation preclude precisely this. And so direct representation of the people is replaced in her work by an indirect "address"; as much as her fiction proposes it, it is also subject to a "return of the repressed."

This polarity then enables us to make an overall assessment of Gordimer's novels in terms of their fundamental historical "fault." We have seen how Gordimer writes from within the overall historical background of a colonial framework; yet also how her work foretells the end of the colonial era. We have seen how Gordimer is contained both socially and historically by the limits of her position within the fractured society of modern apartheid; yet also how the deepest address of her work is towards the people, in a complex attempt to overcome that fracture. There may be problems concealed in too simple an identification of "realism" with "popularity"; yet it is also understandable how a perfect realism, in representing truth, totality and justice, might perfectly represent the cause of the people. In this light we may borrow the equation for a moment, for it allows us to appreciate what is perhaps the deepest feature of Gordimer's work, proceeding directly from her "split position," and to view it, moreover, as a matter of both form and content. In formal terms, measured against the long colonial history of South Africa on the one hand, and the specific class and race structures of modern apartheid on the other, this feature appears as a settler or fractured realism. And measured as a matter of content, it emerges as a settler or fractured populism. The "populist" feature is itself of some significance. For the writer in Gordimer's position there is, by force of historical circumstances, an address to a largely undifferentiated black world. This in itself is an indication of just how far she is divided from that world, even as she approaches. Still, she is there approaching, across the paths of her own time and place, the broken landscape of her historical environment.

Notes

1. Claude Lévi-Strauss, *Tristes Tropiques,* trans. John and Doreen Weightman (1973; Harmondsworth: Penguin, 1976), pp. 68–9. Lévi-Strauss is discussing here the influences that led towards his becoming an anthropologist. Besides geology, the two other major ones were, perhaps significantly for this chapter, Freud and Marx.

2. This term is an adapted version of that proposed by Fredric Jameson as the "political unconscious"; see his *The Political Unconscious: Narrative as a Socially Symbolic Act* (London: Methuen, 1981). Jameson has a much broader agenda and a different kind of focus than mine, but I am indebted to him for setting off the central concerns of this section.

3. Appendix (1973) to "The novel and the nation," p. 52. This is given as a correction to Gordimer's earlier view in the original text of the article that "there is little reason why a straightforward novel of events in which the protagonists are black men should not be written just as authentically by a white writer as by a black one" (p. 44).

4. Alex La Guma, interviewed by Robert Serumaga in D. Duerden and C. Pieterse (eds.), *African Writers Talking* (London: Heinemann, 1972), p. 92.

5. Ezekiel Mphahlele, quoting from his MA thesis, "The non-European character in South African English fiction," in *Down Second Avenue*, p. 196.

6. "It's difficult to decide my identity," in Essop Patel (ed.), *The World of Nat Nakasa*, introduction by Nadine Gordimer (Johannesburg: Ravan/Bateleur, 1975), p. 77.

7. "Relevance and commitment," pp. 2, 12.

8. The title piece of *Something Out There* (London: Cape, 1984).

9. See Chapter 1, page 24.

10. It is perhaps significant that "Is there nowhere else we can meet?" heads the short stories that Gordimer selected for *No Place Like*, although she points out in the introduction to that volume that it could only have come from a very specific time.

11. See Sigmund Freud, *The Interpretation of Dreams*, ed. A. Richards, trans. J. Strachey (Harmondsworth: Penguin, 1976), esp. ch. 6, "The dream work."

12. Jameson has stressed the need for the conception of a "political unconscious" to transcend the categories of individuality in favour of the social or collective. See *The Political Unconscious*, p. 68.

13. See for example both Conor Cruise O'Brien, "Waiting for revolution," *New York Review of Books*, 25 October 1979, pp. 27–31, and R. W. Johnson, "Growing up to martyrdom," *New Society*, 14 June 1979, pp. 657–8, on *Burger's Daughter*.

14. Jean-Paul Sartre, *What is Literature?*, trans. Bernard Frechtman, introduction by David Caute (London: Methuen, 1967), ch. 3.

15. Ibid., p. 68.

16. See Gramsci, *Prison Notebooks*, ed. and trans. Quintin Hoare and Geoffrey Nowell Smith (London: Lawrence & Wishart, 1971), pp. 5–14. The notion of what an "organic intellectual" might be in South Africa is, on the other hand, not entirely unproblematic. As Gramsci's formulation anticipates, with increasing class differentiation in the black world itself, there is, and is bound to be, differentiation amongst its intellectuals.

17. See Miriam Tlali, *Amandla* (Johannesburg: Ravan, 1980); Mongane Serote, *To Every Birth its Blood* (Johannesburg: Ravan, 1981); and Mbulelo Vizikhungo Mzamane, *The Children of Soweto* (London: Longman, 1982).

18. "A writer in South Africa," p. 28.

19. See, for example, Alan Lomberg, "Withering into the truth: the romantic realism of Nadine Gordimer," *English in Africa*, vol. 3, no. 1 (March 1976), pp. 1–12.

20. *Walter Benjamin*, p. 161. In passing, Eagleton too links this irony with Freudian theory and the possibility of an historical "unconscious."

21. Stephen Gray, *Southern African Literature*, ch. 5, "The rise and fall of the colonial hunter," esp. pp. 108–9.

22. Bertolt Brecht, "Popularity and realism," in Bloch *et al, Aesthetics and Politics*, p. 80.

23. Ibid.

24. Ibid. There are few enough issues on which Brecht and Lukács were agreed, but this it seems was one of them; for Lukács, too, the "truth-telling" of realism intrinsically favoured the people. On the other hand, the two were not all *that* much agreed; for Lukcs this overall realism of effect could be achieved only by a containing realism of mode, or representational realism. For Brecht modal diversity was a basic component of his method in the attempt to construct a "popular" art.

25. Jeremy Cronin, "To learn how to speak. . . .," *Inside* (Johannesburg: Ravan, 1983), p. 58. Cronin was a political prisoner for seven years, and his remarkable volume is a rare record of his experiences. Though his voice never deviates from the highly personal, it also speaks through and for many "inside."

INDEX

DATE DUE